Praise for *Number Talks . . .*

Time and time again, middle and high school teachers encounter students who lack fluency with small numbers, operations sense, and conceptual understanding of place value; the lack of these foundational concepts is a major obstacle to understanding integers, rational numbers, and algebra. The number talks in this resource have incredible importance for the development of mathematical proficiency and are appropriate and important experiences for teachers to provide for their students.

—Cathy Humphreys, coauthor of *Connecting Mathematical Ideas*

No other resource has impacted my students' ability to work flexibly with numbers in the way that *Number Talks* has. It has been truly transformational! Not only are my students more computationally fluent, but so am I. We have all grown as mathematicians.

—Donna Boucher, coauthor of *Guided Math Workshop*, blogger at Math Coach's Corner, and educational consultant

For years I struggled to help my students who were unable to master algorithms. *Number Talks* has been nothing less than transformative! *Number Talks* has helped my students develop confidence in their mathematical abilities. I especially love the growth of confidence in my girls. I've even had parents ask me to teach them *Number Talks* strategies.

—Bridget Anderson, first-grade teacher, Curtis Elementary, Rialto, California

Sherry Parrish outlines the very best way to teach math to young children and gives educators access to the ideas and methods that they will need. This book is a valuable resource for anyone who cares about children's mathematical development.

—Jo Boaler, professor, Stanford University, and author of *What's Math Got to Do With It? Helping Children Learn to Love Their Least Favorite Subject*

Using number talks helps teachers listen to and follow their students' thinking and also deepens their own understanding of the mathematics they teach. Routinely using number talks is an important way to launch into inquiry-based mathematics teaching. In this resource, Sherry Parrish provides a wealth of sample number talks that can be used in sequence to address important mathematical ideas.

—Ann Dominick, Presidential Awardee for Elementary Math and former Alabama Teacher of the Year

NUMBER TALKS

WHOLE NUMBER COMPUTATION

- More than 850 purposefully designed number talks
- Streaming video featuring 19 number talks filmed in actual classrooms

SHERRY PARRISH

Math Solutions
Sausalito, California, USA

INCLUDES VIDEO STREAMING

Math Solutions
One Harbor Drive, Suite 101
Sausalito, California, USA 94965
www.mathsolutions.com

ISBN-13: 978-1-935099-62-8
ISBN-10: 1-935099-62-0

Math Solutions is a division of Houghton Mifflin Harcourt.

Editor: Jamie Ann Cross
Production: Melissa L. Inglis-Elliott/Denise A. Botelho
Cover design: Wanda Espana/Wee Design Group
Interior design: Susan Barclay/Barclay Design
Composition: MPS Limited
Cover and interior images: South Shades Crest Elementary School, Hoover, Alabama.
Videographer: Friday's Films, www.fridaysfilms.com

Printed in the United States of America.
5   6   7   8   9   10   0014   23   22   21   20   19   18   17
4510003438

To my husband and children
who now believe there is no "1" to carry.

A Message from Math Solutions

We at Math Solutions believe that teaching math well calls for increasing our understanding of the math we teach, seeking deeper insights into how students learn mathematics, and refining our lessons to best promote students' learning.

Math Solutions shares classroom-tested lessons and teaching expertise from our faculty of professional development consultants as well as from other respected math educators. Our publications are part of the nationwide effort we've made since 1984 that now includes

- more than five hundred face-to-face professional development programs each year for teachers and administrators in districts across the country;

- professional development books that span all math topics taught in kindergarten through high school;

- videos for teachers and for parents that show math lessons taught in actual classrooms;

- on-site visits to schools to help refine teaching strategies and assess student learning; and

- free online support, including grade-level lessons, book reviews, inservice information, and district feedback, all in our Math Solutions Online Newsletter.

For information about all of the products and services we have available, please visit our website at *www.mathsolutions.com.* You can also contact us to discuss math professional development needs by calling (800) 868-9092 or by sending an email to *info@mathsolutions.com.*

We're always eager for your feedback and interested in learning about your particular needs. We look forward to hearing from you.

Brief Contents

SECTION IV: The Facilitator's Guide

Contents

SECTION III: Student Thinking and Number Talks in the 3–5 Classroom

SECTION IV: The Facilitator's Guide

Acknowledgments

This book is the culmination of classroom reflections, thoughtful conversations, and encounters with educators and students who have challenged and refined my thinking about what it means to be mathematically powerful.

I am forever grateful to Patty Lofgren and Cathy Humphreys for challenging me as a learner; Connie Kamii for coaching me as a teacher to trust that children can invent; Marilyn Burns for opportunities to wonder why; and Ann Dominick Hardin for planting the initial seeds of questions that changed my practice and for walking with me every step of the way. Your passion and dedication to know and learn math with understanding have inspired the journey.

Many thanks to Carolyn Felux and Jamie Cross for believing in this project and for their timeless commitment to bring this resource to fruition—you have graced this project with wisdom, encouragement, and joy; Melissa Inglis-Elliott for masterfully crafting the whole from the individual parts; Perry Pickert and Friday's Films for listening to the heart of this book in order to capture its intent in film; and to the students, teachers, and administrators of South Shades Crest Elementary for doing what you do best—learning and loving math.

Finally, I thank my husband, Jimmy, for believing in miracles.

How to Use This Resource

Talking About Number Talks
Why Number Talks?
Author Clip A.1

In an interview with the author, Sherry Parrish shares why number talks are an essential component in today's classrooms and how number talks provide equity and access in learning and build mathematically powerful students.

To view this video clip, scan the QR code or access via mathsolutions.com/ NTWNCA1

Number Talks: Whole Number Computation was created in response to the requests of teachers—teachers who want to implement number talks but are unsure of how to begin and teachers who are seasoned in this art of instruction but desire additional support in crafting purposeful problems. The primary purpose of the book is to help teachers begin or refine their use of number talks with whole numbers in the strand of number and operations. The video clips give readers the opportunity to access authentic classroom number talks with kindergarten through fifth-grade students. The video clips also provide a visual platform for teachers to reflect on their current practices and target essential understandings from their readings.

Regardless of where you are in your number talk journey, it is important to establish a common understanding of number talks before immersing yourself in this resource. Number talks can be best described as classroom conversations around purposefully crafted computation problems that are solved mentally. The problems in a number talk are designed to elicit specific strategies that focus on number relationships and number theory. Students are given problems in either a whole- or small-group setting and are expected to mentally solve them accurately, efficiently, and flexibly. By sharing and defending their solutions and strategies, students have the opportunity to collectively reason about numbers while building connections to key conceptual ideas in mathematics. A typical classroom number talk can be conducted in five to fifteen minutes.

Overview of *Number Talks*

While *Number Talks* is designed to be read from cover to cover, it is crafted in such a way as to provide differentiation for the range of learners. To accomplish this goal, the book is organized into the following sections.

Reference Tables

Five reference tables provide ease in locating common student computation strategies by grade level, featured number talks, classroom video clips by grade level or chapter, and connections to the Common Core State Standards for Mathematics.

Section I: Understanding Number Talks

Chapters 1 and 2 discuss the key components of number talks and how to establish essential procedures and expectations for their implementation.

Section II: Student Thinking and Number Talks in the K–2 Classroom

Chapters 3 and 4 concentrate on the goals of K–2 number talks, common student strategies used by primary students, and crafting number talks to target specific strategies.

Section III: Student Thinking and Number Talks in the 3–5 Classroom

Chapters 5 and 6 focus on the operations of addition and subtraction with third-, fourth-, and fifth-grade students. The number talk goals for intermediate students are addressed and accompanied by common addition and subtraction strategies for these grade levels. Classroom student–teacher dialogue examples are included in addition to suggested number talks to elicit specific strategies.

Chapters 7 and 8 address multiplication and division strategies for intermediate students, goals for these operations, and specific number-talk sequences to build proficiency with commonly used strategies.

Section IV: The Facilitator's Guide

While the book may be used as an independent resource, it is also structured to provide a framework for professional learning communities or to provide professional development opportunities through grade-level teams, individual schools, or districts. Chapter 9 allows guided navigation through authentic classroom footage by grade-level video clips. The chapter also offers a new set of discussion questions (different from the Classroom Links sections throughout the other chapters) for each video clip.

Appendices

- Appendix A, "Author's Video Reflections," is a collection of author commentaries for the classroom number talks featured in the video clips.

- Appendix B, "Questions and Answers," contains commonly asked questions and answers about implementing classroom number talks.

- Appendix C, "Suggested Grade-Level Resources," provides a repertoire of grade-level resources to assist the classroom teacher in building meaningful, inquiry-based math tasks.

- Appendix D, "Reproducible Templates," provides the reader with templates for making tools to assist student thinking in number talks, such as rekenreks and five- and ten-frames.

Overview of the Video Clips

Classroom Clips

In Chapters 1 through 8, readers have an opportunity to view video clips of actual classroom number talks through the Classroom Links sections, a series of guided questions and reflections crafted specifically to address the ideas from each chapter. Readers also have the option of reading the author's commentary on each Classroom Link (see Appendix A: "Author's Video Reflections.") Note that these Classroom Links questions differ from the discussion questions featured in Chapter 9, which can be used in addition to the Classroom Links questions.

Teacher Clips

Clips of interviews with each teacher can be viewed as well (see Section IV, "The Facilitator's Guide.")

Author Clips

Interview clips of the author can be viewed (see the beginning of this section, Chapter 9, and Appendix A).

How to Access Online Video Clips

Readers have several options for accessing the video clips. Either scan the QR code (with a QR code reader app of your choice) that appears within the video clip section in the text or enter the corresponding URLs in your browser. If you would like to access all the clips at once, follow these instructions:

1. Go to mathsolutions.com/myvideos and click or tap the Create New Account button at the bottom of the Log In form.
2. Create an account, even if you have created one with Math Solutions bookstore. You will receive a confirmation email when your account has been created.
3. Once your account has been created, you will be taken to the Product Registration page. Click Register on the product you would like to access (in this case, *Number Talks: Whole Number Computation*).
4. Enter key code **NTWNC** and click or tap the Submit Key Code button.
5. Click or tap the Complete Registration button.
6. To access videos at any time, visit your account page.

How Number Talks Support the Common Core State Standards for Mathematics

Overview

As my own mathematics teaching practice shifted from a teaching-by-telling approach to a teaching and learning philosophy built upon the principles of Piaget and Kamii, my expectations for my students also shifted. Instead of asking them to memorize procedures, I began to expect them to reason, make sense, and construct strategies built upon numerical relationships. Our classroom was transformed from a didactic, static instructional environment to one characterized by listening, reasoning, justifying, applying patterns, and communicating our conjectures and generalizations. Number talks were at the heart of this personal and classroom transformation and served as a catalyst for my students and me to begin developing the mathematical dispositions and habits of mind for learning, doing, and applying mathematics. We were utilizing the Common Core's eight Standards for Mathematical Practice—before they officially existed—to explore, investigate, analyze, and lay a foundation for reasoning with numbers.

The Common Core's Standards for Mathematical Content and Practice require us to take our students deeper and build a strong foundation:

> *These Standards are not intended to be new names for old ways of doing business. They are a call to take the next step. It is time for states to work together to build on lessons learned from two decades of standards-based reforms. It is time to recognize that these standards are not just promises to our children, but promises we intend to keep. (CCSS, 2010)*

Implementation of the Standards for Mathematical Content and Practice provides a lens with which we can examine our own practices for shifts we may need to make in our approach to teaching mathematics. Number talks are an accessible way to reach deep into and draw upon the Standards for Mathematical Content and Practice to promote numerical reasoning and mathematically powerful students.

> Number talks are an accessible way to reach deep into and draw upon the Standards for Mathematical Content and Practice to promote numerical reasoning and mathematically powerful students.

Number talks are firmly grounded in the dispositions and processes of the Standards for Mathematical Practice while simultaneously addressing content standards in two domains: "Operations and Algebraic Thinking" and "Number and Operations in Base Ten." The intent of *Number Talks: Whole Number Computation* is not to teach strategies but to provide a platform for students to invent, construct, and make sense of important foundations in number. As classroom communities engage in number talks, content and practice standards are intertwined in a purposeful, intentional way that allows students a voice in their learning and understanding.

The Standards for Mathematical Practice

As we look at the Common Core's eight Standards for Mathematical Practice, we can envision how students incorporate them as they engage in classroom number talks. Throughout this resource you will find video segments highlighted to illustrate specific mathematical practices and to exhibit how classroom number talks provide a vehicle for students to develop these habits of mind for doing and learning mathematics. While the standards will be discussed as individual practices, in this resource they also are viewed as interdependent with no lines of division among them:

> Throughout this resource you will find video segments highlighted to illustrate specific mathematical practices and to exhibit how classroom number talks provide a vehicle for students to develop these habits of mind for doing and learning mathematics.

1. Make sense of problems and persevere in solving them.

2. Reason abstractly and quantitatively.

3. Construct viable arguments and critique the reasoning of others.

4. Model with mathematics.

5. Use appropriate tools strategically.

6. Attend to precision.

7. Look for and make use of structure.

8. Look for and express regularity in repeated reasoning.

The Standards for Mathematical Content*

"Counting and Cardinality," "Operations and Algebraic Thinking," and "Number and Operations in Base Ten" are the key Common Core domains addressed in *Number Talks: Whole Number Computation*. The following table outlines the CCSS domains and standards incorporated in *Number Talks*:

Domain	Grade	Content Standard Clusters
Counting and Cardinality	K	Know number names and the count sequence.
		Count to tell the number of objects.
		Compare numbers.
Operations and Algebraic Thinking	K	Understand addition, and understand subtraction.
	1	Represent and solve problems involving addition and subtraction.
		Understand and apply properties of operations and the relationship between addition and subtraction.
		Add and subtract within 20.
		Work with addition and subtraction equations.
	2	Represent and solve problems involving addition and subtraction.
		Add and subtract within 20.
		Work with equal groups of objects to gain foundations for multiplication.
	3	Represent and solve problems involving multiplication and division.
		Understand properties of multiplication and the relationship between multiplication and division.
		Multiply and divide within 100.
		Solve problems involving the four operations, and identify and explain patterns in arithmetic.

(continued)

	4	Use the four operations with whole numbers to solve problems.
		Gain familiarity with factors and multiples.
		Generate and analyze patterns.
	5	Write and interpret numerical expressions.
		Analyze patterns and relationships.
Number and Operations in Base Ten	**K**	Work with numbers 11–19 to gain foundations for place value.
	1	Extend the counting sequence.
		Understand place value.
		Use place value understanding and properties of operations to add and subtract.
	2	Understand place value.
		Use place value understanding and properties of operations to add and subtract.
	3	Use place value understanding and properties of operations to perform multi-digit arithmetic.
	4	Generalize place value understanding for multi-digit whole numbers.
		Use place value understanding and properties of operations to perform multi-digit arithmetic.
	5	Understand the place value system.
		Perform operations with multi-digit whole numbers and with decimals to hundredths.

*National Governors Association Center for Best Practices and the Council of Chief State School Officers. 2010. *Common Core State Standards Initiative: Common Core State Standards for Mathematics*. Washington, DC. www.corestandards.org/assets/ccssi-introduction.pdf.

The purposeful progression of the standards embedded in these domains serves to aid students in building conceptual understanding and procedural fluency. One progression to carefully note is the distinction among strategies, algorithms, and the standard algorithm and how each progression is carefully designed to help students build understanding and fluency. Classroom number talks provide a collaborative forum for students to

- invent strategies;

- generalize individual strategies into personal algorithms; and

- build a conceptual bridge to the standard algorithm.

Lastly, throughout this resource you will find video segments highlighted to illustrate specific Standards for Mathematical Content and to demonstrate how number talks provide a vehicle for students to develop and utilize the core foundations of mathematics.

> Throughout this resource you will find video segments highlighted to illustrate specific Standards for Mathematical Content and to demonstrate how number talks provide a vehicle for students to develop and utilize the core foundations of mathematics.

Strategies Table

The following strategies are featured in this resource and listed here for quick reference.

Category	Strategy/Tool	K	1	2	3	4	5	Page Number
Addition	Counting All/Counting On	•	•	•				46, 50, 59, 60, 121
	Doubles/Near-Doubles		•	•	•	•	•	51, 60, 172, 341, 343
	Making Tens		•	•	•	•	•	51, 61, 172, 341, 343, 344
	Making Landmark or Friendly Numbers		•	•	•	•	•	22, 46, 62, 171, 346
	Breaking Each Number into Its Place Value		•	•	•	•	•	23, 51, 63, 164, 171, 343, 344, 346
	Compensation		•	•	•	•	•	23, 62, 165, 173, 342
	Adding Up in Chunks		•	•	•	•	•	47, 64, 164, 173, 344, 345

(continued)

Strategies Table

Category	Strategy/Tool	K	1	2	3	4	5	Page Number
Subtraction	Adding Up		•	•	•	•	•	48, 54, 55, 65, 166, 167, 175, 349, 350, 367
	Removal or Counting Back		•	•	•	•	•	47, 55, 66, 176, 206, 349, 350, 367
	Place Value and Negative Numbers			•	•	•	•	177
	Adjusting One Number to Create an Easier Problem				•	•	•	167, 179, 349
	Keeping a Constant Difference				•	•	•	178, 348, 350
Multiplication	Repeated Addition or Skip Counting				•	•	•	238, 239, 242, 245, 265, 351, 352, 353
	Making Landmark or Friendly Numbers				•	•	•	242, 247, 360, 362
	Partial Products				•	•	•	242, 248, 352, 353, 354, 359, 361
	Doubling and Halving				•	•	•	250, 361, 362
	Breaking Factors into Smaller Factors				•	•	•	252, 362
Division	Repeated Subtraction or Sharing/Dealing Out				•	•	•	254, 255, 256, 257, 287
	Partial Quotients				•	•	•	258
	Multiplying Up				•	•	•	258, 293
	Proportional Reasoning				•	•	•	259

Number Talks Table

The following number talks are featured in this resource and listed here for quick reference.

Number Talk	Strategy/Tool	K	1	2	3	4	5	Page Number
Fluency with 3	Dot Images	•						71
	Five-Frames	•						90
	Rekenreks	•						83
Fluency with 4	Dot Images	•						72
	Five- and Ten-Frames	•						90
	Rekenreks	•						83
Fluency with 5	Dot Images	•						73
	Ten-Frames	•						91
	Rekenreks	•						84

(continued)

Number Talks Table

Number Talk	Strategy/Tool	K	1	2	3	4	5	Page Number
Fluency with 6	Dot Images	•	•					74
	Ten-Frames	•	•					92
	Rekenreks	•	•					84
Fluency with 7	Dot Images	•	•					76
	Ten-Frames	•	•					93
	Rekenreks	•	•					85
Fluency with 8	Dot Images	•	•					77
	Ten-Frames	•	•					94
	Rekenreks	•	•					86
Fluency with 9	Dot Images	•	•					78
	Ten-Frames	•	•					95
	Rekenreks	•	•					87
Fluency with 10	Dot Images	•	•	•				80
	Ten-Frames	•	•	•				96
	Rekenreks	•	•	•				88

Number Talk	Strategy/Tool	K	1	2	3	4	5	Page Number
Addition: Counting All/ Counting On	Dot Images		•					98
	Double Ten-Frames		•					103
	Rekenreks		•					101
	Number Sentences		•					106
Addition: Doubles/Near-Doubles	Double Ten-Frames		•					109
	Rekenreks		•					107
	Number Sentences		•	•	•	•	•	111, 121, 193
Addition: Making Tens	Double Ten-Frames		•					114
	Rekenreks		•					112
	Number Sentences		•	•	•	•	•	117, 125, 185
Addition	Making Landmark or Friendly Numbers		•	•	•	•	•	118, 129, 189
	Breaking Each Number into Its Place Value		•	•	•	•	•	133, 197
	Compensation			•	•	•	•	137
	Adding Up in Chunks			•	•	•	•	141, 201

(continued)

Number Talks Table

Number Talk	Strategy/Tool	K	1	2	3	4	5	Page Number
Subtraction	Adding Up			•	•	•	•	146, 207
	Removal			•	•	•	•	150, 212
	Counting Back			•	•	•	•	206
	Place Value and Negative Numbers			•	•	•	•	217
	Adjusting One Number to Create an Easier Problem				•	•	•	221
	Keeping a Constant Difference				•	•	•	226
Multiplication	Making Landmark or Friendly Numbers				•	•	•	267
	Partial Products				•	•	•	272
	Doubling and Halving				•	•	•	276
	Breaking Factors into Smaller Factors				•	•	•	282
Division	Partial Quotients				•	•	•	288
	Multiplying Up				•	•	•	293
	Proportional Reasoning					•	•	298

Video Clips by Chapter

(continued)

Chapter	Clip Number/Focus	Page Number	Grade
5	3.1 Addition: $38 + 37$	174	3
5	5.6 Subtraction: $1000 - 674$	181	5
6	None		
7	5.2 Multiplication: 32×15	231	5
7	3.7 Array Discussion: 8×25	234	3
7	5.4 Array Discussion: $150 \div 15, \ 300 \div 15$	236	5
7	3.6 Doubling and Halving: $4 \times 7, \ 2 \times 14$	241	3
7	3.5 Multiplication String: 7×7	245	3
7	5.1 Associative Property: 12×15	253	5
7	5.5 Division String: $496 \div 8$	261	5
8	None		
9	K.1 Ten-Frames and Dot Cards K.2 Rekenreks K.3 Counting Book	309 310 310	K
9	2.1 Ten-Frames: $8 + 6$ 2.2 Addition: $16 + 15$ 2.3 Addition: $26 + 27$	314 314 315	2
9	3.1 Addition: $38 + 37$ 3.2 Addition: $59 + 13$ 3.3 Subtraction: $70 - 59$ 3.4 Subtraction: $70 - 34$ 3.5 Multiplication String: 7×7 3.6 Doubling and Halving: $4 \times 7, \ 2 \times 14$ 3.7 Array Discussion: 8×25	319 319 320 321 321 322 323	3

Video Clips by Grade

Clip Number/Focus	K	Grade 2	Grade 3	Grade 5	Page Number
A.1 Why Number Talks	•	•	•	•	xvii
A.2 Using Number Talks for Professional Learning	•	•	•	•	304
A.3 Number Talks: Teachers as Learners	•	•	•	•	337
K.1 Ten-Frames and Dot Cards	•				36, 309
K.2 Rekenreks	•				42, 310
K.3 Counting Book	•				49, 310
T.K Kindergarten: Erin Keenan	•				306
2.1 Ten-Frames: 8 + 6		•			43, 314
2.2 Addition: 16 + 15		•			58, 314
2.3 Addition: 26 + 27		•			59, 315
T.2 Second Grade: Galey Thomas		•			311
3.1 Addition: 38 + 37			•		24, 174, 319
3.2 Addition: 59 + 13			•		158, 319
3.3 Subtraction: 70 − 59			•		161, 320

(continued)

Clip Number/Focus	K	Grade 2	Grade 3	Grade 5	Page Number
3.4 Subtraction: $70 - 34$			•		6, 321
3.5 Multiplication String: 7×7			•		245, 321
3.6 Doubling and Halving: $4 \times 7,\ 2 \times 14$			•		241, 322
3.7 Array Discussion: 8×25			•		234, 323
T.3 Third Grade: Jann Montgomery			•		316
5.1 Associative Property: 12×15				•	253, 326
5.2 Multiplication: 32×15				•	231, 327
5.3 Multiplication: 16×35				•	17, 328
5.4 Array Discussion: $150 \div 15,\ 300 \div 15$				•	236, 328
5.5 Division String: $496 \div 8$				•	261, 329
5.6 Subtraction: $1000 - 674$				•	181, 330
T.5 Fifth Grade: Lee Ann Davidson				•	324

Teaching with the Common Core State Standards for Mathematics: Video Clip Connections

Clip Number	Grade Level	Domain	Clusters for Common Core State Standards for Mathematical Content
K.1 **Ten-Frames and Dot Cards**	K	Counting and Cardinality	Know number names and the count sequence. (K.CC.2) Count to tell the number of objects. (K.CC.4, K.CC.5) Compare numbers. (K.CC.6)
		Operations and Algebraic Thinking	Understand addition, and understand subtraction. (K.OA.3)
K.2 **Rekenreks**	K	Counting and Cardinality	Know number names and the count sequence. (K.CC.2) Count to tell the number of objects. (K.CC.4, K.CC.5) Compare numbers. (K.CC.6)
		Operations and Algebraic Thinking	Understand addition, and understand subtraction. (K.OA.3)
K.3 **Counting Book**	K	Counting and Cardinality	Know number names and the count sequence. (K.CC.2) Count to tell the number of objects. (K.CC.4, K.CC.5) Compare numbers. (K.CC.6)
		Operations and Algebraic Thinking	Understand addition, and understand subtraction. (K.OA.3)

(continued)

Clip Number	Grade Level	Domain	Clusters for Common Core State Standards for Mathematical Content
2.1 Ten-Frames: 8 + 6	1	Operations and Algebraic Thinking	Represent and solve problems involving addition and subtraction. (1.OA.1) Understand and apply properties of operations and the relationship between addition and subtraction. (1.OA.3) Add and subtract within 20. (1.OA.5, 1.OA.6) Work with addition and subtraction equations. (1.OA.7, 1.OA.8)
		Number and Operations in Base Ten	Understand place value. (1.NBT.2)
	2	Operations and Algebraic Thinking	Represent and solve problems involving addition and subtraction. (2.OA.1) Add and subtract within 20. (2.OA.2)
		Number and Operations in Base Ten	Use place value understanding and properties of operations to add and subtract. (2.NBT.5, 2.NBT.9)
2.2 Addition: 16 + 15	1	Operations and Algebraic Thinking	Understand and apply properties of operations and the relationship between addition and subtraction. (1.OA.B.3) Work with addition and subtraction equations. (1.OA.D.7, 1.OA.D.8)
		Number and Operations in Base Ten	Understand place value. (1.NBT.B.2) Use place value understanding and properties of operations to add and subtract. (1.NBT.C.4, 1.NBT.C.5)
	2	Operations and Algebraic Thinking	Represent and solve problems involving addition and subtraction. (2.OA.A.1) Add and subtract within 20. (2.OA.B.2)

Clip Number	Grade Level	Domain	Clusters for Common Core State Standards for Mathematical Content
		Number and Operations in Base Ten	Use place value understanding and properties of operations to add and subtract. (2.NBT.B.5, 2.NBT.B.6, 2.NBT.B.9)
2.3 Addition: 26 + 27	1	Operations and Algebraic Thinking	Understand and apply properties of operations and the relationship between addition and subtraction. (1.OA.B.3) Work with addition and subtraction equations. (1.OA.D.7, 1.OA.D.8)
		Number and Operations in Base Ten	Understand place value. (1.NBT.B.2) Use place value understanding and the properties of operations to add and subtraction. (1.NBT.C.4, 1.NBT.C.5)
	2	Operations and Algebraic Thinking	Represent and solve problems involving addition and subtraction. (2.OA.A.1) Add and subtract within 20. (2.OA.B.2)
		Number and Operations in Base Ten	Use place value understanding and properties of operations to add and subtract. (2.NBT.B.5, 2.NBT.B.6, 2.NBT.B.9)
3.1 Addition: 38 + 37	2	Operations and Algebraic Thinking	Represent and solve problems involving addition and subtraction. (2.OA.A.1) Add and subtract within 20. (2.OA.B.2)
		Number and Operations in Base Ten	Use place value understanding and properties of operations to add and subtract. (2.NBT.B.5, 2.NBT.B.6, 2.NBT.B.9)
	3	Number and Operations in Base Ten	Use place value understanding and properties of operations to perform multi-digit arithmetic. (3.NBT.A.1, 3.NBT.A.2)
3.2 Addition: 59 + 13	2	Operations and Algebraic Thinking	Represent and solve problems involving addition and subtraction. (2.OA.A.1) Add and subtract within 20. (2.OA.B.2)

(continued)

Clip Number	Grade Level	Domain	Clusters for Common Core State Standards for Mathematical Content
	3	Number and Operations in Base Ten	Use place value understanding and properties of operations to perform multi-digit arithmetic. (3.NBT.A.1, 3.NBT.A.2)
3.3 Subtraction: 70 − 59	2	Operations and Algebraic Thinking	Represent and solve problems involving addition and subtraction. (2.OA.A.1) Add and subtract within 20. (2.OA.B.2)
		Number and Operations in Base Ten	Use place value understanding and properties of operations to add and subtract. (2.NBT.B.5, 2.NBT.B.7, 2.NBT.B.9)
	3	Number and Operations in Base Ten	Use place value understanding and properties of operations to perform multi-digit arithmetic. (3.NBT.A.1, 3.NBT.A.2)
3.4 Subtraction: 70 − 34	2	Operations and Algebraic Thinking	Represent and solve problems involving addition and subtraction. (2.OA.A.1) Add and subtract within 20. (2.OA.B.2)
		Number and Operations in Base Ten	Use place value understanding and properties of operations to add and subtract. (2.NBT.B.5, 2.NBT.B.7, 2.NBT.B.9)
	3	Number and Operations in Base Ten	Use place value understanding and properties of operations to perform multi-digit arithmetic. (3.NBT.A.1, 3.NBT.A.2)
3.5 Multiplication String: 7×7	3	Operations and Algebraic Thinking	Represent and solve problems involving multiplication and division. (3.OA.A.1, 3.OA.A.3, 3.OA.A.4) Understand properties of multiplication and the relationship between multiplication and division. (3.OA.B.5) Multiply and divide within 100. (3.OA.C.7) Solve problems involving the four operations, and identify and explain patterns in arithmetic. (3.OA.D.9)

Clip Number	Grade Level	Domain	Clusters for Common Core State Standards for Mathematical Content
3.6 Doubling and Halving: $4 \times 7, 2 \times 14$	3	Operations and Algebraic Thinking	Represent and solve problems involving multiplication and division. (3.OA.A.1, 3.OA.A.3, 3.OA.A.4) Understand properties of multiplication and the relationship between multiplication and division. (3.OA.B.5) Multiply and divide within 100. (3.OA.C.7) Solve problems involving the four operations, and identify and explain patterns in arithmetic. (3.OA.D.9)
		Number and Operations in Base Ten	Use place value understanding and properties of operations to perform multi-digit arithmetic. (3.NBT.A.3)
5.1 Associative Property: 12×15	4	Operations and Algebraic Thinking	Use the four operations with whole numbers to solve problems. (4.OA.A.1, 4.OA.A.2, 4.OA.A.3) Gain familiarity with factors and multiples. (4.OA.B.4)
		Number and Operations in Base Ten	Generalize place value understanding for multi-digit whole numbers. (4.NBT.A.1, 4.NBT.A.2) Use place value understanding and properties of operations to perform multi-digit arithmetic. (4.NBT.B.5) Understand the place value system. (5.NBT.A.1, 5.NBT.A.2)
	5	Operations and Algebraic Thinking	Write and interpret numerical expressions. (5.OA.A.1)
		Number and Operations in Base Ten	Understand the place value system. (5.NBT.A.1, 5.NBT.A.2) Perform operations with multi-digit whole numbers and with decimals to hundredths. (5.NBT.B.5)
5.2 Multiplication: 32×15	4	Operations and Algebraic Thinking	Use the four operations with whole numbers to solve problems. (4.OA.A.1, 4.OA.A.2, 4.OA.A.3)

(continued)

Clip Number	Grade Level	Domain	Clusters for Common Core State Standards for Mathematical Content
		Number and Operations in Base Ten	Generalize place value understanding for multi-digit whole numbers. (4.NBT.A.1, 4.NBT.A.2) Use place value understanding and properties of operations to perform multi-digit arithmetic. (4.NBT.B.5)
	5	Operations and Algebraic Thinking	Write and interpret numerical expressions. (5.OA.A.1)
		Number and Operations in Base Ten	Understand the place value system. (5.NBT.A.1, 5.NBT.A.2) Perform operations with multi-digit whole numbers and with decimals to hundredths. (5NBT.B.5, 5.NBT.B.6, 5.NBT.B.7)
5.3 Multiplication: 16 × 35	4	Operations and Algebraic Thinking	Use the four operations with whole numbers to solve problems. (4.OA.A.1, 4.OA.A.2, 4.OA.A.3)
		Number and Operations in Base Ten	Generalize place value understanding for multi-digit whole numbers. (4.NBT.A.1, 4.NBT.A.2) Use place value understanding and properties of operations to perform multi-digit arithmetic. (4.NBT.B.5)
	5	Operations and Algebraic Thinking	Write and interpret numerical expressions. (5.OA.A.1)
		Number and Operations in Base Ten	Understand the place value system. (5.NBT.A.1, 5.NBT.A.2) Perform operations with multi-digit whole numbers and with decimals to hundredths. (5NBT.B.5, 5.NBT.B.6, 5.NBT.B.7)
5.4 Array Discussion: 150 ÷ 15, 300 ÷ 15	4	Operations and Algebraic Thinking	Use the four operations with whole numbers to solve problems. (4.OA.A.1, 4.OA.A.2, 4.OA.A.3)

Clip Number	Grade Level	Domain	Clusters for Common Core State Standards for Mathematical Content
		Number and Operations in Base Ten	Generalize place value understanding for multi-digit whole numbers. (4.NBT.A.1, 4.NBT.A.2) Use place value understanding and properties of operations to perform multi-digit arithmetic. (4.NBT.B.5)
	5	Number and Operations in Base Ten	Understand the place value system. (5.NBT.A.1, 5.NBT.A.2) Perform operations with multi-digit whole numbers and with decimals to hundredths. (5.NBT.B.5, 5.NBT.B.6, 5.NBT.B.7)
5.5 Division String: $496 \div 8$	**4**	Operations and Algebraic Thinking	Use the four operations with whole numbers to solve problems. (4.OA.A.1, 4.OA.A.2, 4.OA.A.3)
		Number and Operations in Base Ten	Generalize place value understanding for multi-digit whole numbers. (4.NBT.A.1, 4.NBT.A.2) Use place value understanding and properties of operations to perform multi-digit arithmetic. (4.NBT.B.5)
	5	Number and Operations in Base Ten	Understand the place value system. (5.NBT.A.1, 5.NBT.A.2) Perform operations with multi-digit whole numbers and with decimals to hundredths. (5.NBT.B.5, 5.NBT.B.6, 5.NBT.B.7)
5.6 Subtraction: $1000 - 674$	**3**	Number and Operations in Base Ten	Use place value understanding and properties of operations to perform multi-digit arithmetic. (3.NBT.A.1, 3.NBT.A.2)
	4	Number and Operations in Base Ten	Generalize place value understanding for multi-digit whole numbers. (4.NBT.A.1, 4.NBT.A.2)
	5	Number and Operations in Base Ten	Perform operations with multi-digit whole numbers and with decimals to hundredths.

Guidelines for Watching Videos of Teaching

The teachers who agreed to be recorded in these videos have complex and challenging classrooms, just like you. When we watch videos of others it is easy to see things that we might do differently. It is then all too easy to move to a critical stance, focusing on what the teacher "should" have done differently. But we have found that such a stance is not helpful for learning.

These videos are not scripted or rehearsed. They are real classroom sessions. Remember that teaching is a complicated activity, in which the teacher is required to do many things at once. As you watch these videos, alone or with others, we recommend following these rules:

1. Assume that there are many things you don't know about the students, the classroom, and the shared history of the teacher and students in the video.

2. Assume good intent and expertise on the part of the teacher. If you cannot understand his or her actions, try to hypothesize what might have motivated him or her.

3. Keep focused on your observations about what students are getting out of the talk and interaction.

4. Keep focused on how the classroom discourse is serving the mathematical goals of the lesson.

Source: From *Talk Moves: A Teacher's Guide for Using Talk Moves to Support the Common Core and More, Third Edition* by Suzanne H. Chapin, Catherine O'Connor, and Nancy Canavan Anderson (Math Solutions, 2013, xxi).

Section I

Understanding Number Talks

CHAPTER 1
What Is a Classroom Number Talk?

Rationale for Number Talks

Recently, during a visit to a second-grade classroom, I watched Melanie subtract 7 from 13. She had written the problem vertically on her paper and began solving it using the standard U.S. algorithm for subtraction.

$$
\begin{array}{r}
0\ 13 \\
\cancel{13} \\
-\ \ 7 \\
\hline
6
\end{array}
$$

I asked Melanie to share her thinking about this problem. She said, "I couldn't take seven from three so I borrowed ten. And I made the one a zero and the three became thirteen. And thirteen minus seven is six."

When asked why she chose to solve the problem this way, Melanie replied, "That's just how you do it when the bottom number is bigger than the top."

In a third-grade classroom, I also observed students using the standard U.S. algorithm to solve the problem $328 - 69$.

$$
\begin{array}{r}
2\ 11\ 18 \\
\cancel{328} \\
-\ \ \ 69 \\
\hline
259
\end{array}
$$

I was curious about their understanding of this process and posed, "When you crossed out the numbers in three hundred twenty-eight and wrote different numbers above it, did you still have an amount that is the same as in three hundred twenty-eight?" The students looked puzzled by this question and collectively replied, "No, you have a different amount, because you have a two, an eleven, and an eighteen. That's why you can minus the six and the nine." Their struggle to make the connection between decomposing or breaking apart 328 into 200 + 110 + 18 was an indication that they did not fully understand the method they had been taught.

Like Melanie and this group of third graders, our classrooms are filled with students and adults who think of mathematics as rules and procedures to memorize without understanding the numerical relationships that provide the foundation for these rules. The teaching of mathematics has been viewed as a discrete set of rules and procedures to be implemented with speed and accuracy but without necessarily understanding the mathematical logic. For some people, learning mathematics as procedures has been successful; but for the majority of our nation, knowledge of mathematical rules has not allowed them to use math confidently in their daily lives. With almost two-thirds of the nation's adult population fearful of mathematics, they have simply said "No" to mathematics and closed the doors to careers that require higher math (Burns 1998).

Today's students often elect not to pursue more complex mathematics courses and careers that require higher math after negative experiences with earlier mathematics and algebra. Their foundation based on memorization crumbles when they are called to generalize arithmetic relationships in algebra courses. Robert Moses, an avid proponent for equity in mathematics, refers to algebra as a gatekeeper with far-reaching effects on an individual's ability to succeed. "So algebra, once solely in place as the gatekeeper for higher math and the priesthood who gained access to it, now is the gatekeeper for citizenship; and people who don't have it are like the people who couldn't read and write in the industrial age" (Moses and Cobb 2001, 14).

While our current understanding and approaches to mathematics may have been sufficient during earlier time periods in the United States, today's information age requires students and adults to develop a deeper understanding of mathematics. Our students must have the ability to reason about quantitative information, possess number sense,

> Our classrooms are filled with students and adults who think of mathematics as rules and procedures to memorize without understanding the numerical relationships that provide the foundation for these rules.

and check for the reasonableness of solutions and answers. We need citizens who are able to discern whether numbers make sense and are applicable to specific situations and who are capable of communicating solutions to problems. Today's mathematics curricula and instruction must focus on preparing students to be mathematically proficient and compute accurately, efficiently, and flexibly.

What does it mean to compute with accuracy, efficiency, and flexibility? *Accuracy* denotes the ability to produce an accurate answer; *efficiency* refers to the ability to choose an appropriate, expedient strategy for a specific computation problem; and *flexibility* means the ability to use number relationships with ease in computation. Take as an example the problem 49 × 5. A student exhibits these qualities in her thinking if she can use the relationship between 49 and 50 to think about the problem as 50 × 5 and then subtract one group of 5 to arrive at the answer of 245. If our goal is to create students who meet the above criteria, we must provide opportunities for them to grapple with number relationships, apply these relationships to computation strategies, and discuss and analyze their reasoning.

> *Accuracy* denotes the ability to produce an accurate answer; *efficiency* refers to the ability to choose an appropriate, expedient strategy for a specific computation problem; and *flexibility* means the ability to use number relationships with ease in computation.

The introduction of number talks is a pivotal vehicle for developing efficient, flexible, and accurate computation strategies that build upon the key foundational ideas of mathematics such as composition and decomposition of numbers, our system of tens, and the application of properties. Classroom conversations and discussions around purposefully crafted computation problems are at the very core of number talks. These are opportunities for the class to come together to share their mathematical thinking. The problems in a number talk are designed to elicit specific strategies that focus on number relationships and number theory. Students are presented with problems in either a whole- or small-group setting and are expected to learn to mentally solve them accurately, efficiently, and flexibly. By sharing and defending their solutions and strategies, students are provided with opportunities to collectively reason about numbers while building connections to key conceptual ideas in mathematics. A typical classroom number talk can be conducted in five to fifteen minutes.

A Number Talk: Key Components

Recently, I had the opportunity to visit Ms. Morton's third-grade classroom where number talks are an integral component of math

Classroom Link: Subtraction: 70 – 34
Classroom Clip 3.4

Before you watch the third-grade number talk for 70 – 34, think about how you would mentally solve this problem.

As you watch the third-grade number talk for 70 – 34, consider:

1. How are students using number relationships to solve the problem?

2. How would you describe the classroom community and environment?

3. Which strategies demonstrate accuracy, efficiency, and flexibility?

4. How are the students' strategies similar to or different from your strategy?

For commentary on the above, see Appendix A: Author's Video Reflections.

To view this video clip, scan the QR code or access via mathsolutions.com /NTWNC34

CCSS

Mathematical Practice 1: Make sense of problems and persevere in solving them.

A cornerstone of a mathematically powerful individual is the ability to make sense of and persevere when solving problems. When problems are introduced at the beginning of a number talk, students look for number relationships to plan their strategies and seek alternate ways to verify their reasoning. Developing flexibility in looking at problems from multiple perspectives builds perseverance as well as provides a system of checks and balances. As students share their answers and strategies, they must evaluate other ideas and approaches. Class discussions around reasonableness of answers and analyzing strategies for sense-making further develop this mathematical disposition.

---

instruction. The third graders are sitting in the front of the classroom while Ms. Morton writes the problem *102 − 76* horizontally on the chalkboard. Within seconds students begin to place their thumbs on their chests, signaling that they have mentally arrived at a solution. Ms. Morton asks, "What answer did you get?" Students raise their hands, and the teacher records all student answers on the chalkboard: *26, 126.* "Who would like to defend their answer?" she poses.

Sylvia says, "I want to defend twenty-six. I used an adding-up strategy. I added four to seventy-six to make eighty, and then added on twenty to get to one hundred, plus two more to get to one hundred two. So the four plus twenty plus two gave me twenty-six."

As Sylvia shares her strategy, Ms. Morton uses an open number line to model Sylvia's thinking. (See Figure 1–1.)

"Did anyone think about this problem in a different way?" questions Ms. Morton.

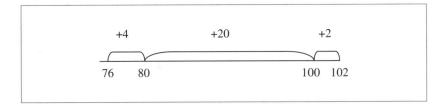

Figure 1–1   *Adding-Up Strategy for 102 − 76*

"I got twenty-six, too, but I did it another way. I added on four to each number to change the problem to one hundred six minus eighty, and I knew that one hundred six minus eighty was twenty-six. And that was easy to solve in my head!" shares Brendan.

$$
\begin{array}{r}
102 + 4 = 106 \\
-\ 76 + 4 = -\ 80 \\
\hline
26
\end{array}
$$

"Do you follow Brendan's strategy? Can we prove it using the number line?" asks Ms. Morton.

"I do," offers Carla. "I think it will always work, because you're keeping the space between the numbers the same."

"What do you mean?" questions Marquez.

"Well, let's say you have the problem five minus three. We know that's going to be two, right? Well, if you add the same amount to both the three and the five, you will still get two when you subtract."

"Let's test Carla's idea," proposes Sierra.

Carla shares, "I'll use the problem five minus three again. If we add one to the five and one to the three, the problem would become six minus four, which still equals two. If we added two to the five and two to the three, then we'd get the problem seven minus five and this still equals two. We could even add three to each of the numbers to make eight minus six, and it still comes out as two!" (See Figure 1–2.)

Melinda jumps up to the number line on the board. "Oh, I get it! You're moving both of the numbers up the same amount on the number line, so the distance between them stays the same! As long

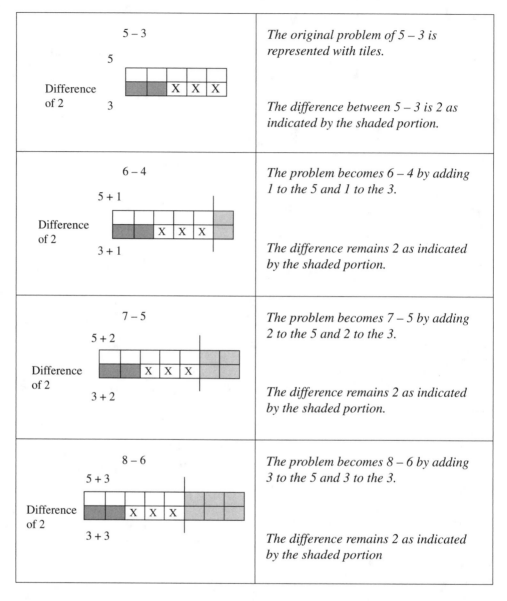

5 – 3 5 Difference of 2 3	*The original problem of 5 – 3 is represented with tiles.* *The difference between 5 – 3 is 2 as indicated by the shaded portion.*
6 – 4 5 + 1 Difference of 2 3 + 1	*The problem becomes 6 – 4 by adding 1 to the 5 and 1 to the 3.* *The difference remains 2 as indicated by the shaded portion.*
7 – 5 5 + 2 Difference of 2 3 + 2	*The problem becomes 7 – 5 by adding 2 to the 5 and 2 to the 3.* *The difference remains 2 as indicated by the shaded portion.*
8 – 6 5 + 3 Difference of 2 3 + 3	*The problem becomes 8 – 6 by adding 3 to the 5 and 3 to the 3.* *The difference remains 2 as indicated by the shaded portion*

Figure 1–2   *Square Tiles to Represent the Constant Difference Strategy for 5 – 3*

as you add the same amount to each number, the difference will stay the same!"

Marquez says, "I see now, but why did you add four to each number in the problem one hundred two minus seventy-six?"

"Because I was trying to get the seventy-six to an even ten of eighty," replies Brendan.

"So, this is a strategy we might want to investigate a little further today after our number talk," responds Ms. Morton. "I noticed that we have two strategies that support the answer of twenty-six for our original problem of one hundred two minus seventy-six. We also have the answer of one hundred twenty-six. Would someone share their thinking about this answer?"

"I don't think it's reasonable," offers Conner, "because seventy-six plus just thirty more puts you over one hundred two."

"Agree," several students chime in while nodding their heads in agreement with Conner.

Robert speaks up, "I disagree with myself, but I'm not sure why my strategy didn't work. I put the problem up and down in my head. I couldn't take six from two, so I went next door to borrow a ten. So I crossed out the zero and made it a nine and made the two a twelve. Twelve minus six is six and nine minus seven is two, and then I brought down the one. That's how I got the answer one hundred twenty-six."

$$
\begin{array}{r}
9\ 12 \\
1\cancel{0}\cancel{2} \\
-\ \ 76 \\
\hline
126
\end{array}
$$

"Oh, I think I see what you're trying to do," offers Amelia. "Are you trying to borrow ten from the one hundred and give it to the two? It's really like breaking up one hundred into ninety and ten or renaming one hundred two to ninety plus twelve."

As an upper-grade elementary teacher, my initial classroom experiences were full of Roberts, and I grew to predict with certainty the errors that would come with regrouping in addition, borrowing in subtraction, multiplying with multidigit numbers, and applying the steps of long division. We would study and practice the procedures for computing with these operations, but students continued to produce answers that were far from reasonable. My students were trying to remember the rules and apply them, but for the majority of them, math simply did not make sense.

For the students in Ms. Morton's classroom, math is about making sense of numerical relationships. They understand place value and can apply this concept in their computation. They can compose and decompose numbers and use these relationships to structure efficient, flexible, and accurate strategies. They know there is a strong connection between addition and subtraction, and they build upon this relationship with adding up on the number line. They understand that subtraction involves finding the difference between quantities. Students are able to defend their thinking and support it with mathematical reasoning and proof.

We can extract several key components of number talks from Ms. Morton's classroom. While each of these components will be discussed separately, they are interdependent and tightly interwoven:

> *Key Components of Number Talks*
>
> 1. Classroom environment and community
>
> 2. Classroom discussions
>
> 3. The teacher's role
>
> 4. The role of mental math
>
> 5. Purposeful computation problems

Classroom Environment and Community

Building a cohesive classroom community is essential for creating a safe, risk-free environment for effective number talks. Students should be comfortable in offering responses for discussion, questioning themselves and their peers, and investigating new strategies. The culture of the classroom should be one of acceptance based on a common quest for learning and understanding. Did you notice how Robert was willing to risk being incorrect with his peers, and how his fellow classmates were committed to working toward a collective understanding?

It takes time to establish a community of learners built on mutual respect, but if you consistently set this expectation from the beginning, students will respond.

Classroom Discussions

During a number talk, the teacher writes a problem on the board and gives the students time to solve the problem mentally. Students start with their fists held to their chests and indicate when they are ready with a solution by quietly raising a thumb. Once students have found an answer, they are encouraged to continue finding efficient strategies while others are thinking. They indicate that they have found other approaches by raising another finger for each solution. This quiet form of acknowledgement allows time for students to think, while the process continues to challenge those who already have an answer. When most of the students have indicated they have a solution and strategy, the teacher calls for answers. All answers—correct and incorrect—are recorded on the board for students to consider.

Students are now given the opportunity to share their strategies and justifications with their peers. The benefits of sharing and discussing computation strategies are highlighted as follows:

> **Benefits of Sharing and Discussing Computation Strategies**
>
> Students have the opportunity to:
>
> 1. Clarify their own thinking.
>
> 2. Consider and test other strategies to see if they are mathematically logical.
>
> 3. Investigate and apply mathematical relationships.
>
> 4. Build a repertoire of efficient strategies.
>
> 5. Make decisions about choosing efficient strategies for specific problems.

Do children come up with incorrect answers in number talks? Absolutely. However, students are asked to defend or justify their answers to prove their thinking to their peers. In number talk classrooms, students have a sense of shared authority in determining whether an answer is accurate. The teacher is not the ultimate authority, and students are expected to think carefully about the solutions and strategies presented.

In number talks, wrong answers are used as opportunities to unearth misconceptions and for students to investigate their thinking and learn from their mistakes. In a number talk classroom, mistakes play an important role in learning. They provide opportunities to question and analyze thinking, bring misconceptions to the forefront, and solidify understanding. Helping students realize that mistakes are opportunities for learning is an important cornerstone in building a learning community.

The Teacher's Role

As educators, we are accustomed to assuming the roles of telling and explaining. Teaching by telling is the method most of us experienced as students, and we have continued to emulate this model in our own practice. Since a goal of number talks is to help students make sense of mathematics by building upon mathematical relationships, our role must shift from being the sole authority in imparting information and confirming correct answers to assuming the interrelated roles of facilitator, questioner, listener, and learner.

> Since the heart of number talks is classroom conversations, it is appropriate for the teacher to move into the role of facilitator.

Since the heart of number talks is classroom conversations, it is appropriate for the teacher to move into the role of facilitator. Keeping the discussion focused on the important mathematics and helping students learn to structure their comments and wonderings during a number talk is essential to ensure that the conversation flows in a meaningful and natural manner. As a facilitator, you must guide the students to ponder and discuss examples that build upon your purposes. By posing such questions as "How does Joey's strategy connect to the ideas in Renee's strategy?" you are leading the conversations to build on meaningful mathematics.

When I began listening to my students' thinking, I realized I had much to learn about students' natural intuitions regarding numbers. Instead of only concentrating on a final, correct answer and one procedure for getting there, I began to broaden my scope to engage in listening to and learning about students' natural thinking through asking open-ended questions. My initial focus of "What answer did you get?" shifted to include "*How* did you get your answer?" I had made an assumption that all of my students solved their computation problems in the way I had taught them. While initially I was only interested in finding out their final answers to a problem such as 16 + 17, my focus broadened to learning about *how* they arrived at their answers and *why*. Did they use the doubles of 15 + 15 to solve 16 + 17, or did they combine the 10s to make 20 and then add the 13 from the total in the ones column? This was information I did not know and could use to help them look at how numbers are interrelated in different operations. By changing my question from "What answer did you get?" to "How did you solve this problem?" I was able to understand how they were making sense of mathematics.

> By changing my question from "What answer did you get?" to "How did you solve this problem?" I was able to understand how they were making sense of mathematics.

The Role of Mental Math

Mental computation is a key component of number talks because it encourages students to build on number relationships to solve problems instead of relying on memorized procedures. One of the purposes of a number talk is for the students to focus on number relationships and use these relationships to develop efficient, flexible strategies with accuracy. When students approach problems without paper and pencil, they are encouraged to rely on what they know and understand about the numbers and how they are interrelated. Mental computation causes them to be efficient with the numbers to avoid holding numerous quantities in their heads.

An example that illustrates this idea is a common strategy for solving the problem 12×49. If students think about multiplying by a multiple of 10, they often change the 49 to 50 and multiply 12×50 for a product of 600. Since they multiplied by one extra group of 12, they subtract 12 for a final answer of 588. This strategy not only exhibits flexibility with the numbers, but is an efficient strategy that produces an accurate answer.

Another rationale for mental computation is to help strengthen students' understanding of place value. By looking at numbers as whole quantities instead of discrete columns of digits, students have to use their knowledge of place value. During initial number talks, problems are often written in a horizontal format to encourage the student's thinking in this realm. As students become accustomed to reasoning about the magnitude of numbers and utilizing place value in their strategies, the teacher may present problems both horizontally and vertically.

A problem such as $199 + 199$ helps illustrate this reasoning. By writing this problem horizontally, you encourage a student to think about and utilize the value of the entire number. A student with a strong sense of number and place value should be able to consider that 199 is close to 200; therefore, 200 + 200 is 400 minus the two extra 1s for a final answer of 398:

$$199 + 199$$
$$\underline{1 + \quad 1}$$
$$200 + 200 = 400$$
$$\underline{- \quad 2}$$
$$398$$

Recording this same problem in a vertical format can encourage students to ignore the magnitude of each digit and its place value. A student who sees each column as a column of ones would not be using real place values in the numbers if they are thinking about 9 + 9, 9 + 9, and 1 + 1:

$$
\begin{array}{r}
1\,|\,1 \\
1\,|\,9\,|\,9 \\
+\ 1\,|\,9\,|\,9 \\
\hline
3\,|\,9\,|\,8
\end{array}
$$

Purposeful Computation Problems

Crafting problems that guide students to focus on mathematical relationships is an essential part of number talks that is used to build mathematical understanding and knowledge. The teacher's goals and purposes for the number talk should determine the numbers and operations that are chosen. Careful planning before the number talk is necessary to design "just right" problems for students.

For example, if the goal is to help students use strategies that build upon using tens, starting with numbers multiplied by 10 followed by problems with 9 in the ones column creates a situation where this type of strategy is important. Problems such as 20×4, 19×4, 30×3, 29×3, 40×6, and 39×6 lend themselves to strategies where students use tens as friendly or landmark numbers. In the problem 19×4, the goal would be for students to think about 20×4 and subtract 4 from the product of 80, because they added on one extra group of 4. The other problems sets are designed to elicit a similar approach. In later number talks the teacher would start with a number with 9 in the ones column without starting with the multiple of 10.

Does this mean that given a well-crafted series of problems, students will always develop strategies that align with the teacher's purpose? No. Numerous strategies exist for any given problem; however, specific types of problems typically elicit certain strategies. Take, for instance, the same 19 × 4 problem that was crafted to target students' thinking using tens. Students could approach this problem in a variety of ways including, but not limited to, the following:

- Break the 19 into 10 + 9; then multiply 10 × 4 and 9 × 4 and combine these products.

- Break the 4 into 2 + 2; then multiply 2 × 19 and 2 × 19 and combine these products.

- Add 19 + 19 + 19 + 19, or add 4 nineteen times.

However, a mixture of random problems such as 39 × 5, 65 − 18, and 148 + 324 do not lend themselves to a common strategy. While this series of problems may be used as practice for mental computation, it does not initiate a common focus for a number talk discussion.

Summary

In this chapter we have looked at how number talks can be a purposeful vehicle for

1. making sense of mathematics;

2. developing efficient computation strategies;

3. communicating mathematically; and

4. reasoning and proving solutions.

In the following chapters, we will investigate how to design purposeful number talks with addition, subtraction, multiplication, and division while building on foundational concepts in arithmetic.

CHAPTER 2

How Do I Prepare for Number Talks?

Establishing Procedures and Setting Expectations: The Four Essentials

While a number talk is designed to be only five to fifteen minutes in duration, the potential for mathematical impact is significant. It is critical that students come ready to think, listen, share, and question themselves and their peers. This concentrated period should be a time of coming together as a community of learners with a common focus and purpose. Building this environment takes time, patience, and consistency. Establishing the following procedures and expectations are essential to number talks:

Four Procedures and Expectations Essential to Number Talks

1. Select a designated location that allows you to maintain close proximity to your students for informal observations and interactions.

2. Provide appropriate wait time for the majority of the students to access the problem.

3. Accept, respect, and consider all answers.

4. Encourage student communication throughout the number talk.

Classroom Link: Multiplication: 16 × 35
Classroom Clip 5.3

Before you watch the fifth-grade number talk for 16 × 35, think about how you would mentally solve this problem.

As you watch the fifth-grade number talk for 16 × 35, consider:

1. How does the teacher facilitate the classroom discussion?

2. What procedures are in place that allow students to share their thinking?

3. What opportunities exist for the teacher to informally assess student understanding?

4. What conditions are present that foster a safe learning community?

5. How is student communication encouraged and valued?

6. How would you describe the teacher's role during the number talk?

For commentary on the above, see Appendix A: Author's Video Reflections.

To view this video clip, scan the QR code or access via mathsolutions.com /NTWNC53

Mathematical Practice 6: Attend to precision.

Often we think of precision as accuracy. While this definition of precision is a goal of number talks, precision also refers to efficiency in solving problems. During number talks discussions, targeting efficiency is critical to help students refine their strategies. Consider a first-grade problem such as 5 + 7. Possible student approaches are:

- Counting All
- Counting On from 5
- Counting On from 7
- Making a quick 10 by decomposing 5 into 2 + 3 and combining the 3 and 7
- Doubles Plus or Minus 2 by adding either (5 + 5) + 2 or (7 + 7) − 2

While each strategy will result in an accurate answer, there is a progression of precision or efficiency. Having conversations during number talks that focus on efficiency allows students to attend to precision.

A fellow student in this fifth-grade clip raises the question of efficiency with a partial products' strategy. As students gain more flexibility with different strategies, we want to continue to encourage them to discern which strategy is most efficient given a specific set of numbers.

1. Select a designated location that allows you to maintain close proximity to your students for informal observations and interactions.

One way to elevate the status of number talk time and signal its importance is to have a specific location in the classroom where the students gather for this purpose. The physical act of moving to a designated space serves as a reminder that the class is transitioning as learners into a unique time of the day. Some teachers choose to use an area in their classroom that is set apart with a large rug; others move to a section of the classroom with a large writing space. I prefer to gather my students close to me on the floor by a whiteboard or chalkboard. While many teachers wish to have their students remain at their desks, I have found that it is easier to build a cohesive community and a focused discussion when students shift away from their regular routines and are removed from typical desk distractions.

Number talks offer an opportunity to glean information about each student's thinking and approach to the problems. Having the children in close proximity allows you to observe whether the students are using or developing an overreliance on certain tools during mental computation. Possible situations to note for second- through fifth-grade students are

- use of fingers for calculations, especially basic facts;
- access to a posted number line or hundreds chart; or
- reliance on the standard U.S. algorithm by writing the problem on the floor or in the air with their fingers.

Positioning yourself in front of your students also allows you to informally assess who is struggling, who readily has an answer, and who is not engaged. Observing student participation during the sharing of strategies will also help in planning appropriate follow-up.

2. Provide appropriate wait time to ensure that the majority of the students have accessed the problem.

> One of the purposes of a number talk is to bring equity to the math classroom. We want *all* students to think; therefore, wait until you see an indication that most students have accessed the problem.

By waiting to collect answers until most of the students have signaled with a quiet thumb that they are ready, you send the message that *all* students are expected to think and contribute during this time. Many students have the misconception that they are not good at math because they are not fast. We can easily reinforce this misconception if we begin gathering answers as soon as the first students are ready.

One reason to establish the protocol of using the quiet thumb signal is to keep all students engaged and thinking. Once students see several hands raised, they are accustomed to stopping their thinking. They know that the teacher will call on those students who already have an answer. One of the purposes of a number talk is to bring equity to the math classroom. We want all students to think; therefore, wait until you see an indication that most students have accessed the problem.

By using appropriate wait time, we also send the message to the students who respond quickly that they need to keep thinking about additional strategies that will work. I encourage students to place a second, third, or fourth finger up to indicate that they have two, three, or four ways to solve the problem. This provides additional challenges to students who may need them while giving everyone time to solve the problem. The aim is not to reward speed, but to focus on thinking about mathematical relationships.

3. All answers are accepted, respected, and considered.

A first step toward establishing a respectful classroom learning community is acceptance of all ideas and answers—regardless of any obvious errors. Rich mathematical discussions cannot occur if this expectation is not in place. We must remember that wrong answers are often rooted in misconceptions, and unless these ideas are allowed to be brought to the forefront, we cannot help students confront their thinking. Students who are in safe learning environments are willing to risk sharing an incorrect answer with their peers in order to grow mathematically. It is important to model and expect the acceptance of all ideas without derogatory comments. As educators we can model this by recording all answers to be considered without giving any verbal or physical expressions that indicate agreement or disagreement with any answer. The teacher may need to practice having a "blank face." Students look to teachers as the source of correct answers. Part of building a safe learning community is to shift this source of knowledge to the students by equipping them to defend the thinking behind their solutions.

If there is a large range of incorrect answers, it would be appropriate to have students discuss which answers are reasonable and which answers could be ruled out based on logic and number sense. This provides an excellent opportunity for students to estimate and further consider the relationships between the numbers.

4. Encourage student communication throughout the number talk.

A successful number talk is rooted in communication. Throughout number talks students may be asked to share individual strategies or respond to others' strategies.

Asking students to think on their own and then turn and talk to someone close to them is an important vehicle for establishing productive conversation around mathematics. Using this Think/Pair/Share technique serves two main purposes: first, all students are immediately involved and engaged, and second, children who are reluctant to speak out in a whole group will be more comfortable articulating their thinking in a smaller venue with a partner.

The Think/Pair/Share approach can be used effectively throughout the number talk. When answers are first shared, students can be asked to turn and talk to a partner about which answers are reasonable or unreasonable and why. This centers the conversation on ways to estimate and how to rule out answers that are unreasonable. After an individual strategy is shared, it would be appropriate to have students Think/Pair/Share and state the strategy in their own words or discuss what they do and do not understand. Posing whether a strategy will work in every situation also provides a time for partner talk and allows an opportunity for students to work together to test other situations.

Providing opportunities for students to articulate their thinking and reasoning is important. It allows students time to reconsider their own ideas, self-correct if needed, and clarify their understandings. The class's role during this period of sharing is to listen carefully and consider the proposed strategies. Initially, this can be difficult for teachers and students alike, because we tend to be locked into our own pathways of thinking. Having the opportunity to ponder other approaches strengthens our own mathematical foundation and understanding.

Stop and consider how you would mentally solve the problem $346 + 127$. Did you use any of the following strategies?

- Picture the numbers stacked on top of each other and solve using the standard U.S. regrouping algorithm:

$$\begin{array}{r} 1 \\ 346 \\ +127 \\ \hline 473 \end{array}$$

- Adjust both addends to make friendly numbers:

$$\begin{array}{r} 346 \quad + \quad 127 \\ +\quad 4 \quad\ + \quad 3 \\ \hline 350 \quad + \quad 130 = 480 \end{array}$$

$$480 - 7 = 473$$

- Expand each number and add like place-value quantities:

$346 + 127$

$300 + 40 + 6 + 100 + 20 + 7$

$300 + 100 = 400$

$40 + 20 = 60$

$6 + 7 = 13$

$400 + 60 + 13 = 473$

- Take an amount from one number and add that amount to the other number (compensation) to make friendlier numbers:

$$346 + 127$$
$$+\ 4 \quad -\ 4$$
$$350 + 123 = 473$$

Were any of these strategies different from the one you used? If so, did you find them more difficult to follow? Flexibility in mathematical thinking develops as we push ourselves and our students to reason through different approaches to problems. Asking students to test a new strategy they have just considered with another problem during a number talk provides an opportunity for them to continue to add strategies to their mathematical toolbox.

We must repeatedly model appropriate ways to respond to other students' strategies. Displaying sample prompts to help students learn how to frame their questions and comments may help them learn how to share their thinking in a productive manner without being negative. Possible prompts to consider are the following:

Sample Prompts

- I agree with _____ because _____.

- I do not understand _____. Can you explain this again?

- I disagree with _____ because _____.

- How did you decide to _____?

Children should clearly hear the message that they are to think about other strategies continually. It is a big idea for students to realize that there are always other possible approaches to solve a problem.

Anticipating How to Record Student Thinking

As students share each computation strategy, the teacher should record individual student thinking in a clear, concise manner that captures the big mathematical ideas presented. The first step in successfully recording student thinking is to anticipate how students will respond. Take time to think through possible strategies for each problem beforehand. This will help you as you gain confidence in listening and following student thinking. Chapters 4, 6, and 8 highlight strategies commonly used by K–2 and 3–5 students; however, many others may arise.

As you anticipate potential strategies for each problem, also consider how you will capture each student's thinking so that others may access the strategy. Consider which mathematical ideas you want to highlight and how you might record the strategies to support those specific concepts. For example, if making tens or utilizing place value is a vital component in the strategy, is there a way to make these ideas stand out in your recording?

We can use the problem 28 + 29 to look at four different strategies and ways to record each:

Four Different Strategies for Solving 28 + 29

① Student's Strategy: Making Landmark or Friendly Numbers	The Strategy as Recorded by the Teacher
Miguel: I knew twenty-five plus twenty-five was fifty, but I knew each number was more than just twenty-five. The twenty-eight had three more, and the twenty-nine had four more.	28 + 29
Teacher: So you knew twenty-eight was the same as twenty-five plus three and twenty-nine was the same as twenty-five plus four?	$(25 + 3) + (25 + 4)$ $(25 + 25) + (3 + 4)$
Miguel: Yes. The twenty-five plus twenty-five gave me fifty and the extra three and four gave me seven more. So I had fifty-seven in all.	$25 + 25 = 50$ $3 + 4 = 7$ $50 + 7 = 57$
② Student's Strategy: Making Landmark or Friendly Numbers	The Strategy as Recorded by the Teacher
Lori: I bumped both of the numbers up to friendly tens.	28 + 29
Teacher: What tens did you change them to?	

Lori: I made both of them a thirty, so thirty plus thirty is sixty. But I knew I had too much, so I minused three and got fifty-seven.

Teacher: How did you know to subtract three?

Lori: Because I added on two to the twenty-eight and one to the twenty-nine and that was three too much.

$$30 + 30 = 60$$

$$
\begin{array}{cc}
28 & 29 \\
+\ 2 & +\ 1 \\
\hline
30 & 30 = 60
\end{array}
$$

$$60 - 3 = 57$$

③ Student's Strategy: Compensation	The Strategy as Recorded by the Teacher

Darius: I wanted to make an easy ten, so I took one from the twenty-eight and gave it to the twenty-nine. That gave me twenty-seven plus thirty.

Teacher: How did you add twenty-seven plus thirty?

Darius: I started at twenty-seven and made three jumps of ten.

Teacher: Why three jumps of ten?

Darius: Because thirty is the same as three tens. So I counted from twenty-seven and went thirty-seven, forty-seven, fifty-seven.

$$
\begin{array}{cc}
28 & 29 \\
-\ 1 & +\ 1 \\
\hline
27 & 30
\end{array}
$$

$$+10 \qquad +10 \qquad +10$$

27　　　　37　　　　47　　　　57

④ Student's Strategy: Breaking Each Number into Its Place Value	The Strategy as Recorded by the Teacher

Peggy: It was easier for me to break the numbers apart and put all of the tens together and then all of the ones.

Teacher: So how did you add it up?

Peggy: I added the twenty plus twenty and got forty and eight plus nine and got seventeen. I knew I had to put the forty and seventeen together next.

$$28 + 29$$

$$(20 + 8) + (20 + 9)$$

$$(20 + 20) + (8 + 9)$$

$$40 + 17$$

(continued)

Teacher: How did you combine those?	
Peggy: Well, seventeen is the same as ten plus seven, so I added that ten to the forty and got fifty. Fifty plus seven is fifty-seven.	$40 + (10 + 7)$ $(40 + 10) + 7$ $50 + 7 = 57$

Classroom Link: Addition: 38 + 37
Classroom Clip 3.1

To view this video clip, scan the QR code or access via mathsolutions.com /NTWNC31

Before you watch the third-grade number talk for 38 + 37, anticipate possible student strategies and how you might record them.

As you watch the third-grade number talk for 38 + 37, consider:

1. How does the teacher's recording of each strategy provide access for the students?

2. Which strategies are easiest for you to understand?

3. Which strategies are more challenging to follow?

4. What mathematical concepts are being addressed during the number talk?

5. How did the teacher bring these ideas to the forefront for the class?

For commentary on the above, see Appendix A: Author's Video Reflections.

Operations and Algebraic Thinking:
Add and subtract within 20.

2.OA.B.2 Fluently add and subtract within 20 using mental strategies. By end of Grade 2, know from memory all sums of two one-digit numbers.

Number and Operations in Base Ten:
Use place value understanding and

As you record student thinking, make sure your notation is mathematically correct. One symbol to watch carefully is the equals sign. The equals sign denotes that the quantities on each side of the sign are equivalent. If we are not careful with this convention, we can easily record mathematically incorrect statements.

For example, when Lori shared, "I made both of them a thirty, so thirty plus thirty is sixty. But I knew I had too much, so I minused three and got fifty-seven" for her 28 + 29 strategy, it would be easy to record $30 + 30 = 60 - 3 = 57$. However, in doing so we would be stating that $30 + 30, 60 - 3$, and 57 are all equivalent. It would be accurate to record $28 + 29 = (30 - 2) + (30 - 1)$ because the expressions on either side of the equals sign are equivalent.

Six Ways to Develop Accountability with Students

It is definitely possible for a student to give an illusion of understanding during number talks. As a teacher, I not only want to keep the goals of accuracy, efficiency, and flexibility in the forefront, but I also want to make sure that I have a system of accountability built into the number talk process to ensure that each student is mentally participating and accessing the proposed strategies. There are numerous ways to incorporate accountability.

> *Six Ways to Develop Accountability*
>
> 1. Ask students to use finger signals to indicate the most efficient strategy.
>
> 2. Keep records of problems posed and the corresponding student strategies.
>
> 3. Hold small-group number talks throughout each week.
>
> 4. Create and post class strategy charts.
>
> 5. Require students to solve an exit problem using the discussed strategies.
>
> 6. Give a weekly computation assessment.

1. Ask students to use finger signals to indicate the most efficient strategy.

While strategies for a specific problem are still posted, have students indicate whether Strategy 1, Strategy 2, and so on is most efficient by signaling to you with their fingers. This not only allows you to make a quick, informal assessment, but it also pulls the discussion back into focus with your goals.

properties of operations to add and subtract.

3.NBT.A.1 Use place value understanding to round whole numbers to the nearest 10 or 100.

3.NBT.A.2 Fluently add and subtract within 1000 using strategies and algorithms based on place value, properties of operations, and/or the relationship between addition and subtraction.

Within the context of a number talk, multiple content standards are addressed. As the third graders share their strategies for adding 38 + 37, they provide us with clear examples of applying their understandings of place value when they break apart 38 and 37 into 30 + 8 and 30 + 7 and combine the tens and ones to efficiently add. Equally important is the use of the commutative and associative properties as the order and the grouping of the numbers are changed. By recording the student's thinking in the following manner, the properties are more clearly highlighted:

$$38 + 37$$
$$(30 + 8) + (30 + 7)$$
$$(30 + 30) + (8 + 7)$$

Flexibility with different efficient strategies and use of number relationships are exhibited as students round the original numbers to friendly tens and remove the "extras." Fluency with adding tens is exhibited as one addend is kept intact while the other is decomposed to quickly add a group of tens.

2. Keep records of problems posed and the corresponding student strategies.

Keep a record of the problems posed and which students offered specific strategies by writing the student's name next to the strategy. This is not only a great tool to share with parents during conferences, but it also helps you keep track of which students are consistently voicing their strategies and which students are rarely participating. Depending on the technological resources available, there are several ways to document this.

If you have access to a document camera, a spiral notebook works well for describing student strategies during number talks. Another option is to capture student strategies using a SMART board and computer. This type of documentation allows you to post number talks to a classroom Web page and provide continuous access to parents. Recording student strategies on overhead transparencies is another means to keep a record of student thinking. Other teachers prefer to use a whiteboard or chalkboard for number talks and transfer the strategies and student names into a notebook.

3. Hold small-group number talks throughout each week.

Incorporating small-group number talks throughout the week provides greater opportunities to focus on individual students. You can group students according to a common mathematical need, by those who need to be challenged beyond regular grade-level concepts, or by those who may be more reluctant to share in front of the whole group. Forming small, intimate groups removes the veil of anonymity and allows you to focus more carefully on individual strengths as well as factors interfering with understanding.

4. Create and post class strategy charts.

Creating and posting class strategy charts serves to support students as they ponder and try new strategies posed by their classmates. (See Figure 2–1.) Similar to anchor charts in reading, class strategy charts provide a reference for students as they work. Engage the students in formulating the strategies that are posted on charts for each of the four operations. Make sure the charts are living documents and can be added to throughout the year as new strategies are shared.

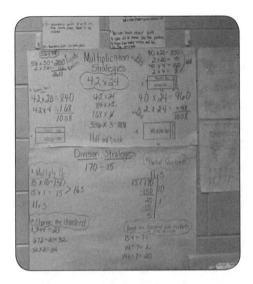

Figure 2–1   *Example of a Class Strategy Chart*

5. Require students to solve an exit problem using the discussed strategies.

As new computation strategies emerge from number talk discussions, you will want to provide students with opportunities to use and test these ideas. Requiring students to solve an exit problem using the strategies discussed encourages them to think through new ideas. I give my students an index card and request that they solve a computation problem using a strategy that was shared on one side, and on the other side they can use any strategy they wish. This allows me to get a quick look at individual understandings and misconceptions, and also helps to direct the choice of problems for our number talk on the next day. These exit cards are never graded since they are used as a formative assessment only.

6. Give a weekly computation assessment.

At the end of each week I give my third- through fifth-grade students a computation assessment consisting of five to ten problems similar to the ones used in our number talks that week. They are required to solve each problem in two ways. This reinforces the expectations in our classroom of accuracy, flexibility, and efficiency.

Gathering Tools to Model Student Strategies

If students have never been asked to reason mentally about numbers or if they are being asked to think about a new concept in computation, then it is important for them to have access to mathematical tools. Number lines and hundreds charts help students think about the magnitude of numbers and patterns in place value. Making sure that manipulatives are available but not imposed is important—especially if a student is having difficulty accessing a problem without using these materials. Color tiles, interlocking cubes, and counters are some possible manipulatives to have on hand. Ten-frames and rekenreks are important tools for the primary grades.

Starting with Five Small Steps

Making the shift toward teaching for understanding can often be overwhelming. Many of us are comfortable with telling students how to solve a problem, but it may be foreign and intimidating not to focus on giving out knowledge. The first time I led my students in a number talk, I had to concentrate on how to ask open-ended questions to elicit students' thinking versus choosing words to demonstrate how to do something. I felt awkward not knowing in advance where their conversations would go. I worried I would not be able to follow my students' thinking if it were to be different from mine. Give yourself the license to be a learner along with your students. You will be surprised how you may grow in your own understanding of mathematics! Remember that you cannot change everything at once, so starting small will be beneficial to you and your students.

Five Small Steps Toward Teaching for Understanding

1. Start with smaller problems to elicit thinking from multiple perspectives.

2. Be prepared to offer a strategy from a previous student.

3. It is all right to put a student's strategy on the back burner.

4. As a rule, limit your number talks to five to fifteen minutes.

5. Be patient with yourself and your students as you incorporate number talks into your regular math time.

1. Start with smaller problems to elicit thinking from multiple perspectives.

Using arrangements of dots is a perfect place to begin. As you show the dot arrangement for a few seconds, ask your students how many dots there are and how they can prove it. Even a simple arrangement, as in the following illustrations, can elicit multiple ways to know how many there are.

Students can prove there are six dots using multiple strategies, such as:

- Three on the top plus three on the bottom

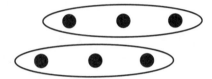

- Three groups of two

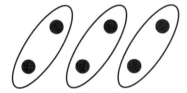

- One triangle of three plus one triangle of three

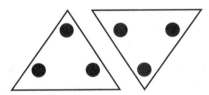

Literature from authors such as Greg Tang and Cindy Neushwander provides similar opportunities to look at multiple perspectives with pictorial representations.

Even basic math facts can be used to establish that there are many ways to view and approach a problem. Let's look at several ways that $6 + 7$ could be solved:

- using doubles ($6 + 6 = 12$ plus one more; $7 + 7 = 14$ minus one);

- making quick tens (6 can be split into 3 + 3 and 3 + 7 = 10 plus three more); and

- counting on or counting all (7, 8, 9, 10, 11, 12, 13).

2. Be prepared to offer a strategy from a previous student.

When I began number talks with my third-grade class, they had never been asked to think about number relationships or to do mental math. As I posed my first problem and allowed plenty of wait time, no thumbs went up. They needed help to know how to enter the conversation. I knew if I offered to show them how I solved the problem, they would look at me as the source of the answers. Instead, I shared a strategy that I had heard from a previous student and asked them to consider whether this was a possible way to solve the problem and whether it would always work. Sometimes it takes hearing alternative strategies before children begin to have the confidence that they can build their own.

3. It is all right to put a student's strategy on the back burner.

> One of the scariest things about leading a number talk is the fear that you will not be able to follow students' thinking or pose the right questions to help them untangle their reasoning.

One of the scariest things about leading a number talk is the fear that you will not be able to follow students' thinking or pose the right questions to help them untangle their reasoning. If I am still struggling to follow a student's logic after having the student restate the strategy, I will ask all of the students to turn and talk to someone about what they understand and questions they can pose to clarify their thinking. As I listen to their conversations, I can get a sense about whether everyone is totally confused or if there is something upon which we can build our thinking. Many times I simply tell the student who is sharing a strategy that I need time to think about it before continuing. Then I circle that strategy and meet with the student privately to work through their thinking. This honors the child's thinking while not slowing down the class conversation.

4. As a rule, limit your number talks to five to fifteen minutes.

I have found that this is one of the most difficult pieces to implement, but it is extremely important. You want your students to be thoroughly engaged during a number talk with their minds focused, so remain cognizant of their attention and adjust accordingly. Many teachers set a timer to help adhere to this time frame.

5. **Finally, be patient with yourself and your students as you incorporate number talks into your regular math time.**

Do not give up when things do not go perfectly well; make adjustments and keep moving forward. You may face resistance initially, but as your students grow in their understanding, there will be payoffs in all areas of their mathematical learning.

Summary

In this chapter we have looked at establishing procedures and expectations for number talks, recording student thinking, creating student accountability, and using tools to model student strategies. In the following chapters we discuss goals for number talks and look at ways to build number fluency and common strategies for addition, subtraction, multiplication, and division.

Student Thinking and Number Talks in the K–2 Classroom

CHAPTER 3

How Do I Develop Specific Strategies in the K–2 Classroom?

Overarching Goals

Numerical reasoning starts from the earliest stages of child development. Stacking blocks, counting objects, and filling containers are examples of beginning ideas of reasoning with numbers. As children transition into kindergarten, it is important to provide opportunities to build a foundation that mathematics is about making sense with numbers and number relationships from the very first day. Number talks in the K–2 classroom are an essential vehicle for laying this foundation and providing the building blocks to develop mathematically powerful students. To accomplish this objective it is important to focus on four overarching goals during number talks:

Four Goals for K–2 Number Talks

1. Developing number sense

2. Developing fluency with small numbers

3. Subitizing

4. Making tens

Developing Number Sense

Number sense is often discussed in math education, but what is it? Fennell and Landis (1994) state, "[Number sense] is an awareness and understanding about what numbers are, their relationships, their magnitude, the relative effect of operating on numbers, including the use of mental

Classroom Link: Ten-Frames and Dot Cards
Classroom Clip K.1

To view this video clip, scan the QR code or access via mathsolutions.com /NTWNCK1

As you watch the kindergarten number talk in which ten-frames and dot cards are used, consider:

1. How does the teacher build student fluency with small numbers?

2. What questions does the teacher pose to build understanding?

3. How are the tools and models used to support the goals of K–2 number talks?

4. What strategies are the students using to build meaning of the numbers?

5. What examples of subitizing, conserving number, and one-to-one correspondence do you notice?

6. What opportunities are created for the students to begin building an understanding of ten?

7. How does the teacher support student communication during the number talk?

For commentary on the above, see Appendix A: Author's Video Reflections.

K.OA.A.3 Decompose numbers less than or equal to 10 into pairs in more than one way, e.g., by using objects or drawings, and record each decomposition by a drawing or equation (e.g., $5 = 2 + 3$ and $5 = 4 + 1$).

K.CC.A.2 Count forward beginning from a given number within the known sequence instead of having to begin at 1.

K.CC.B.4 Understand the relationship between numbers and quantities; connect counting to cardinality.

The use of dot cards and ten-frames in a primary number talk provides an opportunity for multiple content standards to be addressed. While one of the primary goals highlighted in this classroom clip is supporting students' reasoning about ways to decompose small quantities, it also provides

mathematics and estimation" (187). Every time you elicit answers to a problem in a number talk and ask students to share whether the proposed solutions are reasonable, you are helping to build number sense. When you ask students to give an estimate before they begin thinking about a specific strategy, you are fostering number sense. As a math coach, I am frequently asked to assess struggling students. Time and time again I have found that the students I interview can rarely give an estimate to a problem. They may be able to apply a memorized procedure, but they cannot discern or justify whether their solution is reasonable. By asking students to estimate an answer before solving a problem and provide evidence that an answer is reasonable, we can help build this essential skill.

Conservation of number and one-to-one correspondence are essential foundations in building number sense for young children. Conservation of number is the understanding that the quantity of a given number of objects remains the same regardless of how it is spatially arranged. If a child is shown a group of marbles arranged in a horizontal line (see Figure 3–1a) and determines there is a quantity of five but must recount the same five marbles when represented in a different arrangement (see Figure 3–1b and c), the child would be considered unable to conserve number. A child who can conserve number will recognize that he still has five marbles without having to recount.

The development of one-to-one correspondence is also necessary in building number sense, meaningful counting, and a foundation for computation. Students who use one-to-one correspondence are able to count a set of objectives while understanding how a given quantity correlates to a specific number. This is not the same as rote counting and matching a number name to an object.

For example in rote counting, a child might count the following set of hearts by moving from one heart to the next, assigning a number name to each. In this example 3 represents the third object and not a set of three. (See Figure 3–2.) If a child has one-to-one correspondence, each number represents a collection or set of objects. Two represents two hearts and three represents a collection of hearts numbered 1, 2, and 3. (See Figure 3–3.)

One-to-one correspondence is understanding that a set of three cookies can be matched to three people, or two gloves can be placed on two hands. Students who have not yet developed one-to-one correspondence will not be able to sustain this relationship. Connecting objects with numbers allows a child to begin to count with understanding.

> opportunities for students to utilize one-to-one correspondence and other counting strategies, develop cardinality, and subitize. The simple questions "How many dots do you see, and how do you see them?" allow the teacher to serve a diverse group of learners with "just right" mathematics while addressing the Standards for Mathematical Content. From one-to-one correspondence to subitizing small quantities, a simple Quick Image number talk with these tools meets a range of needs.

> Conservation of number and one-to-one correspondence are essential foundations in building number sense for young children.

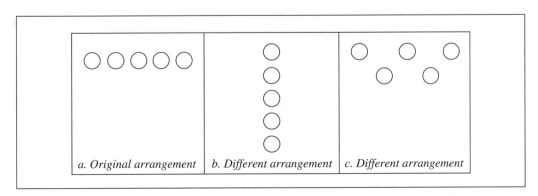

| a. Original arrangement | b. Different arrangement | c. Different arrangement |

Figure 3–1   *Original and Different Arrangements*

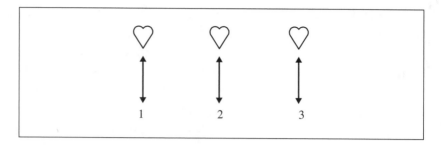

Figure 3–2   *Rote Counting*

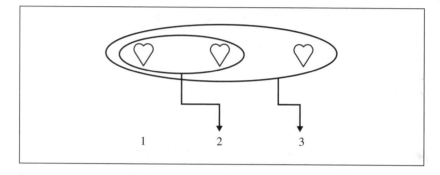

Figure 3–3   *One-to-One Correspondence*

Developing Fluency with Small Numbers

Developing fluency with small numbers is an important goal of number talks at the primary level. Often fluency with numbers is compared to knowing basic facts; however, fluency is much more than fact recall. Fluency is knowing how a number can be composed and decomposed and using that information to be flexible and efficient with solving problems. Consider the string of numbers $5 + 7 + 8$. Knowing that 7 can be decomposed into $5 + 2$ in order to think about the problem as $5 + (5 + 2) + 8$ allows access to making quick tens. The problem can then be solved as $(5 + 5) + (2 + 8)$ through the associative property. In the primary grades students work toward building fluency for the numbers 1 through 6, and then the numbers 7 through 10 (Richardson 2002). Number talks provide opportunities to help students use and develop fluency.

Subitizing

Just as important as building fluency is the ability to *subitize*, or immediately recognize a collection of objects as a single unit. Looking at the arrangement of pips on a die and being able to instantly know there are five pips without counting is an example of subitizing. Rolling two dice and automatically recognizing that one die displays a 3 and the other die exhibits a 5 are examples of subitizing. Number talks that use dot images, five- and ten-frames, or rekenreks provide opportunities for children to build recognition of numbers and their parts. Subitizing is an important component of computation at the lower grades.

Making Tens

Making groups of ten provides a link to developing and understanding place value and our system of tens. Understanding that ten ones can also be thought of as a single entity of one 10 is a critical understanding to begin building in the primary grades. Students need many opportunities to count objects and organize them into groups of ten to begin constructing an understanding of place value. Equally important is presenting questions that ask students to consider how many more are needed to have a group of ten. This helps students build an understanding of how to compose and decompose 10.

There are many natural ways to create situations that encourage students to organize objects into units of ten and think about fluency with this amount.

Ways to Create Situations That Encourage Students to Organize Objects into Units of Ten

- Use a weekly classroom estimation jar to give students an opportunity to initially build a sense of estimation by making predictions. After predictions are made, empty the contents of the jar and prompt students to organize the objects into groups of five and ten for easy counting.

- Incorporate five- and ten-frames into calendar time by charting the number of days students are in school with dots on the frames.

- Have students use interlocking cubes to build a tower to match their height. Count the number of cubes used by grouping by tens.

- Let students help organize classroom materials into packages of ten for easy distribution.

Using Models and Tools to Anchor Student Strategies to Goals

Models and tools such as dot images, rekenreks, five- and ten-frames, and number lines can be used in number talks to help students build understanding. Incorporating these visuals into number talks helps provide a visual link to the relationships being investigated.

Dot Images

Showing students an organized arrangement of dots for a few seconds and then asking them to share how many they see encourages subitizing and fluency. Look at the following dot image.

How many dots do you see? *How* did you see them?

Did you see the arrangement as:

	Doubles +1 (4 + 4) + 1
	Doubles +1 (4 + 4) + 1
	Doubles − 1 (5 + 5) − 1

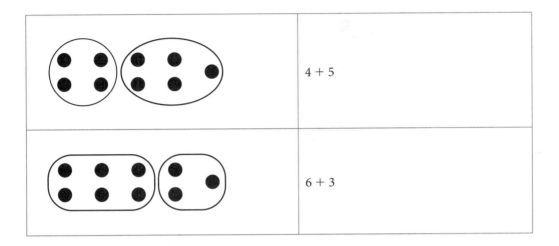

	4 + 5
	6 + 3

Incorporating dot images into classroom number talks provides opportunities for students to work on counting, seeing numbers in a variety of ways, subitizing, and learning combinations.

Rekenreks

Rekenreks originated in the Netherlands and have been widely used in other countries to help students reason about numbers, subitize, build fluency, and compute using number relationships (Fosnot and Dolk, 2001). The rekenrek is composed of two rows of stringed beads with five beads of one color and five beads of another color on each row. They are colored in groups of five to help students "see" or subitize the quantity of five. The teacher has the option of using only one row of beads at a time to build fluency up to ten or using both rows to work on fluency with numbers up to twenty.

The bead arrangement on the left side of the rekenrek shown below could be used to build fluency to thirteen using either of the following strategies.

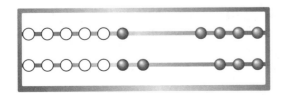

Mathematical Practice 5: Use appropriate tools strategically.

Number talks are primarily designed to focus on building computation strategies from a mental math perspective. However, there are instances where physical or mental tools are used to provide additional cognitive support or to specifically address the content. Rekenreks may be incorporated into a primary number talk to provide an opportunity for the teacher to target counting strategies, subitizing, composing and decomposing small numbers, and so on. Students may have access to a class number line or hundreds chart to provide support during computation. The teacher can also choose to use a ten-frame or a number line to model students' strategies during a number talk.

Often number talk discussions serve as a springboard for the class to engage in further investigation of ideas that arise during the talk. For example, if a student uses the strategy of doubling and halving to solve a multiplication problem, the student may wonder if the same strategy will work with odd numbers. This is an excellent opportunity for students to work with partners to explore and test this idea using calculators, color tiles, or other tools.

Doubles or Near-Doubles (for example, $(6 + 6) + 1$; $(7 + 7) - 1$):

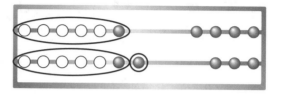

Making Tens (for example, $(5 + 5) + 3$):

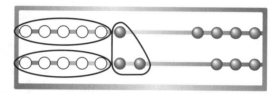

 Classroom Link: Rekenreks
Classroom Clip K.2

To view this video clip, scan the QR code or access via mathsolutions.com/NTWNCK2

As you watch the kindergarten number talk in which rekenreks are used, consider:

1. What instructional strategies does the teacher use to engage the students in the mathematics?

2. How does the teacher use rekenreks as a tool to build fluency with small numbers?

3. What role does the game "Can You Guess My Way?" play in the number talk?

4. What mathematical understandings and misconceptions are being addressed?

5. How does the rekenrek provide opportunities for differentiation within the number talk?

For commentary on the above, see Appendix A: Author's Video Reflections.

Five-Frames/Ten-Frames

Five- and ten-frames can be used as a single row of five (five-frame) or two rows of five (ten-frame), or putting two ten-frames together provides the opportunity to work with numbers to twenty. Like rekenreks, ten-frames can be used to foster fluency, subitizing, working with place value, and computing with addition and subtraction. Frames are also arranged to capitalize on subitizing to five as half of ten. Varying the questions posed to students can change the purpose and focus of each ten-frame.

Questions such as, "How many did you see? How do you see seven?" help students build fluency with targeted numbers. By posing, "How

Classroom Link: Ten-Frames: 8 + 6
Classroom Clip 2.1

As you watch the second-grade number talk for the 8 + 6 sequence, consider:

1. How does the teacher build student fluency with small numbers using ten-frames?

2. What questions does the teacher use to build understanding about decomposing and composing numbers?

3. How are the double ten-frames used to support the goals of K–2 number talks?

4. What strategies are the students using to build meaning of the numbers?

5. What opportunities are created for the students to understand and use 10 as a unit?

6. How do the students demonstrate composing and decomposing numbers?

For commentary on the above, see Appendix A: Author's Video Reflections.

To view this video clip, scan the QR code or access via mathsolutions.com /NTWNC21

Mathematical Practice 4: Model with mathematics.

When we think about modeling with mathematics, visual models such as arrays, number lines, ten-frames,

many more do we need to make ten? How many are left after removing three?" the focus shifts to computation.

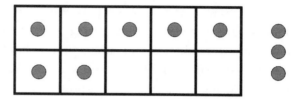

Number Lines

A number line can be an important tool for discussing and modeling strategies in addition and subtraction. It allows the students to visualize the action of the operation and the magnitude of the numbers and the distance moved. Primary students are still building an understanding of numbers, so it is important to explicitly model the distance moved by drawing in actual jumps made. We can demonstrate how to correctly use this tool with the problem 8 + 9. (See Figure 3–4.)

The number line is also an excellent tool for modeling subtraction strategies. We can revisit some of the subtraction strategies previously discussed with the problem 14 – 7:

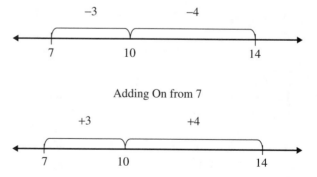

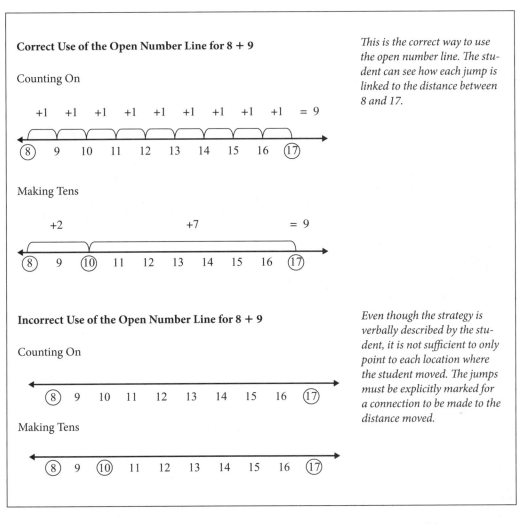

Correct Use of the Open Number Line for 8 + 9

Counting On

This is the correct way to use the open number line. The student can see how each jump is linked to the distance between 8 and 17.

Making Tens

Incorrect Use of the Open Number Line for 8 + 9

Counting On

Even though the strategy is verbally described by the student, it is not sufficient to only point to each location where the student moved. The jumps must be explicitly marked for a connection to be made to the distance moved.

Making Tens

Figure 3-4   *Correct and Incorrect Ways to Use the Open Number-Line Model*

Hundred Chart

The hundred chart helps students count, model addition and subtraction strategies, and notice important ideas and patterns about our system of tens. The following examples demonstrate possible ways to incorporate a hundred chart during number talks.

1	2	3	4	5	6	7	8	9	10
11	12	13	14	15	16	17	18	19	20
21	22	23	24	25	26	27	28	29	30
31	32	33	34	35	36	37	38	39	40
41	42	43	44	45	46	47	48	49	50
51	52	53	54	55	56	57	58	59	60
61	62	63	64	65	66	67	68	69	70
71	72	73	74	75	76	77	78	79	80
81	82	83	84	85	86	87	88	89	90
91	92	93	94	95	96	97	98	99	100

Counting On

$5 + 6$

$5 + 6 = 11$

Using the hundred chart provides opportunities for discussions about efficiency in counting on from the larger or smaller addend and thinking about how many more numbers to the nearest ten.

1	2	3	4	5	6	7	8	9	10
11	12	13	14	15	16	17	18	19	20
21	22	23	24	25	26	27	28	29	30
31	32	33	34	35	36	37	38	39	40
41	42	43	44	45	46	47	48	49	50
51	52	53	54	55	56	57	58	59	60
61	62	63	64	65	66	67	68	69	70
71	72	73	74	75	76	77	78	79	80
81	82	83	84	85	86	87	88	89	90
91	92	93	94	95	96	97	98	99	100

Decomposing to Make a Landmark or Friendly Number

$19 + 8$

$19 + (1 + 7)$

$19 + 1 = 20$

$20 + 7 = 27$

1	2	3	4	5	6	7	8	9	10
11	12	13	14	15	16	17	18	19	20
21	22	23	24	25	26	27	28	29	30
31	32	33	34	35	36	37	38	39	40
41	42	43	44	45	46	47	48	49	50
51	52	53	54	55	56	57	58	59	60
61	62	63	64	65	66	67	68	69	70
71	72	73	74	75	76	77	78	79	80
81	82	83	84	85	86	87	88	89	90
91	92	93	94	95	96	97	98	99	100

Adding Up in Chunks

27 + 24

27 + (20 + 3 + 1)

27 + 20 = 47

47 + 3 = 50

50 + 1 = 51

1	2	3	4	5	6	7	8	9	10
11	12	13	14	15	16	17	18	19	20
21	22	23	24	25	26	27	28	29	30
31	32	33	34	35	36	37	38	39	40
41	42	43	44	45	46	47	48	49	50
51	52	53	54	55	56	57	58	59	60
61	62	63	64	65	66	67	68	69	70
71	72	73	74	75	76	77	78	79	80
81	82	83	84	85	86	87	88	89	90
91	92	93	94	95	96	97	98	99	100

Removal or Counting Back

53 − 21

53 − (10 + 10 + 1)

53 − 10 = 43

43 − 10 = 33

33 − 1 = 32

1	2	3	4	5	6	7	8	9	10
11	12	13	14	15	16	17	18	19	20
21	22	23	24	25	26	27	28	29	30
31	32	33	34	35	36	37	38	39	40
41	42	43	44	45	46	47	48	49	50
51	52	53	54	55	56	57	58	59	60
61	62	63	64	65	66	67	68	69	70
71	72	73	74	75	76	77	78	79	80
81	82	83	84	85	86	87	88	89	90
91	92	93	94	95	96	97	98	99	100

+1

Adding Up

$61 - 38$

$38 + 2 = 40$

$40 + 10 = 50$

$50 + 10 = 60$

$60 + 1 = 61$

$61 - 38 = 23$

Using Real-Life Contexts

Once I began incorporating number talks as a regular component of my math instruction, I stopped showing students how to solve a computation problem. Instead, I provided story problems that incorporated new operations and encouraged students to make sense of the problems and the numbers. Using a real-life context as a springboard for mathematical thinking serves to help students in three main ways.

Three Benefits of Using Real-Life Contexts

1. A real-life context engages students in mathematics that is relevant to them.

2. A real-life context attaches meaning to the numbers.

3. A real-life context helps students access the mathematics.

Classroom Link: Counting Book
Classroom Clip K.3

As you watch the kindergarten number talk in which a counting book is used, consider:

1. How does the literature provide a context for thinking about number fluency?

2. What role do the teacher's questions play in helping students build number sense?

3. What math concepts are addressed during this number talk?

4. What strategies are the students using to build meaning with the numbers?

5. How does the teacher use student responses to address the commutative property?

6. What can the teacher learn about her students' understandings from this number talk?

For commentary on the above, see Appendix A: Author's Video Reflections.

To view this video clip, scan the QR code or access via mathsolutions.com /NTWNCK3

1. A real-life context engages students in mathematics that is relevant to them.

By crafting story problems that are intertwined in content that matters to students, you create a need for them to want to know. Designing problems around classroom parties, recess time, games, reading goals, or schoolwide projects naturally draws students into the mathematics.

2. A real-life context attaches meaning to the numbers.

A story-problem context allows students to envision a mental image of the mathematics. In contrast, problems that utilize only bare numbers require students to have a previous understanding of the operation and create their own mental images of the numerical actions.

3. A real-life context helps students access the mathematics.

A story-problem context provides multiple points of entry for students and allows them access to the math. A context also gives students a framework for deciding if an answer is reasonable. Real-world situations may also provide opportunities for students to notice commonalities between previously solved problems and a new problem.

Using a Context with Addition

Consider the problem 19 + 18. When embedded in the following story problem, 19 + 18 can be used to introduce second graders to addition with regrouping.

Student representations using the specified context open the door for students to invent their own strategies for solving 19 + 18. Common first strategies are described in the chart following the story problem.

> *Mr. Hamby's and Ms. Lamont's second-grade classrooms are going to the zoo. Mr. Hamby's classroom has 19 students, and Ms. Lamont's has 18. How many students will go on the field trip?*

Four Different Strategies for Solving 19 + 18

① Student's Strategy: Counting On by Ones	The Strategy as Recorded by the Teacher
Matthew: I put the nineteen in my head and counted up. **Teacher:** How did you count? **Matthew:** By ones.	19 20 21 22 23 24 25 26 27 28 29 30 31 32 33 34 35 36 37

② Student's Strategy: Counting On in Chunks	The Strategy as Recorded by the Teacher
Sylvia: I took the eighteen and broke it apart into ten plus eight. Then I added ten to the nineteen and got twenty-nine.	19 + 18 19 + (10 + 8) 19 + 10 = 29

I wasn't sure what twenty-nine plus eight was so I broke the eight into one plus seven.	29 + 8 29 + (1 + 7)
Teacher: Why did you choose to break eight into a one and a seven?	
Sylvia: Because I knew if I added one more to twenty-nine I would get an easy ten of thirty, and thirty plus seven would be thirty-seven.	29 + 1 = 30 30 + 7 = 37
③ **Student's Strategy: Doubles/Near-Doubles**	**The Strategy as Recorded by the Teacher**
Nick: I know doubles so I changed nineteen and eighteen to twenty plus twenty and got forty. I had to take three away and that got me to thirty-seven.	$\begin{array}{r} 19 + 18 \\ +1 \quad +2 \\ \hline 20 + 20 = 40 \end{array}$
Teacher: Why did you need to take three away?	40 − 3 = 37
Nick: Since I added one extra to nineteen and two extras to eighteen, I had to take these away.	
④ **Student's Strategy: Breaking Each Number into Its Place Value and Making Tens Combined**	**The Strategy as Recorded by the Teacher**
Denise: I broke all of the numbers apart. I broke nineteen into ten plus nine and eighteen into ten plus eight. Then I put all of my tens together and all of my ones together to get twenty plus seventeen.	19 + 18 (10 + 9) + (10 + 8) (10 + 10) + (9 + 8) 20 + 17
Teacher: How did you add the twenty and seventeen?	20 + (10 + 7) (20 + 10) + 7
Denise: I broke my seventeen into ten plus seven and put the ten and twenty together. That gave me thirty plus seven, which was thirty-seven.	30 + 7 = 37

Notice how the teacher uses the student-invented strategies to facilitate student thinking without telling them how to solve the problem. The recording of each strategy serves as an opportunity to capture important mathematical ideas in this problem (fluency with small numbers, combining tens, associative property, and commutative property) and continues to help students attach meaning to the numbers.

Using a Context for Subtraction

Many of us learned that subtraction was taking away an amount from a given quantity. While subtraction can involve removing an amount or taking it away, it also includes: finding the difference between numbers, comparing numbers, and looking at part-to-whole relationships. By incorporating subtraction problems in a contextual situation, we can help students come to understand each type of subtraction as well as develop a toolbox of efficient strategies. The context of a subtraction problem not only determines the type of subtraction (comparison, part-to-whole, or removal) but can also influence the strategy used.

Creating a word problem that implies distance also gives students a mental image and action of counting up or moving forward from the smaller number to the larger number. The following problem is an example of a context that implies distance for 50 – 17.

> *Martha's goal is to walk 50 laps on the school track. She has already walked 17 laps. How many more laps does Martha need to walk to reach her goal?*

The scenario alone creates a mental picture and action of moving forward from seventeen to reach fifty and lends itself to the student solving the problem in this manner.

Other examples of contextual problems to promote Adding Up for subtraction are shown on the next page. Notice how each problem uses numbers that are relatively far apart, and the context implies a distance to be bridged by starting with a part and working toward the whole.

Contextual Problems to Promote Adding Up for Subtraction

- *Paul plans to read 40 pages each day. So far, he has read only 16 pages. How many more pages does Paul need to read today to reach his goal?*

- *Rebekah wants to buy a video game that costs $52. She has saved $6 so far. How much more money does Rebekah need before she can buy the game?*

- *If Ms. Cain's class raises $80 for new books for the library, the students will receive a pizza party. So far the students have raised $12. How much more money do they need to reach their goal?*

To help your students be successful with this and other strategies, introduce the computation problems embedded in a context.

Discussing Efficiency

As students better understand the mathematics of an operation, number talks are used to investigate different strategies, test whether they will always work for any set of numbers, and discuss efficiency. By keeping each strategy posted for the duration of the number talk, students have an opportunity to discuss efficiency as well as similarities and differences between strategies. If each strategy is labeled with a number (such as 1, 2, 3, 4), the teacher can ask students to use a hand signal to quietly indicate which strategy they consider to be the most efficient. This allows the teacher to glean information about which students are struggling to use tens and friendly numbers, break apart numbers, or manipulate numbers with ease.

Using the previously reviewed problem, 19 + 18, the teacher could lead the class in a brief class discussion about efficiency as indicated by the following classroom narrative.

> If each strategy is labeled with a number (such as 1, 2, 3, 4), the teacher can ask students to use a hand signal to quietly indicate which strategy they consider to be the most efficient.

> *Classroom Example: Discussing Efficiency Using Strategies for 19 + 18*
>
> **Teacher:** I noticed there were a lot of signals for Strategy 3, Nick's strategy. Could someone share why you thought this was the most efficient strategy?
>
> **Bonita:** He made it a simpler problem. That makes it quicker.
>
> **Luis:** Yes. Adding tens is easy!
>
> **William:** It wasn't as much to keep up with in my head. I tried the first strategy, but I kept getting all of the jumps mixed up.
>
> **Teacher:** Sounds like you agree that using doubles is a good, efficient strategy. Let's test out your thinking with one more problem, 26 + 25.

Having conversations about efficient subtraction strategies is equally important. Let's take a moment to look at four student strategies for the problem 31 − 14, followed by a classroom efficiency discussion.

Four Student Strategies for 31 − 14

① Student's Strategy: Adding Up	The Strategy as Recorded by the Teacher
Maleka: I thought about a number line and counted up to thirty-one. **Teacher:** How did you count up? **Maleka:** I started with the fourteen and counted up by ones. **Teacher:** How many jumps of one did you make to get to thirty-one? **Maleka:** Seventeen. **Teacher:** Is it hard to keep up with how many jumps you made? **Maleka:** Kind of. I had to go back and count them in my head.	 14 15 16 17 18 19 20 21 22 23 24 25 26 27 28 29 30 31

② Student's Strategy: Adding Up	The Strategy as Recorded by the Teacher
Alexandra: I counted up, too, but in a different way. **Teacher:** How did you count up? **Alexandra:** First, I added one to fourteen to get to fifteen. Then I added five more to get to twenty. And twenty plus ten is thirty. One more jump and I got to thirty-one. **Teacher:** So how much did you add to fourteen to get to thirty-one? **Alexandra:** Seventeen.	
③ Student's Strategy: Counting Back	The Strategy as Recorded by the Teacher
Scott: I counted back. I started with thirty-one and counted back fourteen and landed on seventeen. **Teacher:** How did you count back? **Scott:** I counted back one at a time. **Teacher:** How did you know when to stop counting back? **Scott:** I had to use my fingers to see when I had used fourteen up.	
④ Student's Strategy: Removal	The Strategy as Recorded by the Teacher
Ann: I figured it out by taking chunks out. **Teacher:** How did you remove the fourteen in chunks? **Ann:** I broke the fourteen into a ten and a one and a three. Then I took ten from the thirty-one and got twenty-one. I still needed to take away four more so I broke the four into a one and a three.	

(continued)

Teacher: Why did you choose to break the four into a one plus three instead of a two plus two?

Ann: Because I could take one from twenty-one easily to get to twenty and then take off three more.

Classroom Example: Discussing Efficiency for 31 – 14

Teacher: I noticed there were a lot of signals for Ann and Alexandra's strategies. Could someone share why you thought these were the most efficient strategies?

Stephen: They both got to friendlier numbers and that made it quicker.

Melanie: It seemed easier to keep up with how much was added when Alexandra used friendly numbers. There weren't as many jumps to count.

Robert: I tried counting back by ones but I got lost. I think Ann's strategy was easier because she used an easy jump of ten and smaller numbers.

Teacher: Sounds like we all agree that using friendly numbers in subtraction is more efficient. Let's test out this idea with one more problem, 50 – 24.

Anticipating Student Thinking

As discussed in Chapter 2, do not be discouraged if you don't quickly access a student's thinking. It takes time to follow a strategy when you hear it for the first time. Students commonly use a limited number of strategies to solve different types of problems, and taking time to think through possible strategies for each problem beforehand will help you gain confidence in listening and following student thinking. As you become more accustomed to these strategies, you will find yourself anticipating your students' thinking and becoming more comfortable with understanding the approaches they have selected.

As you anticipate potential strategies for each problem, also consider how you will capture each student's thinking so other students may access the strategy. Consider which mathematical ideas you want to highlight and how you might record the strategy to emphasize those specific concepts. For example, if making tens or utilizing place value is an important component in the strategy, make sure these ideas stand out in your recording.

Many teachers and other adults are surprised that students can invent ways to solve a problem. I have found, however, that by laying the foundation for making sense of number relationships, students are quite capable of inventing efficient strategies. There are many opportunities to help students build upon number relationships.

Ways to Help Students Build upon Number Relationships

- Ask students to estimate before they compute. This helps them build a sense of quantity and magnitude and provides a platform for them to judge the reasonableness of an answer. Many students who do not have number sense struggle to estimate; they choose to compute first and then provide an estimate. To help students build sense of number, teachers can provide a range of estimates from which to choose. For example, before students compute the problem 29 + 19, give them a list of possible estimates from which to choose, such as 20, 30, 40, 50, 60, 70, and 80.

- Locate numbers on a hundreds chart and discuss how close or far the number is to the nearest ten.

- Encourage students to think of equivalent representations for numbers by composing and decomposing quantities. Understanding that 30 can be represented as 20 + 10, 19 + 11, 15 + 15, 40 − 10, and so on, is critical to building number relationships.

- Provide opportunities for students to analyze a set of numbers and form generalizations, which builds an understanding of relationships and interdependence among quantities. By using the following two sets of numbers, students can consider how the sets are alike, different, what other numbers would fit in each set, and so on.

    Set A: 2, 4, 6, 8, 10, 12

    Set B: 12, 14, 16, 18, 20, 22

Operations and Algebraic Thinking: Understand and apply properties of operations and the relationship between addition and subtraction.

1.OA.B.3 Apply properties of operations as strategies to add and subtract.

Number and Operations in Base Ten: Use place value understanding and properties of operations to add and subtract.

1.NBT.B.2 Understand that the two digits of a two-digit number represent amounts of tens and ones.

2.NBT.B.5 Fluently add and subtract within 100 using strategies based on place value, properties of operations, and/or the relationship between addition and subtraction.

Within the context of a number talk, multiple content standards are addressed. As the second graders share their strategies for adding 16 + 15, they provide us with clear examples of applying their understandings of place value when they break apart 16 and 15 into 10 + 6 and 10 + 5 and combine the tens and ones to efficiently add. Equally important is the use of the commutative and associative properties as the order and the grouping of the numbers are changed. By recording the student's thinking in the following manner, the properties are more clearly highlighted.

16 + 15

(10 + 6) + (10 + 5)

(10 + 10) + (6 + 5)

Classroom Link: Addition: 16 + 15
Classroom Clip 2.2

To view this video clip, scan the QR code or access via mathsolutions.com /NTWNC22

Before you watch the second-grade number talk for 16 + 15, anticipate possible student strategies and how you might record them.

As you watch the second-grade number talk for 16 + 15, consider:

1. How does the teacher record each strategy to provide access for the class?

2. Which strategies are easiest for you to understand?

3. Which strategies are more challenging to follow?

4. What mathematical concepts are being built upon during the number talk?

5. How did the teacher bring these ideas to the forefront for the class?

For commentary on the above, see Appendix A: Author's Video Reflections.

An Introduction to Common Addition Strategies

The following strategies represent a valued collection of mathematical ideas from kindergarten, first-, and second-grade students. Do not be quick to discount them because the recording takes up writing space; the students solved them very quickly using only mental math. Each strategy is "named" to help you better understand its foundation; however, in my classroom strategies were often named for the students who invented them.

Classroom Link: Addition: 26 + 27
Classroom Clip 2.3

Before you watch the second-grade number talk for 26 + 27, anticipate possible student strategies and how you might record them.

As you watch the second-grade number talk for 26 + 27, consider:

1. How does the teacher record each strategy to provide access for the class?

2. Which strategies are easiest for you to understand?

3. Which strategies are more challenging to follow?

4. What mathematical concepts are being built upon during the number talk?

5. How did the teacher bring these ideas to the forefront for the class?

For commentary on the above, see Appendix A: Author's Video Reflections.

To view this video clip, scan the QR code or access via mathsolutions.com /NTWNC23

Mathematical Practice 7: Look for and make use of structure.

Our number system is composed of multiple structures such as place value, class inclusion (numbers embedded in numbers), compensation, and so on. When students decompose numbers, use place value, and compensate, they are looking for and using structure. When they apply the use of properties, they are using structure. When teachers ask students to consider how strategies are similar or different, structure is again being utilized.

A number string provides opportunities for students to notice and apply structure during computation. Consider the following number string for doubles and near doubles:

$$15 + 15$$
$$16 + 17$$
$$25 + 25$$
$$26 + 27$$

This purposeful string highlights a mathematical situation that helps students notice a number of structures: place value, the relationship between

Eight Common Strategies for Addition

(A-1) Addition Strategy: Counting All

Counting every number is an addition strategy used primarily by kindergarten and beginning first-grade students. Students who use this strategy are not yet able to add on from either addend. They cannot visualize and hold a number in their mind; instead they must mentally build every number quantity.

(continued)

doubles and near doubles, and numbers embedded in numbers (class inclusion). As the teacher records student strategies for this series of problems, the structure of properties can also be addressed. If the student solves 26 + 27 by decomposing each addend as a number relating to 25, we can see the commutative and associative properties utilized.

$$26 + 27$$
$$(25 + 1) + (25 + 2)$$
$$(25 + 25) + (1 + 2)$$
$$50 + 3$$

8 + 9 1, 2, 3, 4, 5, 6, 7, 8, 9, 10, 11, 12, 13, 14, 15, 16, 17	The student literally starts with 1 and counts up to 17 using every number. Using models to help the student keep track of their location when counting is helpful.

(A-2) Addition Strategy: Counting On

Counting On is a transitional strategy used primarily in first and early-second grade. The student starts with one of the numbers and counts on from this point. When students are able to conceptualize a number, they will transition from Counting All to Counting On. It is tempting to show or tell students this strategy in an attempt to move them to a more efficient strategy. However, if students don't construct this strategy for themselves, it becomes a magical procedure without any foundation.

8 + 9 8 . . . 9, 10, 11, 12, 13, 14, 15, 16, 17 or 9 . . . 10, 11, 12, 13, 14, 15, 16, 17	It is not unusual to hear students say, "I put the eight in my head and counted up nine more." From an efficiency standpoint, it is important to note whether the student counts on from the smaller or larger number.

(A-3) Addition Strategy: Doubles/Near-Doubles

Beginning as early as kindergarten, children are able to recall sums for many doubles. This strategy capitalizes on this strength by adjusting one or both numbers to make a double or near-doubles combination.

(continued)

$8 + 9$	The student could choose from several doubles/near-doubles combinations to solve this problem:
$8 + (8 + 1)$ $(8 + 8) + 1$ $16 + 1 = 17$	$8 + 8$ Using this double requires the student to decompose 9 into $8 + 1$.
$\begin{array}{r} 8 + 9 \\ +1 \\ \hline 9 + 9 = 18 \\ -1 \\ \hline 17 \end{array}$	$9 + 9$ Using this double requires the student to add an extra 1 and then subtract it from the total.
$\begin{array}{r} 8 \; + \; 9 \\ +2 \; + +1 \\ \hline 10 \; + \; 10 = 20 \\ -3 \\ \hline 17 \end{array}$	$10 + 10$ Using this double requires the student to add 3 extra and then subtract the extra 3 from the total.

(A-4) Addition Strategy: Making Tens

Developing fluency with number combinations that make ten is an important focus in the primary grades. Beginning around second grade, students should be able to break numbers apart quickly to make ten. The focus of this strategy is to be able to utilize fluency with ten to expedite adding. Being able to take numbers apart with ease, or fluency, is the key to using this strategy. Several examples can help us consider how this strategy can be efficient and effective.

$8 + 9$ $(7 + 1) + 9$ $7 + (1 + 9)$ $7 + 10 = 17$ or	By changing the 8 to a $7 + 1$ the student can restructure the problem to create a combination of 10 with $1 + 9$.

(continued)

$8 + 9$ $8 + (2 + 7)$ $(8 + 2) + 7$ $10 + 7 = 17$	The student could also choose to make a 10 by breaking apart the 9 into $7 + 2$ and combining the 2 with the 8 to create 10.

(A-5) Addition Strategy: Making Landmark or Friendly Numbers

Landmark or friendly numbers are numbers that are easy to use in mental computation. Fives, multiples of ten, as well as monetary amounts such as twenty-five and fifty are examples of numbers that fall into this category. Students may adjust one or all addends by adding or subtracting amounts to make a friendly number.

$23 + 48$ $\underline{ + 2}$ $23 + 50 = 73$ $\underline{-2}$ 71	In this example only the 48 is adjusted to make an easy landmark number. The extra 2 that was added on must be subtracted.

(A-6) Addition Strategy: Compensation

The goal of compensation is to manipulate the numbers into easier, friendly numbers to add. When compensating, students will remove a specific amount from one addend and give that exact amount to the other addend to make friendlier numbers. Taking from one addend and giving the same quantity to the other addend to maintain the total sum is a big mathematical idea in addition. This strategy will often begin to emerge in the second semester of first grade as a way to make doubles and tens.

(continued)

A. $\quad 8 \;+\; 6$ $\quad\; -1 \quad +1$ $\quad\;\; 7 \;+\; 7 = 14$	Example A demonstrates a first grader's Compensation strategy for making a double.
B. $\quad 18 \;+\; 23$ $\quad +2 \quad -2$ $\quad\; 20 \;+\; 21 = 41$	In Example B, the student changes 18 to the friendly number of 20. Notice how 2 was subtracted from the 23 and then added to the 18.
C. $\quad 36 \;+\; 9$ $\quad -1 \quad +1$ $\quad\; 35 \;+\; 10 = 45$	Example C demonstrates that Compensation can be used to make an easy 10. Choosing which number to adjust is an important student decision that is linked to the student's thinking about efficiency.

(A-7) Addition Strategy: Breaking Each Number into Its Place Value

Once students begin to understand place value, this is one of the first strategies they utilize. Each addend is broken into expanded form and like place value amounts are combined. When combining quantities, children typically work left to right because it maintains the magnitude of the numbers.

$24 + 38$ $(20 + 4) + (30 + 8)$	Each addend is broken into its place value.
$20 + 30 = 50$	Tens are combined.
$4 + 8 = 12$	Ones are combined.
$50 + 12 = 62$	Totals are added from the previous sums.

(continued)

(A-8) **Addition Strategy: Adding Up in Chunks**

This strategy is similar to the Breaking Each Number into Its Place Value strategy except the focus is on keeping one addend whole and adding the second number in easy-to-use chunks. This strategy is slightly more efficient than the Breaking Each Number into Its Place Value strategy, since you are not breaking apart every number.

A. $45 + 28$ $45 + (20 + 8)$ $45 + 20 = 65$ $65 + 8 = 73$	In Example A, 45 is kept whole while 28 is broken into its place value and added in parts to the 45.
B. $45 + 28$ $(40 + 5) + 28$ $40 + 28 = 68$ $68 + 5 = 73$	Example B demonstrates that either number can be kept whole. This time the 28 is kept intact while 45 is broken into combinations that make the problem easier to solve.

An Introduction to Common Subtraction Strategies

An appropriate time to begin introducing students to subtraction is around the end of first grade and the beginning of second grade. Usually during this time frame students are beginning to understand the importance of tens, how to break numbers apart for addition strategies, and how to reason more confidently with numbers. Students are often ready to begin using their understanding of addition to lay a foundation for reasoning with subtraction. The stronger a student is with addition, the better she is able to access subtraction.

Two ideas to consider when crafting number talks to encourage the Adding Up strategy for subtraction are: 1) keep the whole (minuend) and the part being subtracted (subtrahend) far apart, and 2) create a context that implies distance.

The farther apart the subtrahend is from the minuend the more likely it is that students will count or add up. The closer the two numbers are,

Encouraging students to invent alternative ways to subtract can seem intimidating at first. Galey Thomas, second-grade teacher, shares a personal account of her classroom experiences with this operation. See Teacher Clip T.2.

the greater the likelihood that students will count back. For example, if the problem is 50 – 47, it would be quite efficient and easy to count back; but, if the problem is 50 – 17, it would be more cumbersome and tedious to count back.

Two Common Strategies for Subtraction

(S-1) Subtraction Strategy: Adding Up

This strategy allows students to build on their strength with addition by adding up from the number being subtracted (subtrahend) to the whole (minuend). When students begin to understand that subtraction is finding the difference between two quantities, they realize that they can add up to compute that distance. The larger the jumps, the more efficient the strategy will be. In thinking about how much more they need to add to reach the whole, students can build upon their knowledge of basic facts, doubles, making ten, and counting on as demonstrated with the following examples.

14 − 7 +1 +1 +1 +1 +1 +1 +1 A. 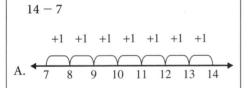 7 8 9 10 11 12 13 14	The open number line is helpful in recording the student's strategy as he adds up by counting each number to 14.
B. 7 + 3 = 10 10 + 4 = 14	Notice how the student first moves to the nearest ten and then navigates from this point.
3 + 4 = 7	The student has found a total difference of 7.
C. 7 + 7 = 14	Using a known fact is also an efficient way to add up to the whole.

(continued)

(S-2) **Subtraction Strategy: Removal or Counting Back**

If students primarily view subtraction as taking away, they will gravitate toward this strategy. Starting with the whole, the subtrahend is removed in parts. The ability to decompose numbers into easy-to-remove parts gives students access to this strategy. Some students will need to count back by ones to the subtrahend; others will remove pieces related to multiples of ten.

A. $65 - 32$ $65 - (10 + 10 + 10 + 2)$ $-2 \quad -10 \quad -10 \quad -10$ 33 35 45 55 65	In Example A, the student has chosen to think about 32 as a combination of three tens and two ones. An open number line is used to show how each part of 32 was removed.
B. $65 - 32$ $65 - (30 + 2)$ $65 - 30 = 35$ $35 - 2 = 33$	Example B demonstrates how the subtrahend can be decomposed into its place-value components and removed accordingly.
C. $65 - 32$ $(10 + 10 + 10 + 10 + 10 + 10 + 1 + 1 + 1 + 1 + 1)$ $(10 + 10 + 10 + \cancel{10 + 10 + 10} + 1 + 1 + 1 + \cancel{1 + 1})$ $10 + 10 + 10 + 3 = 33$	Example C shows how the student has broken the 65 into six tens and five ones before removing 32. The remaining numbers total 33.

Summary

In this chapter, we have looked at the overarching goals during number talks, addition and subtraction student strategies, and tools and models to help support student mathematical understanding in K–2 classrooms. In the following chapter we explore how to use number talks to develop specific strategies in the K–2 classroom.

CHAPTER 4

How Do I Design Purposeful Number Talks in the K–2 Classroom?

Overview

In this chapter, K–2 number talks are organized in three grade-level sections:

- Kindergarten fluency number talks
- First-grade addition number talks
- Second-grade addition and subtraction number talks

The kindergarten fluency number talks are organized by *tools*: dot cards, rekenreks, and five- and ten-frames. The first-grade and second-grade number talks are organized by *operations* and *strategies*.

Although the number talks are categorized by grade level, they should not be used as rigid structures but as fluid components based on student need. That said, fluency number talks should be used to build a strong foundation before moving into number talks that focus on computation.

CONTENTS

Kindergarten Number Talks

Number talks at the kindergarten level are designed to provide students with opportunities for counting, building fluency with small numbers, and developing the concepts of one-to-one correspondence and conservation of number.

Dot images, rekenreks, and five- and ten-frames are used during number talks to provide a context for reasoning with numbers. When using these tools, recording number sentences to match student thinking is often helpful. This will help create a bridge from the geometric model to the numerical model. For example, show the student the following dot image and ask, "How many dots do you see?" Connect the child's thinking to a number sentence by circling the dot arrangement the child describes and writing a correlating number sentence. (See Figure 4–1.)

Give careful thought to the visual and spatial arrangements of the geometric models. The design layout has the potential either to open student thinking to multiple strategies or to inhibit reasoning. The arrangement of the five triangles for the previous problem lends itself to the student looking at solutions from a variety of perspectives. However, if we arranged the triangles in a single row, we would most likely not elicit similar responses. (See Figure 4–2.)

Equally important is using the opportunity to build quick recognition of the groupings of dots or images associated with a specific number such as on a die. When shown briefly for only two to three seconds, dot images are an excellent vehicle for fostering unitizing. Limiting the students' viewing time of the image encourages students to look at the dots in groupings instead of counting them one by one.

Kindergarten number talks to build fluency for the numbers 3 through 10 are organized by tools—dot images, rekenreks, five- and ten-frames—to allow flexibility in moving between numbers. If you are using dot images to address fluency with the number 3 and find this quantity is too easy for your students, you can easily adjust to dot image number talks that focus on the numbers 4 or 5. Listen to your students' thinking to guide your number talk decisions.

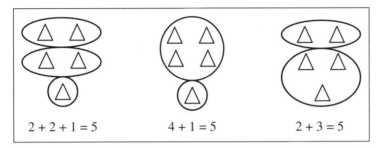

Figure 4–1   *Number Sentences to Describe Students' Strategies for the Number 5*

Figure 4–2   *Single-Row Arrangement for the Number 5*

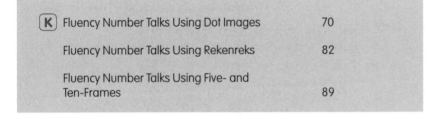

NUMBER TALKS

K

For more on using dot images, see page 40.

Fluency Number Talks Using Dot Images

As discussed in Chapter 3, dot images are an important tool to help students build a visual link to composing and decomposing small numbers. Incorporating dot images into classroom number talks provides opportunities for students to work on counting, seeing numbers in a variety of ways, subitizing, and learning number combinations. In addition, dot images address the core goals of K–2 number talks.

Instructions

The following dot image number talks are each designed to be used in a single session, in any order. Dot image number talks consist of three to five problems, each sequentially labeled A, B, C, and so on. The sequence of problems within a given number talk allows students to apply the strategies from previous problems to subsequent problems or provides opportunities for students to reason with the same quantity from multiple perspectives. This provides an opportunity to informally assess whether the student is unitizing a specific amount and conserving number.

As each problem is shown, ask students, "How many dots do you see? How do you see them?"

Dot images with . . .

The Number 3	71	The Number 7	76
The Number 4	71	The Number 8	77
The Number 5	72	The Number 9	79
The Number 6	74	The Number 10	80

Dot Images with the Number 3

As each number talk is shown, ask students, "How many dots do you see? How do you see them?"

String

NUMBER TALKS

K

The problems within each string should be presented in sequential order (A, B, C, and so on).

String

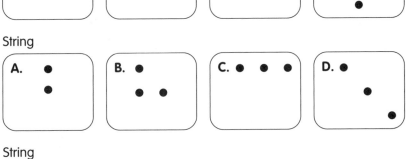

String

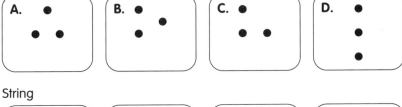

String

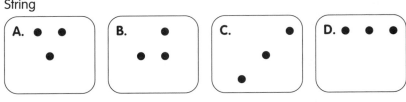

Dot Images with the Number 4

As each number talk is shown, ask students, "How many dots do you see? How do you see them?"

String

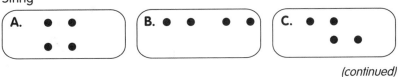

(continued)

The problems within each string should be presented in sequential order (A, B, C, and so on).

(Dot Images with the Number 4, continued)

String

A. • • • •   B. • • • •   C. • • • •

String

A. • B. • • • C. • •
   •   •   • •
   •
   •

String

A. • • •   B. • •   C. • • •
     •   • •
                               • •

String

A. • • • •   B. •   C. • • •
                  • • •   •

String

A. • •   B. • •   C. • •
     •   • •   • •

Dot Images with the Number 5

As each number talk is shown, ask students, "How many dots do you see? How do you see them?"

String

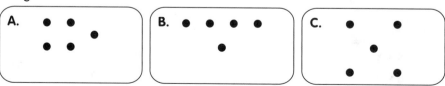

(continued)

(Dot Images with the Number 5, continued)

String

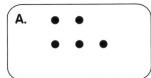 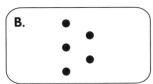 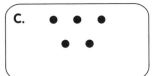

String

The problems within each string should be presented in sequential order (A, B, C, and so on).

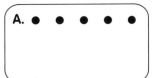  

String

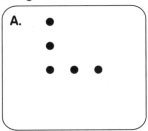 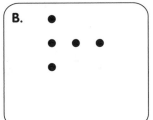 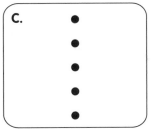

String

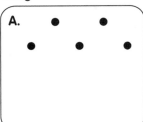 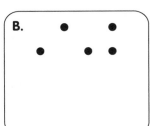 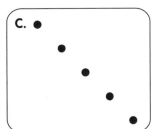

String

See Classroom Clip K.1: Ten-Frames and Dot Cards.

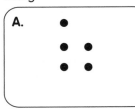 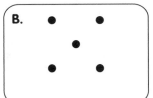 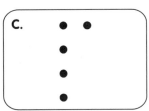

NUMBER TALKS

K

The problems within each string should be presented in sequential order (A, B, C, and so on).

Dot Images with the Number 6

As each number talk is shown, ask students, "How many dots do you see? How do you see them?"

String

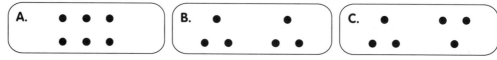

String

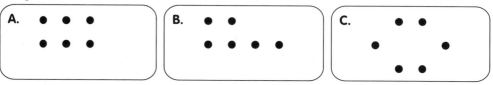

String

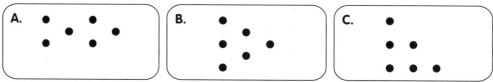

String

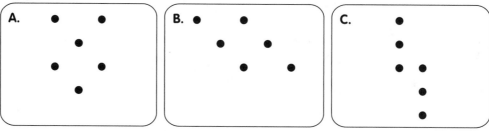

String

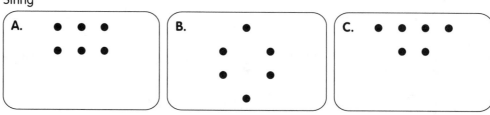

(continued)

(Dot Images with the Number 6, continued)

String

String

String

String

NUMBER TALKS

The problems within each string should be presented in sequential order (A, B, C, and so on).

Dot Images with the Number 7

As each number talk is shown, ask students, "How many dots do you see? How do you see them?"

String

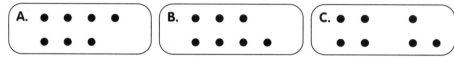

String

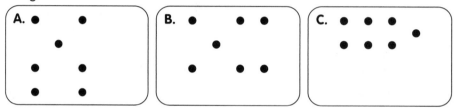

String

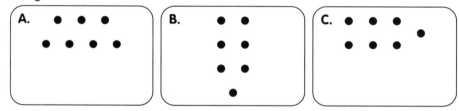

String

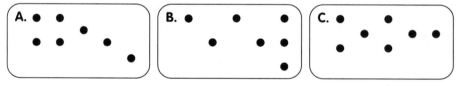

String

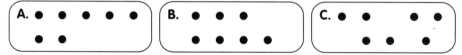

String

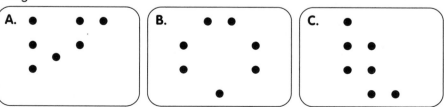

(continued)

(Dot Images with the Number 7, continued)

String

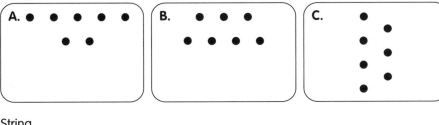

String

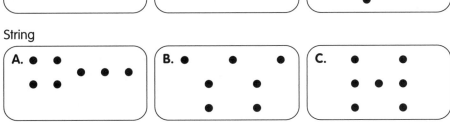

NUMBER TALKS

The problems within each string should be presented in sequential order (A, B, C, and so on).

Dot Images with the Number 8

As each number talk is shown, ask students, "How many dots do you see?
How do you see them?"

String

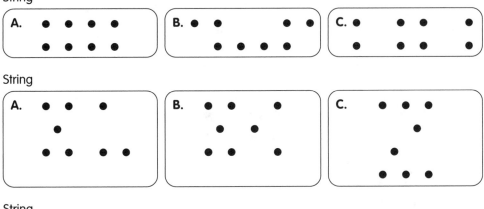

String

String

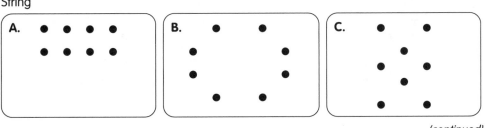

(continued)

NUMBER TALKS

K

(Dot Images with the Number 8, continued)

String

A.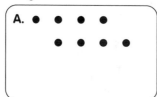

B.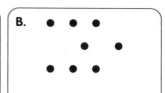

C.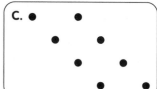

String

A.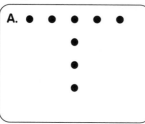

B.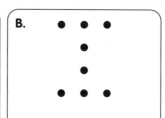

C.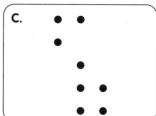

String

A.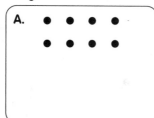

B.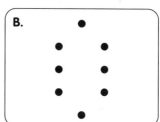

C.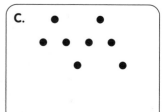

String

A.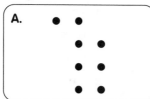

B.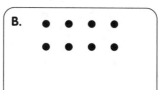

C.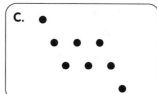

String

A.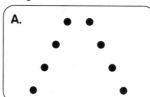

B.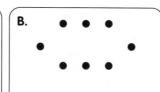

C.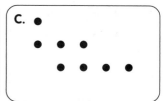

(continued)

(Dot Images with the Number 8, continued)

String

A. 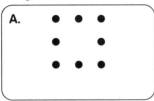 B. 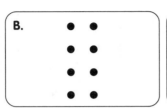 C.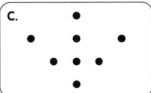

Dot Images with the Number 9

As each number talk is shown, ask students, "How many dots do you see? How do you see them?"

The problems within each string should be presented in sequential order (A, B, C, and so on).

String

A. 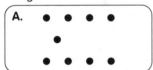 B.  C.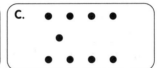

String

A. 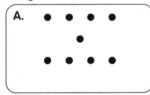 B. 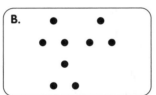 C.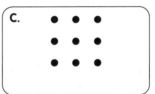

String

A. 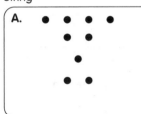 B. 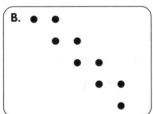 C.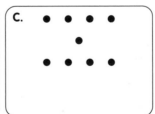

String

A. 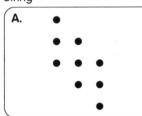 B. 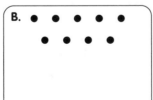 C.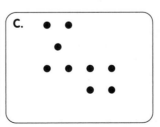

(continued)

79

NUMBER TALKS

K

The problems within each string should be presented in sequential order (A, B, C, and so on).

See Classroom Clip K.1: Ten-Frames and Dot Cards.

(Dot Images with the Number 9, continued)

String

A.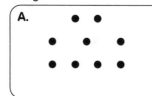

B.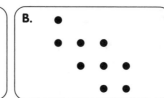

C.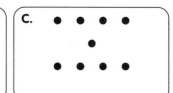

String

A.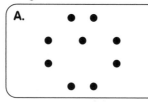

B.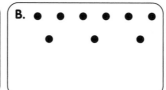

C.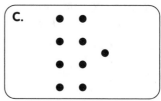

String

A.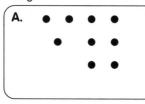

B.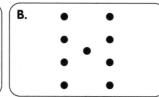

C.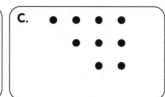

Dot Images with the Number 10

As each number talk is shown, ask students, "How many dots do you see? How do you see them?"

String

A.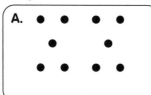

B.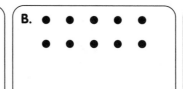

C.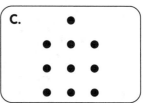

String

A.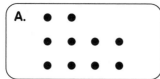

B.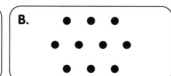

C.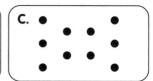

(Dot Images with the Number 10, continued)

String

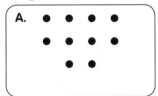 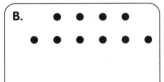 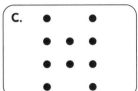

String

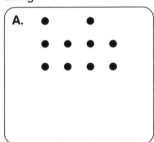 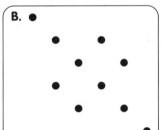 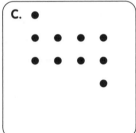

String

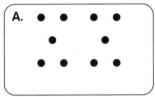 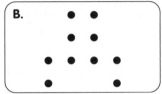 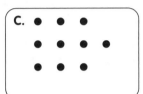

String

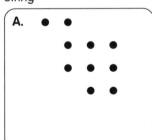 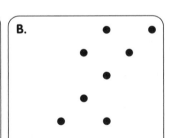 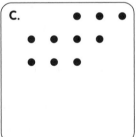

String

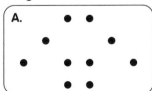 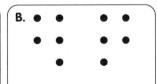 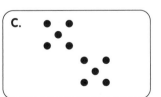

NUMBER TALKS

K

NUMBER TALKS

K

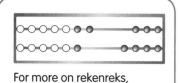

For more on rekenreks, see Chapter 3, page 41.

See Appendix D for directions for making a rekenrek.

Fluency Number Talks Using Rekenreks

As discussed in Chapter 3, rekenreks are an important tool to help students reason about numbers, subitize, build fluency, and compute using number relationships (Fosnot and Dolk 2001). The rekenrek comprises two rows of stringed beads, with five beads of one color and five beads of another color on each row. They are colored in groups of five to help students "see" or subitize the quantity of five. The teacher has the option of using only one row of beads at a time to build fluency up to ten or using both rows to work on fluency with numbers up to twenty. (See Appendix D for directions for making a rekenrek.)

Instructions

The following rekenrek number talks are each designed to be used in a single session, in any order. Rekenrek number talks consist of three to five problems, each sequentially labeled A, B, C, and so on. The sequence of problems within a given number talk allows students to apply strategies from previous problems to subsequent problems or provides opportunities for students to reason with the same quantity from multiple perspectives. This provides an opportunity to informally assess whether the student is unitizing a specific amount and conserving number.

As each problem is shown on a rekenrek, ask students, "How many beads do you see? How do you see them?"

Rekenreks with . . .

The Number 3	83	The Number 7	85
The Number 4	83	The Number 8	86
The Number 5	84	The Number 9	87
The Number 6	84	The Number 10	88

Rekenreks with the Number 3

As each number talk is shown on a rekenrek, ask students, "How many beads do you see? How do you see them?"

NUMBER TALKS

K

A. 0 on top
2 on bottom

B. 1 on top
2 on bottom

C. 3 on top
0 on bottom

D. 2 on bottom
3 on top

A. 1 on top
1 on bottom

B. 2 on top
1 on bottom

C. 1 on top
2 on bottom

D. 0 on top
3 on bottom

A. 3 on top
0 on bottom

B. 2 on top
1 on bottom

C. 0 on top
3 on bottom

The problems within each string should be presented in sequential order (A, B, C, and so on).

Rekenreks with the Number 4

As each number talk is shown on a rekenrek, ask students, "How many beads do you see? How do you see them?"

A. 2 on top
2 on bottom

B. 4 on top
0 on bottom

C. 3 on top
1 on bottom

A. 3 on top
1 on bottom

B. 1 on top
3 on bottom

C. 2 on top
2 on bottom

A. 1 on top
3 on bottom

B. 2 on top
2 on bottom

C. 4 on top
0 on bottom

See Classroom Clip K.2: Rekenreks.

NUMBER TALKS

K

The problems within each string should be presented in sequential order (A, B, C, and so on).

See Classroom Clip K.2: Rekenreks.

Rekenreks with the Number 5

As each number talk is shown on a rekenrek, ask students, "How many beads do you see? How do you see them?"

A. 2 on top
   2 on bottom

B. 2 on top
   3 on bottom

C. 1 on top
   4 on bottom

D. 0 on top
   5 on bottom

A. 2 on top
   3 on bottom

B. 3 on top
   2 on bottom

C. 4 on top
   1 on bottom

D. 5 on top
   0 on bottom

A. 1 on top
   4 on bottom

B. 0 on top
   5 on bottom

C. 3 on top
   2 on bottom

D. 4 on top
   1 on bottom

Rekenreks with the Number 6

As each number talk is shown on a rekenrek, ask students, "How many beads do you see? How do you see them?"

A. 3 on top
   3 on bottom

B. 4 on top
   2 on bottom

C. 3 on top
   3 on bottom

D. 2 on top
   4 on bottom

A. 6 on top
   0 on bottom

B. 5 on top
   1 on bottom

C. 4 on top
   2 on bottom

D. 3 on top
   3 on bottom

A. 1 on top
   5 on bottom

B. 2 on top
   4 on bottom

C. 3 on top
   3 on bottom

D. 0 on top
   6 on bottom

Rekenreks with the Number 7

As each number talk is shown on a rekenrek, ask students, "How many beads do you see? How do you see them?"

The problems within each string should be presented in sequential order (A, B, C, and so on).

A. 3 on top
3 on bottom

B. 3 on top
4 on bottom

C. 4 on top
3 on bottom

D. 7 on top
0 on bottom

A. 4 on top
4 on bottom

B. 3 on top
4 on bottom

C. 3 on top
3 on bottom

D. 3 on top
4 on bottom

A. 5 on top
0 on bottom

B. 5 on top
2 on bottom

C. 4 on top
3 on bottom

D. 2 on top
5 on bottom

A. 3 on top
3 on bottom

B. 6 on top
1 on bottom

C. 5 on top
2 on bottom

D. 7 on top
0 on bottom

A. 3 on top
3 on bottom

B. 2 on top
5 on bottom

C. 4 on top
4 on bottom

D. 3 on top
4 on bottom

A. 0 on top
7 on bottom

B. 1 on top
6 on bottom

C. 2 on top
5 on bottom

D. 3 on top
4 on bottom

NUMBER TALKS

K

The problems within each string should be presented in sequential order (A, B, C, and so on).

Rekenreks with the Number 8

As each number talk is shown on a rekenrek, ask students, "How many beads do you see? How do you see them?"

A. 4 on top
4 on bottom

B. 3 on top
5 on bottom

C. 4 on top
4 on bottom

D. 5 on top
3 on bottom

A. 3 on top
3 on bottom

B. 3 on top
5 on bottom

C. 4 on top
4 on bottom

D. 5 on top
3 on bottom

A. 2 on top
4 on bottom

B. 2 on top
6 on bottom

C. 4 on top
4 on bottom

D. 6 on top
2 on bottom

A. 8 on top
0 on bottom

B. 7 on top
1 on bottom

C. 6 on top
2 on bottom

D. 5 on top
3 on bottom

A. 5 on top
5 on bottom

B. 5 on top
3 on bottom

C. 6 on top
2 on bottom

D. 7 on top
1 on bottom

A. 3 on top
5 on bottom

B. 4 on top
4 on bottom

C. 2 on top
6 on bottom

D. 1 on top
7 on bottom

Rekenreks with the Number 9

As each number talk is shown on a rekenrek, ask students, "How many beads do you see? How do you see them?"

NUMBER TALKS

The problems within each string should be presented in sequential order (A, B, C, and so on).

A. 4 on top
4 on bottom

B. 4 on top
5 on bottom

C. 5 on top
5 on bottom

D. 5 on top
4 on bottom

A. 9 on top
0 on bottom

B. 8 on top
1 on bottom

C. 7 on top
2 on bottom

D. 6 on top
3 on bottom

A. 4 on top
5 on bottom

B. 3 on top
6 on bottom

C. 2 on top
7 on bottom

D. 1 on top
8 on bottom

A. 5 on top
5 on bottom

B. 4 on top
5 on bottom

C. 5 on top
4 on bottom

D. 4 on top
4 on bottom

A. 3 on top
6 on bottom

B. 6 on top
3 on bottom

C. 5 on top
4 on bottom

D. 8 on top
0 on bottom

A. 2 on top
7 on bottom

B. 7 on top
2 on bottom

C. 4 on top
5 on bottom

D. 3 on top
6 on bottom

NUMBER TALKS

K

The problems within each string should be presented in sequential order (A, B, C, and so on).

Rekenreks with the Number 10

As each number talk is shown on a rekenrek, ask students, "How many beads do you see? How do you see them?"

A. 5 on top
5 on bottom

B. 4 on top
6 on bottom

C. 3 on top
7 on bottom

D. 2 on top
8 on bottom

A. 6 on top
4 on bottom

B. 5 on top
5 on bottom

C. 4 on top
6 on bottom

D. 5 on top
5 on bottom

A. 7 on top
3 on bottom

B. 5 on top
5 on bottom

C. 6 on top
4 on bottom

D. 7 on top
3 on bottom

A. 5 on top
5 on bottom

B. 4 on top
6 on bottom

C. 3 on top
7 on bottom

D. 2 on top
8 on bottom

A. 2 on top
8 on bottom

B. 1 on top
9 on bottom

C. 0 on top
10 on bottom

D. 2 on top
8 on bottom

A. 10 on top
0 on bottom

B. 9 on top
1 on bottom

C. 8 on top
2 on bottom

D. 7 on top
3 on bottom

Fluency Number Talks Using Five- and Ten-Frames

As discussed in Chapter 3, five- and ten-frames can be used as a single row of five (five-frame), two rows of five (ten-frame), or as two ten-frames together to provide the opportunity to work with numbers to twenty. Like rekenreks, ten-frames can be used to foster fluency, subitize, work with place value, and compute with addition and subtraction. Frames are also arranged to capitalize on subitizing to five as half of ten. (See Appendix D for five- and ten-frame templates.)

Varying the questions posed to students can change the purpose and focus of each ten-frame. Questions such as, "How many did you see?" and "How do you see seven?" help students build fluency with targeted numbers. Asking, "How many more do we need to make ten?" and "How many are left after removing three?" shifts the focus to computation.

Instructions

The following five- and ten-frame number talks are each designed to be used in a single session, in any order. Five- and ten-frame number talks consist of three to five problems, each sequentially labeled A, B, C, and so on. The sequence of problems within a given number talk allows students to apply the strategies from previous problems to subsequent problems.

The focus for the numbers 3 to 9 is to ask students, "How many dots do you see? How do you see them?" With frames for the number 10, the question shifts to, "How many more to make ten?"

For more on using five- and ten-frames, see page 43.

See Appendix D for five- and ten-frame templates.

Frames with . . .

The Number 3	90	The Number 7	93
The Number 4	90	The Number 8	94
The Number 5	91	The Number 9	95
The Number 6	92	The Number 10	96

NUMBER TALKS

K

> The problems within each string should be presented in sequential order (A, B, C, and so on).

Five-Frames with the Number 3

As each number talk is shown, ask students, "How many dots do you see? How do you see them?"

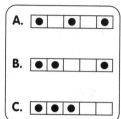

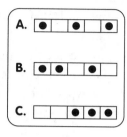

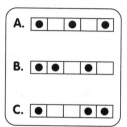

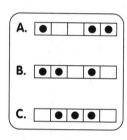

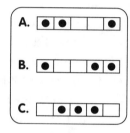

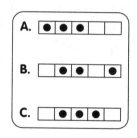

Five- and Ten-Frames with the Number 4

As each number talk is shown, ask students, "How many dots do you see? How do you see them?"

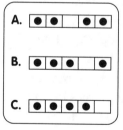

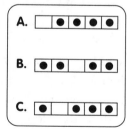

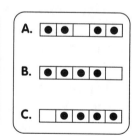

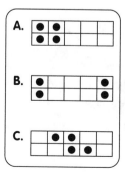

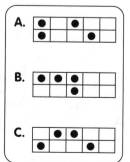

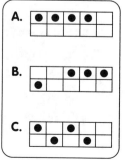

Ten-Frames with the Number 5

As each number talk is shown, ask students, "How many dots do you see? How do you see them?"

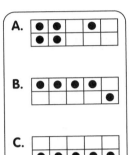

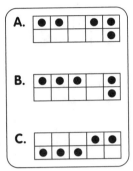

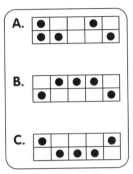

The problems within each string should be presented in sequential order (A, B, C, and so on).

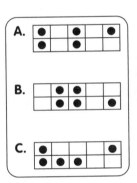

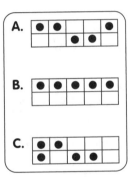

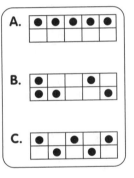

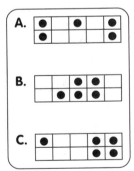

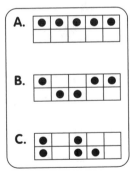

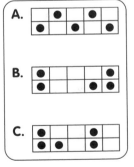

See Classroom Clip K.1: Ten-Frames and Dot Cards.

NUMBER TALKS

K

The problems within each string should be presented in sequential order (A, B, C, and so on).

Ten-Frames with the Number 6

As each number talk is shown, ask students, "How many dots do you see? How do you see them?"

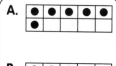

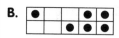

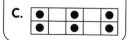

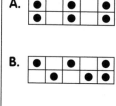

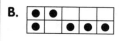

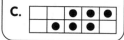

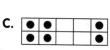

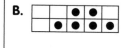

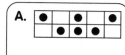

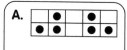

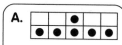

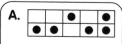

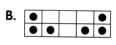

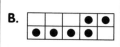

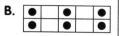

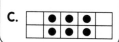

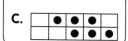

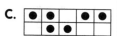

Ten-Frames with the Number 7

As each number talk is shown, ask students, "How many dots do you see? How do you see them?"

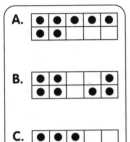

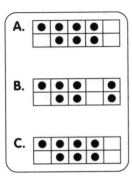

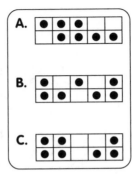

The problems within each string should be presented in sequential order (A, B, C, and so on).

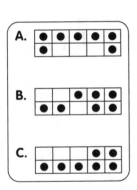

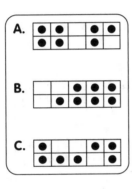

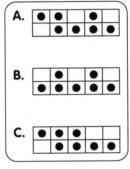

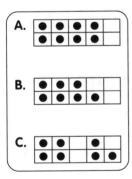

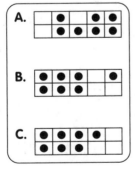

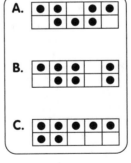

See Classroom Clip K.1: Ten-Frames and Dot Cards.

NUMBER TALKS

K

The problems within each string should be presented in sequential order (A, B, C, and so on).

Ten-Frames with the Number 8

As each number talk is shown, ask students, "How many dots do you see? How do you see them?"

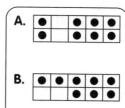
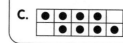
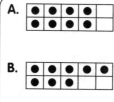
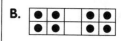
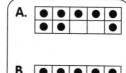
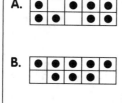
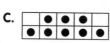
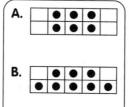
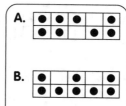
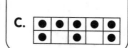
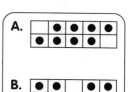
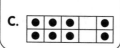
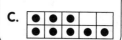

Ten-Frames with the Number 9

As each number talk is shown, ask students, "How many dots do you see? How do you see them?"

NUMBER TALKS

K

A.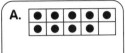

B.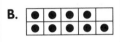

C.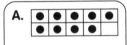

A.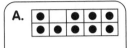

B.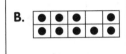

C.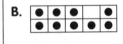

A.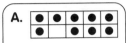

B.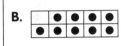

C.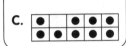

The problems within each string should be presented in sequential order (A, B, C, and so on).

A.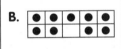

B.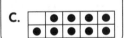

C.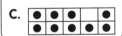

A.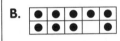

B.

C.

A.

B.

C.

A.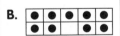

B.

C.

A.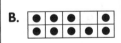

B.

C.

A.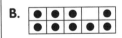

B.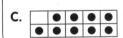

C.

The problems within each string should be presented in sequential order (A, B, C, and so on).

Ten-Frames with the Number 10

As each number talk is shown, ask students, "How many more do we need to make ten?"

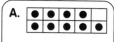

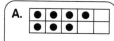

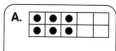

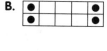

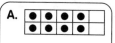

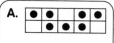

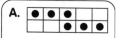

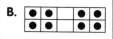

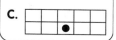

First-Grade Number Talks

1

Addition Number Talks

Number talks at the first-grade level are designed to provide students with opportunities to continue to build fluency with numbers up to ten and develop beginning addition strategies. Dot images, rekenreks, and five- and ten-frames may be used during number talks to provide a context for reasoning with numbers. When using these tools, recording number sentences to match student thinking is often helpful.

The following first-grade number talks are organized by common addition strategies and tools.

NUMBER TALKS
GRADE

1

For more on Counting All/
Counting On, see pages
59–60.

Addition: Counting All/Counting On: Dot Images

Instructions

The following dot image number talks are each designed to be used in a single session, in any order. Dot image number talks consist of three to five problems, each sequentially labeled A, B, C, and so on. The sequence of problems within a given number talk allows students to apply the strategies from previous problems to subsequent problems. As each problem is shown, ask students, "How many dots do you see? How do you see them?"

Note that using two sets of dot images for each number talk provides an opportunity for students to unitize one quantity and count on.

Counting All/Counting On: Dot Images

As each number talk is shown, ask students, "How many dots do you see?
How do you see them?"

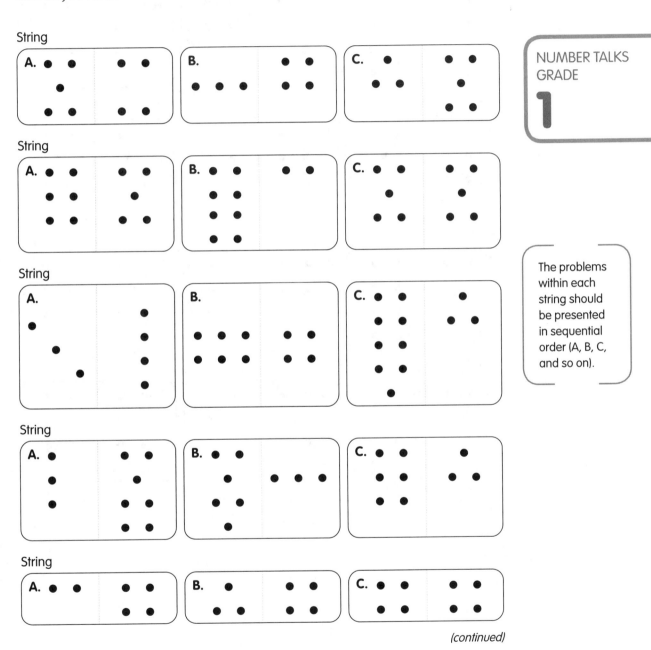

String

String

String

String

String

NUMBER TALKS
GRADE

1

The problems
within each
string should
be presented
in sequential
order (A, B, C,
and so on).

(continued)

(Counting All/Counting On: Dot Images, continued)

NUMBER TALKS
GRADE
1

A.
B.
C.

String

A.
B.
C.

String

A.
B.
C.

String

A.
B.
C.

Addition: Counting All/Counting On: Rekenreks

Instructions

As discussed in Chapter 3, rekenreks are an important tool to help students reason about numbers, subitize, build fluency, and compute using number relationships (Fosnot and Dolk 2001). (See Appendix D for directions for making a rekenrek.)

The following rekenreks number talks are each designed to be used in a single session, in any order. Rekenrek number talks consist of three to five problems, each sequentially labeled A, B, C, and so on. The sequence of problems within a given number talk allows students to apply the strategies from previous problems to subsequent problems.

As each problem is shown on a rekenrek, ask students, "How many beads do you see? How do you see them?"

NUMBER TALKS
GRADE

1

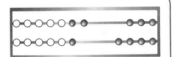

For more on rekenreks, see Chapter 3, page 41.

See Appendix D for directions for making a rekenrek.

Counting All/Counting On: Rekenreks

As each number talk is shown on a rekenrek, ask students, "How many beads do you see? How do you see them?"

NUMBER TALKS
GRADE

1

The problems within each string should be presented in sequential order (A, B, C, and so on).

A. 4 on top
   3 on bottom

B. 5 on top
   2 on bottom

C. 6 on top
   1 on bottom

A. 5 on top
   5 on bottom

B. 5 on top
   7 on bottom

C. 5 on top
   9 on bottom

A. 6 on top
   6 on bottom

B. 6 on top
   4 on bottom

C. 6 on top
   8 on bottom

A. 10 on top
   1 on bottom

B. 9 on top
   2 on bottom

C. 8 on top
   3 on bottom

A. 9 on top
   3 on bottom

B. 9 on top
   4 on bottom

C. 9 on top
   5 on bottom

A. 8 on top
   2 on bottom

B. 8 on top
   4 on bottom

C. 8 on top
   6 on bottom

A. 10 on top
   10 on bottom

B. 10 on top
   5 on bottom

C. 10 on top
   8 on bottom

A. 9 on top
   1 on bottom

B. 9 on top
   2 on bottom

C. 9 on top
   4 on bottom

A. 7 on top
   3 on bottom

B. 7 on top
   5 on bottom

C. 7 on top
   8 on bottom

Addition: Counting All/Counting On: Double Ten-Frames

Instructions

As discussed in Chapter 3, ten-frames are an important tool to help students reason about numbers, subitize, build fluency, work with place value, and compute with addition and subtraction. (See Appendix D for a ten-frame template.)

The following ten-frames number talks are each designed to be used in a single session, in any order. Frames number talks consist of three to five problems, each sequentially labeled A, B, C, and so on. The sequence of problems within a given number talk allows students to apply the strategies from previous problems to subsequent problems.

As each problem is shown, ask students, "How many dots do you see? How do you see them?"

NUMBER TALKS GRADE

1

For more on using ten-frames, see page 43.

Counting All/Counting On: Double Ten-Frames

When the focus is on the numbers 3 to 9, ask students, "How many dots do you see? How do you see them?" When the focus is on the number 10, the question shifts to, "How many more to make ten?"

NUMBER TALKS
GRADE

1

The problems within each string should be presented in sequential order (A, B, C, and so on).

See Classroom Clip 2.1: Ten-Frames: 8 + 6.

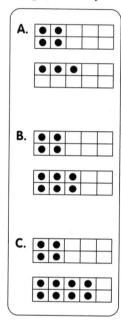
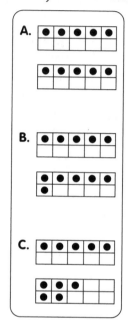
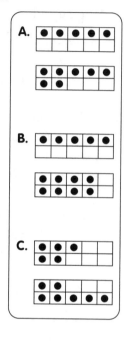
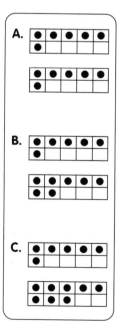
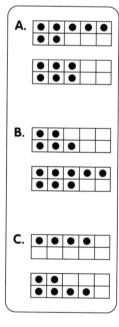
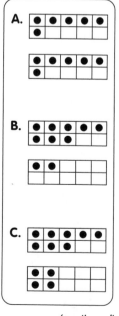

(continued)

(Counting All/Counting On: Double Ten-Frames, continued)

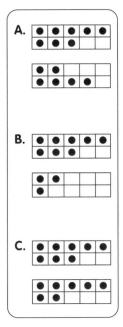

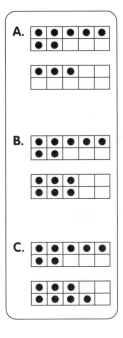

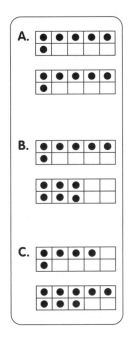

NUMBER TALKS
GRADE

1

Addition: Counting All/Counting On:
Number Sentences

Instructions

The following number talks are each designed to be used in a single session, in any order. These number talks consist of three to five problems. The sequence of problems within a given number talk allows students to apply strategies from previous problems to subsequent problems.

NUMBER TALKS
GRADE

1

Counting All/Counting On: Number Sentences

3 + 6	4 + 6	9 + 1
3 + 7	7 + 4	9 + 3
3 + 8	4 + 8	9 + 5
	4 + 9	9 + 7

For more on
Counting All/
Counting On,
see pages
59–60.

6 + 4	7 + 3	9 + 11
6 + 6	7 + 7	9 + 13
6 + 8	7 + 9	9 + 15
6 + 9	7 + 5	

5 + 5	8 + 2	11 + 5
5 + 7	8 + 5	12 + 4
5 + 9	8 + 7	13 + 3
	8 + 9	

Addition: Doubles/Near-Doubles: Rekenreks

Instructions

As discussed in Chapter 3, rekenreks are an important tool to help students reason about numbers, subitize, build fluency, and compute using number relationships (Fosnot and Dolk 2001). (See Appendix D for directions for making a rekenrek.)

The following rekenreks number talks are each designed to be used in a single session, in any order. Rekenrek number talks consist of three to five problems, each sequentially labeled A, B, C, and so on. The sequence of problems within a given number talk allows students to apply the strategies from previous problems to subsequent problems.

As each problem is shown on a rekenrek, ask students, "How many beads do you see? How do you see them?"

NUMBER TALKS GRADE

1

For more on rekenreks, see Chapter 3, page 41.

See Appendix D for directions for making a rekenrek.

Doubles/Near-Doubles: Rekenreks

As each number talk is shown on a rekenrek, ask students, "How many beads do you see? How do you see them?"

NUMBER TALKS
GRADE

1

The problems within each string should be presented in sequential order (A, B, C, and so on).

A. 3 on top
3 on bottom

B. 4 on top
3 on bottom

C. 3 on top
2 on bottom

A. 4 on top
4 on bottom

B. 5 on top
4 on bottom

C. 4 on top
3 on bottom

A. 5 on top
5 on bottom

B. 6 on top
5 on bottom

C. 5 on top
4 on bottom

A. 6 on top
6 on bottom

B. 7 on top
6 on bottom

C. 6 on top
5 on bottom

A. 7 on top
7 on bottom

B. 8 on top
7 on bottom

C. 7 on top
6 on bottom

A. 8 on top
8 on bottom

B. 9 on top
8 on bottom

C. 8 on top
7 on bottom

(continued)

(Doubles/Near-Doubles: Rekenreks, continued)

A. 9 on top
  9 on bottom

B. 10 on top
  9 on bottom

C. 10 on top
  10 on bottom

A. 5 on top
  5 on bottom

B. 7 on top
  5 on bottom

C. 5 on top
  5 on bottom

D. 5 on top
  3 on bottom

A. 6 on top
  6 on bottom

B. 8 on top
  6 on bottom

C. 6 on top
  6 on bottom

D. 6 on top
  4 on bottom

NUMBER TALKS
GRADE

1

Addition: Doubles/Near-Doubles: Double Ten-Frames

Instructions

As discussed in Chapter 3, ten-frames are an important tool to help students reason about numbers, subitize, build fluency, and work with place value, and compute with addition and subtraction. (See Appendix D for a ten-frame template.)

The following ten-frames number talks are each designed to be used in a single session, in any order. Frames number talks consist of three to five problems, each sequentially labeled A, B, C, and so on. The sequence of problems within a given number talk allows students to apply the strategies from previous problems to subsequent problems.

As each problem is shown, ask students, "How many dots do you see? How do you see them?"

For more on using ten-frames, see page 43.

See Appendix D for a ten-frame template.

Doubles/Near Doubles: Double Ten-Frames

As each number talk is shown, ask students, "How many dots do you see? How do you see them?"

NUMBER TALKS
GRADE

1

The problems within each string should be presented in sequential order (A, B, C, and so on).

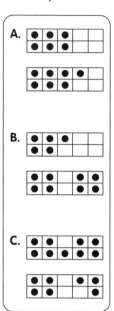

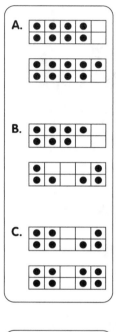

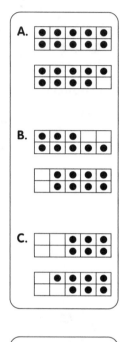

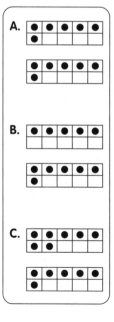

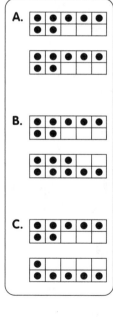

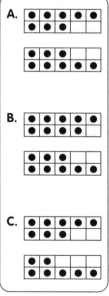

Addition: Doubles/Near-Doubles: Number Sentences

Instructions

The following number talks are each designed to be used in a single session, in any order. Each number talk consists of three to five problems. The sequence of problems within a given number talk allows students to apply strategies from previous problems to subsequent problems.

NUMBER TALKS
GRADE

1

Doubles/Near Doubles: Number Sentences

2 + 2	7 + 7	12 + 12
2 + 3	7 + 6	12 + 13
3 + 3	7 + 8	13 + 13
3 + 4	8 + 8	13 + 14

For more on Doubles/Near-Doubles, see page 60.

4 + 4	8 + 8	15 + 15
4 + 3	8 + 9	15 + 16
3 + 3	9 + 9	14 + 14
3 + 4	9 + 10	14 + 15

5 + 5	10 + 10	20 + 20
5 + 6	10 + 11	19 + 19
6 + 6	11 + 11	19 + 18
6 + 7	11 + 12	18 + 18
	12 + 12	18 + 17

NUMBER TALKS
GRADE

1

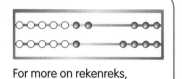

For more on rekenreks,
see Chapter 3, page 41.

See Appendix D for
directions for making a
rekenrek.

Addition: Making Tens: Rekenreks

Instructions

As discussed in Chapter 3, rekenreks are an important tool to help students reason about numbers, subitize, build fluency, and compute using number relationships (Fosnot and Dolk 2001). (See Appendix D for directions for making a rekenrek.)

The following rekenreks number talks are each designed to be used in a single session, in any order. Rekenrek number talks consist of three to five problems, each sequentially labeled A, B, C, and so on. The sequence of problems within a given number talk allows students to apply strategies from previous problems to subsequent problems.

As each problem is shown on a rekenrek, ask students, "How many beads do you see? How do you see them?"

Making Tens: Rekenreks

As each number talk is shown on a rekenrek, ask students, "How many beads do you see? How do you see them?"

A. 5 on top
    5 on bottom

B. 5 on top
    6 on bottom

C. 7 on top
    5 on bottom

A. 5 on top
    5 on bottom

B. 5 on top
    7 on bottom

C. 5 on top
    9 on bottom

A. 8 on top
    2 on bottom

B. 8 on top
    3 on bottom

C. 8 on top
    4 on bottom

A. 10 on top
    0 on bottom

B. 9 on top
    1 on bottom

C. 9 on top
    2 on bottom

A. 9 on top
    1 on bottom

B. 9 on top
    3 on bottom

C. 9 on top
    5 on bottom

A. 7 on top
    3 on bottom

B. 7 on top
    4 on bottom

C. 7 on top
    5 on bottom

A. 8 on top
    2 on bottom

B. 8 on top
    4 on bottom

C. 8 on top
    6 on bottom

A. 7 on top
    3 on bottom

B. 7 on top
    6 on bottom

C. 7 on top
    9 on bottom

A. 6 on top
    4 on bottom

B. 6 on top
    6 on bottom

C. 6 on top
    8 on bottom

NUMBER TALKS
GRADE

The problems within each string should be presented in sequential order (A, B, C, and so on).

NUMBER TALKS
GRADE

1

For more on using ten-frames, see page 43.

See Appendix D for a ten-frame template.

Addition: Making Tens: Double Ten-Frames

Instructions

As discussed in Chapter 3, ten-frames are an important tool to help students reason about numbers, subitize, build fluency, and work with place value, and compute with addition and subtraction. (See Appendix D for a ten-frame template.)

The following ten-frames number talks are each designed to be used in a single session, in any order. Frames number talks consist of three to five problems, each sequentially labeled A, B, C, and so on. The sequence of problems within a given number talk allows students to apply the strategies from previous problems to subsequent problems.

Making Tens: Double Ten-Frames

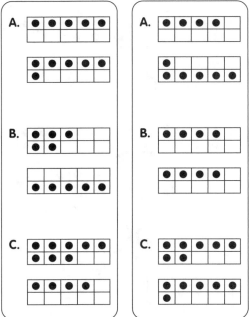
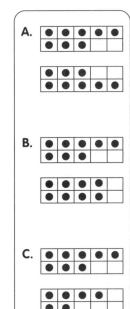

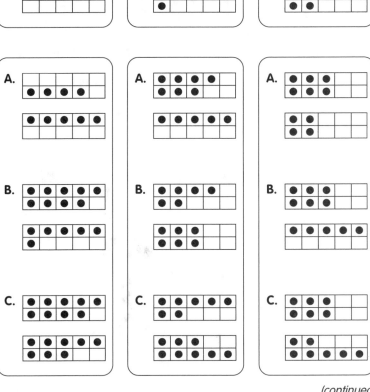

(continued)

NUMBER TALKS
GRADE
1

(Making Tens: Double Ten-Frames, continued)

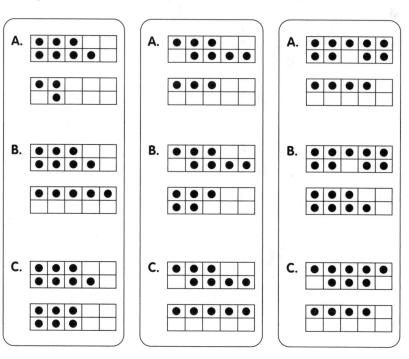

Addition: Making Tens: Number Sentences

Instructions

The following number talks, each designed to be used in a single session, in any order, consist of three to five problems. The sequence of problems within a given number talk allows students to apply strategies from previous problems to subsequent problems.

NUMBER TALKS GRADE

1

Making Tens: Number Sentences

$9 + 1$	$5 + 5$	$8 + 2$
$9 + 3 + 1$	$5 + 5 + 4$	$8 + 3 + 2$
$9 + 5 + 1$	$5 + 3 + 5$	$2 + 5 + 8$

$3 + 7$	$4 + 6$	$1 + 8 + 9$
$7 + 5 + 3$	$4 + 6 + 4$	$9 + 3 + 1$
$3 + 6 + 7$	$6 + 5 + 4$	$1 + 6 + 9$

For more on Making Tens, see page 61.

$5 + 5$	$2 + 8$	$5 + 5 + 8$
$5 + 6 + 5$	$2 + 5 + 8$	$3 + 4 + 6$
$4 + 5 + 5$	$8 + 6 + 2$	$4 + 5 + 6 + 5$

Addition: Making Landmark or Friendly Numbers

Instructions

The following number talks, each designed to be used in a single session, in any order, consist of three to five problems. The sequence of problems within a given number talk allows students to apply strategies from previous problems to subsequent problems.

The following number sentences are designed to encourage students to adjust one or all of the addends by adding or subtracting amounts to make a friendlier number.

NUMBER TALKS
GRADE

1

Making Landmark or Friendly Numbers

For more on Making Landmark or Friendly Numbers, see page 62.

$9 + 1$	$6 + 4$	$8 + 2$
$9 + 1 + 4$	$6 + 4 + 3$	$8 + 2 + 11$
$9 + 5$	$6 + 7$	$8 + 13$
$9 + 6$	$6 + 10$	$8 + 15$
	$6 + 9$	

$8 + 2$	$10 + 12$	$20 + 5$
$8 + 2 + 4$	$9 + 12$	$19 + 1 + 4$
$8 + 6$	$9 + 15$	$19 + 5$
$8 + 5$		$19 + 8$

$7 + 3$	$10 + 10$	$20 + 20$
$7 + 3 + 3$	$9 + 9$	$19 + 20$
$7 + 6$	$9 + 8$	$19 + 19$
$7 + 9$		

Second-Grade Number Talks

The following number talks are designed to elicit and foster specific computation strategies. While each strategy possesses distinct characteristics, often similarities overlap. For example, many of the strategies build on changing numbers to landmark or friendly numbers; this is a similarity. The difference lies in *how* the landmark or friendly number is created. This subtle difference is the essence of the strategy.

As you begin to implement number talks in your classroom, start with small numbers that are age and grade-level appropriate. Using small numbers serves two purposes: 1) students can focus on the nuances of the strategy instead of the magnitude of the numbers, and 2) students are able to build confidence in their mathematical abilities. As students' understanding of different strategies develops, you can gradually increase the size of the numbers. When the numbers become too large, students will rely on less efficient strategies, such as Counting All, or resort to paper and pencil, thereby losing the focus on developing mental strategies.

Each series of number talks is organized by specific strategies and categories. The categories are a suggested sequence to delineate beginning number talks to advanced number talks. They do not represent student math ability levels, but a scaffolding of problems from easier to more difficult problems.

Category Key

1. Category 1 represents introductory number talks that more readily encourage a specific strategy.

2. Category 2 talks are crafted for students who are successfully using the selected strategy.

3. Category 3 provides opportunities for students to use and extend the targeted strategy.

NUMBER TALKS GRADE

2

Addition Number Talks

The following number talks are crafted to elicit specific addition strategies; however, you may find that students also share other efficient methods. Keep in mind that the overall purpose is to help students build a toolbox of efficient strategies based on numerical reasoning. The ultimate goal of number talks is for students to compute accurately, efficiently, and flexibly.

Addition: Counting All/Counting On

Instructions

Counting All and Counting On are entry-level strategies for addition. Since we want to encourage students to move toward more efficient methods for adding, we do not present specific number talks to foster this strategy with second-grade students. If students share this method as their strategy, honor their thinking; however, always make connections to more efficient strategies.

For more on Counting All/Counting On, see pages 59–60.

NUMBER TALKS
GRADE

2

Addition: Doubles/Near-Doubles

Instructions

The following number talks consist of three or more sequential problems. The sequence of problems within a given number talk allows students to apply strategies from previous problems to subsequent problems. These number talk problems may be used in two ways:
- selected at random from each category; or
- navigated in a systematic order by selecting problems with smaller numbers from a specific category, then building to larger numbers.

For more on Doubles/Near-Doubles, see page 60.

Category 1	122
Category 2	123
Category 3	124

Category 1: Doubles/Near-Doubles

The following number talks consist of doubles using basic facts up to 10.

> Category 1 represents introductory number talks that more readily encourage a specific strategy.

NUMBER TALKS GRADE 2

3 + 3 3 + 4 3 + 2	6 + 6 6 + 5 6 + 7	6 + 6 6 + 5 6 + 7
3 + 3 3 + 4 3 + 2	6 + 6 6 + 5 6 + 7	9 + 9 9 + 8 9 + 10
4 + 4 4 + 3 4 + 5	7 + 7 7 + 6 7 + 8	10 + 10 10 + 9 9 + 9
5 + 5 5 + 4 5 + 6	8 + 8 8 + 7 8 + 9	7 + 7 7 + 9 7 + 5

Category 2: Doubles/Near-Doubles

The following number talks consist of doubles using numbers between 10 and 20.

Category 2 talks are crafted for students who are successfully using the selected strategy.

11 + 11
12 + 12
11 + 12
11 + 10

14 + 14
13 + 13
14 + 13
14 + 15

18 + 18
20 + 20
18 + 19
18 + 17

NUMBER TALKS GRADE

2

12 + 12
13 + 13
12 + 11
12 + 13

15 + 15
16 + 16
15 + 14
15 + 16

19 + 19
20 + 20
19 + 18
19 + 20

13 + 13
14 + 14
13 + 12
13 + 14

16 + 16
17 + 17
16 + 15
16 + 17

15 + 15
15 + 17
15 + 13
15 + 16

See Classroom Clip 2.2: Addition: 16 + 15.

Category 3: Doubles/Near-Doubles

The following number talks consist of doubles with numbers between 20 and 50 and with 100.

20 + 20	30 + 30	45 + 45
19 + 19	29 + 29	46 + 45
19 + 21	29 + 28	46 + 46
19 + 17	29 + 31	44 + 46

25 + 25	35 + 35	50 + 50
24 + 25	35 + 36	49 + 49
25 + 26	34 + 35	48 + 49
24 + 26	36 + 37	48 + 48
		49 + 51

25 + 25	40 + 40	100 + 100
25 + 26	39 + 39	99 + 99
25 + 28	39 + 38	99 + 98
24 + 27	39 + 41	99 + 97

Addition: Making Tens

Instructions

The following number talks consist of three or more sequential problems. The sequence of problems within a given number talk allows students to apply strategies from previous problems to subsequent problems. These number talk problems may be used in two ways:

- selected at random from each category; or
- navigated in a systematic order by selecting problems with smaller numbers from a specific category, then building to larger numbers.

Category 1	126
Category 2	127
Category 3	128

For more on Making Tens, see page 61.

NUMBER TALKS
GRADE

2

Category 1: Making Tens

The following number talks include two numbers that make a quick ten.

NUMBER TALKS
GRADE

2

$7 + 3$
$7 + 5 + 3$
$3 + 6 + 7$

$5 + 5$
$5 + 6 + 5$
$5 + 9 + 5$

$9 + 5 + 1$
$8 + 9 + 1$
$1 + 4 + 9$

$8 + 2$
$2 + 4 + 8$
$8 + 3 + 2$

$9 + 1$
$9 + 7 + 1$
$1 + 6 + 9$

$2 + 5 + 8$
$4 + 7 + 6$
$5 + 5 + 8$

$6 + 4$
$4 + 9 + 6$
$6 + 8 + 4$

$3 + 5 + 7$
$6 + 5 + 4$
$2 + 9 + 8$

$3 + 8 + 7$
$9 + 1 + 2$
$4 + 9 + 6$

Category 2: Making Tens

The following number talks include problems with two pairs of numbers that make a quick ten.

$4 + 6 + 8 + 2$
$9 + 3 + 1 + 7$
$5 + 6 + 5 + 4$

$3 + 8 + 2 + 7$
$4 + 4 + 6 + 6$
$9 + 1 + 1 + 9$

$5 + 3 + 5 + 4 + 7$
$9 + 5 + 8 + 2 + 1$
$4 + 5 + 6 + 3 + 7$

NUMBER TALKS
GRADE

2

$3 + 9 + 7 + 1$
$2 + 9 + 8 + 1$
$6 + 4 + 3 + 7$

$5 + 7 + 3 + 5$
$2 + 5 + 5 + 8$
$6 + 6 + 4 + 4$

$3 + 8 + 5 + 5 + 2$
$9 + 1 + 6 + 3 + 4$
$7 + 4 + 3 + 2 + 8$

$4 + 8 + 2 + 6$
$1 + 9 + 2 + 8$
$5 + 3 + 7 + 5$

$3 + 7 + 8 + 2$
$1 + 1 + 9 + 9$
$3 + 7 + 7 + 3$

$2 + 6 + 8 + 3 + 4$
$9 + 3 + 1 + 5 + 5$
$4 + 8 + 6 + 2 + 7$

Category 3: Making Tens

The following number talks require students to decompose at least one number to make a quick ten.

NUMBER TALKS
GRADE

2

9 + 1	8 + 2	7 + 3
9 + 1 + 4	8 + 2 + 3	7 + 3 + 2
9 + 5	8 + 5	7 + 5
9 + 8	8 + 4	7 + 6

10 + 5	10 + 5	10 + 6
9 + 5	8 + 5	7 + 6
10 + 7	10 + 7	10 + 4
9 + 7	8 + 7	7 + 4

9 + 3	8 + 2	7 + 3
9 + 5	8 + 5	7 + 6
9 + 8	8 + 4	7 + 4
9 + 9	8 + 7	7 + 5

10 + 14	10 + 12	10 + 13
9 + 14	8 + 12	7 + 13
10 + 23	10 + 23	10 + 25
9 + 23	8 + 23	7 + 25

Addition: Making Landmark or Friendly Numbers

Instructions

The following number talks consist of three or more sequential problems. The sequence of problems within a given number talk allows students to apply strategies from previous problems to subsequent problems. These number talk problems may be used in two ways:

- selected at random from each category; or
- navigated in a systematic order by selecting problems with smaller numbers from a specific category, then building to larger numbers.

Category 1	130
Category 2	131
Category 3	132

For more on Making Landmark or Friendly Numbers, see page 62.

NUMBER TALKS GRADE

2

Category 1: Making Landmark or Friendly Numbers

The following number talks include single-digit numbers that are one away from a landmark or friendly number.

$10 + 2$	$29 + 1$	$60 + 7$
$9 + 2$	$29 + 5$	$59 + 1 + 6$
$9 + 5$	$29 + 13$	$59 + 7$
$9 + 8$	$29 + 24$	$59 + 12$
$9 + 9$	$29 + 29$	$59 + 22$

$20 + 5$	$40 + 4$	$70 + 8$
$19 + 5$	$39 + 4$	$69 + 1 + 7$
$19 + 7$	$39 + 15$	$69 + 8$
$19 + 8$	$39 + 39$	$69 + 13$

$19 + 1$	$49 + 1$	$80 + 4$
$19 + 15$	$49 + 8$	$79 + 1 + 3$
$19 + 27$	$49 + 16$	$79 + 4$
$19 + 18$	$49 + 27$	$79 + 14$

Category 2: Making Landmark or Friendly Numbers

The following number talks consist of computation problems in which one addend is two away from a multiple of ten or a landmark number.

10 + 5
8 + 2 + 3
8 + 5
8 + 7
8 + 12

30 + 5
28 + 2 + 3
28 + 5
28 + 7
28 + 16

60 + 3
58 + 2 + 1
58 + 3
58 + 14
58 + 26

NUMBER TALKS
GRADE
2

8 + 2
8 + 14
8 + 25
8 + 36

40 + 4
38 + 2 + 2
38 + 4
38 + 13
38 + 27

70 + 7
68 + 2 + 5
68 + 7
68 + 15
68 + 26

18 + 2
18 + 2 + 13
18 + 15
18 + 23

50 + 6
48 + 2 + 4
48 + 6
48 + 13
48 + 25

80 + 5
78 + 2 + 3
78 + 5
78 + 15
78 + 17

Category 3: Making Landmark or Friendly Numbers

The following number talks consist of computation problems in which both addends are one or more away from a multiple of ten or a landmark number. The farther the addends are from landmark numbers, the more challenging the strategy.

NUMBER TALKS
GRADE

2

See Classroom Clip 2.3: Addition: 26 + 27.

10 + 20	25 + 25	20 + 30
9 + 19	26 + 25	19 + 29
9 + 29	26 + 26	18 + 28
9 + 39	26 + 27	19 + 26

10 + 20	30 + 30	30 + 50
9 + 18	29 + 29	29 + 49
10 + 30	28 + 29	28 + 48
9 + 28	28 + 28	29 + 48

20 + 20	20 + 20	50 + 50
19 + 19	19 + 19	49 + 49
19 + 29	18 + 19	49 + 48
19 + 39	18 + 29	48 + 48

Addition: Breaking Each Number into Its Place Value

Instructions

The following number talks consist of three or more sequential problems. The sequence of problems within a given number talk allows students to apply strategies from previous problems to subsequent problems. These number talk problems may be used in two ways:

- selected at random from each category; or
- navigated in a systematic order by selecting problems with smaller numbers from a specific category, then building to larger numbers.

Category 1	134
Category 2	135
Category 3	136

For more on Breaking Each Number into Its Place Value, see page 63.

NUMBER TALKS GRADE

2

Category 1 represents introductory number talks that more readily encourage a specific strategy.

NUMBER TALKS
GRADE

2

Category 1: Breaking Each Number into Its Place Value

The following number talks are composed of smaller two-digit numbers that do not require regrouping.

10 + 10	20 + 20	28 + 11
10 + 11	23 + 25	14 + 35
12 + 13	24 + 21	22 + 15
14 + 15	22 + 26	18 + 31

12 + 17	20 + 30	36 + 22
15 + 14	21 + 32	12 + 37
13 + 16	26 + 33	13 + 14
11 + 17	27 + 31	24 + 32

10 + 20	10 + 30	18 + 31
11 + 22	13 + 31	23 + 14
14 + 23	33 + 16	37 + 12
15 + 21	18 + 31	32 + 25

Category 2: Breaking Each Number into Its Place Value

The following number talks encourage students to combine the ten from the ones column with the tens from the tens column. The two-digit numbers remain smaller in magnitude.

Category 2 talks are crafted for students who are successfully using the selected strategy.

10 + 10 + 10
13 + 17
18 + 12
16 + 14

15 + 27
23 + 18
17 + 25
16 + 27

25 + 35
32 + 28
36 + 27
26 + 24

NUMBER TALKS GRADE

2

13 + 18
16 + 15
17 + 14
12 + 19

22 + 18
15 + 26
17 + 28
16 + 26

17 + 33
24 + 38
16 + 38
37 + 18

15 + 18
17 + 16
14 + 18
15 + 17

26 + 28
23 + 27
27 + 25
28 + 24

27 + 15
35 + 26
17 + 33
25 + 38

Category 3: Breaking Each Number into Its Place Value
The following number talks consist of numbers of greater magnitude.

NUMBER TALKS
GRADE
2

38 + 58
67 + 17
44 + 38
25 + 66

13 + 58
47 + 16
36 + 25
73 + 18

74 + 18
58 + 28
37 + 26
46 + 38

58 + 26
34 + 57
78 + 25
39 + 46

53 + 28
44 + 18
36 + 38
17 + 55

26 + 45
38 + 17
28 + 42
53 + 38

18 + 42
27 + 66
35 + 48
62 + 28

42 + 28
63 + 18
55 + 27
34 + 26

37 + 38
28 + 47
66 + 28
45 + 47

Addition: Compensation

Instructions

When students understand that you can compensate in addition (remove a specific quantity from one addend and add that same quantity to another addend) without altering the sum, they can begin to construct powerful mental computation strategies from this concept. It is not sufficient to tell students that this will always work; they need to have opportunities to test and prove this idea. Initially you may wish to have students use manipulatives to provide proof for their ideas. Numerical fluency (composing and decomposing numbers) is a key component of this strategy.

The following number talks consist of three or more sequential problems. The sequence of problems within a given number talk allows students to apply strategies from previous problems to subsequent problems. These number talk problems may be used in two ways:

- selected at random from each category; or
- navigated in a systematic order by selecting problems with smaller numbers from a specific category, then building to larger numbers.

Category 1	138
Category 2	139
Category 3	140

For more on Compensation, see page 62.

NUMBER TALKS
GRADE

2

NUMBER TALKS
GRADE

2

Category 1: Compensation

The following number talks focus on using compensation as a strategy for basic facts and combinations to 25 by removing 1 from one addend and adding it to the other addend. For example, 5 + 9 can be changed to 4 + 10 by removing 1 from the 5 and adding it to the 9.

5 + 5	3 + 9	16 + 9
4 + 6	9 + 5	9 + 12
6 + 6	7 + 9	15 + 9
5 + 7	9 + 6	13 + 9

7 + 7	2 + 9	16 + 4
6 + 8	4 + 9	19 + 4
8 + 8	6 + 9	6 + 19
7 + 9	9 + 8	19 + 3

10 + 10	9 + 7	14 + 9
9 + 11	4 + 9	9 + 7
12 + 12	9 + 6	15 + 9
11 + 13	8 + 9	19 + 6

Category 2: Compensation

The following number talks focus on adding and subtracting 1 *using larger numbers.*

$$19 + 6$$
$$9 + 16$$
$$9 + 26$$
$$29 + 6$$

$$17 + 19$$
$$9 + 18$$
$$13 + 9$$
$$16 + 19$$

$$29 + 19$$
$$29 + 23$$
$$28 + 29$$
$$23 + 19$$

NUMBER TALKS
GRADE

2

$$7 + 19$$
$$5 + 29$$
$$39 + 8$$
$$49 + 6$$

$$29 + 31$$
$$29 + 16$$
$$19 + 26$$
$$19 + 19$$

$$39 + 7$$
$$49 + 8$$
$$39 + 16$$
$$41 + 19$$

$$11 + 19$$
$$9 + 29$$
$$21 + 9$$
$$19 + 18$$

$$16 + 14$$
$$19 + 21$$
$$26 + 24$$
$$29 + 31$$

$$35 + 29$$
$$36 + 34$$
$$49 + 23$$
$$49 + 49$$

Category 3: Compensation

The following number talks are designed to make easier number combinations by adding and subtracting 2 or more.

4 + 8	27 + 18	13 + 17
8 + 6	38 + 24	23 + 27
8 + 5	18 + 22	33 + 37
7 + 8	48 + 16	43 + 47

8 + 7	17 + 23	28 + 45
17 + 8	22 + 28	53 + 18
13 + 17	35 + 27	38 + 47
17 + 18	38 + 36	17 + 78

27 + 28	23 + 48	18 + 63
28 + 16	17 + 24	37 + 38
37 + 18	47 + 24	67 + 28
23 + 28	17 + 37	48 + 52

Addition: Adding Up in Chunks

For more on Adding Up in Chunks, see page 64.

Instructions

Around midyear in second grade, we want students to be able to add multiples of ten to any number with ease. Adding up numbers in chunks builds on this idea by encouraging students to keep one number whole while adding "chunks" of the second addend. An open number line or hundreds chart is a helpful tool to use when discussing this strategy.

The following number talks consist of three or more sequential problems. The sequence of problems within a given number talk allows students to apply strategies from previous problems to subsequent problems. These number talk problems may be used in two ways:

- selected at random from each category; or
- navigated in a systematic order by selecting problems with smaller numbers from a specific category, then building to larger numbers.

NUMBER TALKS GRADE

2

Category 1	142
Category 2	143
Category 3	144

Category 1 represents introductory number talks that more readily encourage a specific strategy.

Category 1: Adding Up in Chunks

The following number talks focus on adding multiples of ten to any number.

$7 + 10$	$23 + 10$	$28 + 10$
$7 + 20$	$23 + 20$	$28 + 50$
$7 + 30$	$23 + 40$	$28 + 30$
$7 + 40$	$23 + 50$	$28 + 40$

$15 + 10$	$36 + 10$	$55 + 10$
$15 + 20$	$36 + 30$	$55 + 20$
$15 + 30$	$36 + 50$	$55 + 30$
$15 + 40$	$36 + 60$	$55 + 40$

$19 + 10$	$39 + 20$	$42 + 10$
$19 + 20$	$39 + 40$	$42 + 20$
$19 + 30$	$39 + 30$	$42 + 40$
$19 + 40$	$39 + 50$	$42 + 50$

Category 2: Adding Up in Chunks

The following number talks build gradually from adding multiples of ten to a number to adding in chunks.

11 + 10
11 + 20
11 + 30
11 + 33

26 + 10
26 + 30
26 + 50
26 + 53

32 + 10
32 + 14
32 + 20
32 + 25

NUMBER TALKS
GRADE

2

16 + 10
16 + 20
16 + 40
16 + 42

35 + 10
35 + 20
35 + 40
35 + 42

44 + 10
44 + 12
44 + 30
44 + 35

24 + 10
24 + 30
24 + 50
24 + 55

57 + 10
57 + 20
57 + 30
57 + 33

53 + 20
53 + 25
53 + 40
53 + 42

Category 3: Adding Up in Chunks

The following number talks pose problems to add up in chunks and then break apart the 1s into friendly combinations. For example, 28 + 24 could be "chunked" as 28 + 20 = 48; 48 + 4 could be added by breaking the 4 apart into 2 + 2. The problem could then be solved as (48 + 2) + 2 = 50 + 2 = 52.

Category 3 provides opportunities for students to use and extend the targeted strategy.

NUMBER TALKS
GRADE

2

18 + 10	29 + 10	57 + 10
18 + 13	29 + 15	57 + 14
18 + 20	29 + 20	57 + 30
18 + 23	29 + 24	57 + 36

16 + 20	38 + 20	17 + 25
16 + 25	38 + 26	28 + 24
16 + 30	38 + 30	36 + 38
16 + 36	38 + 33	37 + 35

17 + 10	45 + 30	44 + 27
17 + 14	45 + 38	48 + 34
17 + 30	45 + 40	55 + 16
17 + 35	45 + 46	58 + 25

Subtraction Number Talks

An appropriate time to begin introducing students to subtraction is around the end of first grade and the beginning of second grade. Usually during this time frame students are starting to understand the importance of tens, how to break apart numbers into place value for addition strategies, and how to reason more confidently with numbers. They are often ready to use their understanding of addition to lay a foundation for reasoning with subtraction. The stronger a student is with addition, the better she will be able to access subtraction.

With subtraction number talks, you will want to carefully choose the numbers for the problems and anchor the problems with a context. The context of a subtraction problem not only determines the type of subtraction (comparison, part-to-whole, or removal), but can also influence the strategy used. This is especially true with the Adding Up and Removal strategies for subtraction where the implied action within the context leads the student to match the action with a mental strategy. (Please refer to Chapter 2 for possible contexts to use with the following subtraction number talks.)

NUMBER TALKS
GRADE

2

| 2 | Adding Up | 146 |
| | Removal | 150 |

Subtraction: Adding Up

For more on Adding Up, see page 65.

NUMBER TALKS
GRADE

2

Instructions

This strategy allows students to build on their strength with addition by adding up from the number being subtracted (subtrahend) to the whole (minuend). The larger the jumps, the more efficient the strategy will be. In thinking about how much more to add to reach the whole, students can build on their knowledge of basic facts, doubles, making ten, and counting on.

The following number talks consist of three or more sequential problems. The sequence of problems within a given number talk allows students to apply strategies from previous problems to subsequent problems. These number talk problems may be used in two ways:

• selected at random from each category; or
• navigated in a systematic order by selecting problems with smaller numbers from a specific category, then building to larger numbers.

Category 1	147
Category 2	148
Category 3	149

Category 1: Adding Up

The following number talks consist of computation problems in which the wholes are multiples of ten.

Category 1 represents introductory number talks that more readily encourage a specific strategy.

$20 - 15$
$20 - 14$
$20 - 12$
$20 - 11$

$30 - 19$
$30 - 14$
$30 - 24$
$30 - 21$

$50 - 39$
$50 - 44$
$50 - 24$
$50 - 33$

NUMBER TALKS
GRADE

2

$20 - 10$
$20 - 9$
$20 - 7$
$20 - 8$

$40 - 34$
$40 - 29$
$40 - 20$
$40 - 18$

$60 - 49$
$60 - 29$
$60 - 39$
$60 - 19$

$30 - 25$
$30 - 23$
$30 - 15$
$30 - 12$

$40 - 32$
$40 - 28$
$40 - 19$
$40 - 24$

$70 - 59$
$70 - 34$
$70 - 49$
$78 - 18$

See Classroom Clip 3.3: Subtraction: $70 - 59$.

Category 2: Adding Up

The following number talks consist of computation problems in which the whole is no longer a multiple of ten and is below fifty.

NUMBER TALKS
GRADE

2

$15 - 9$	$23 - 19$	$44 - 39$
$17 - 9$	$23 - 16$	$44 - 35$
$14 - 9$	$23 - 14$	$44 - 29$
$16 - 9$	$23 - 9$	$44 - 25$

$21 - 10$	$31 - 29$	$41 - 34$
$21 - 9$	$31 - 26$	$41 - 28$
$21 - 7$	$31 - 24$	$41 - 24$
$21 - 8$	$31 - 15$	$41 - 19$

$25 - 19$	$32 - 28$	$23 - 19$
$25 - 16$	$32 - 25$	$33 - 19$
$25 - 18$	$32 - 19$	$42 - 29$
$25 - 9$	$32 - 15$	$41 - 18$

Category 3: Adding Up

The following number talks consist of a mixture of numbers that lend themselves to the Adding Up strategy.

$20 - 14$	$50 - 24$	$80 - 39$
$24 - 19$	$50 - 39$	$80 - 68$
$22 - 13$	$56 - 28$	$81 - 49$
$26 - 17$	$56 - 17$	$81 - 58$

$30 - 15$	$60 - 49$	$90 - 79$
$33 - 19$	$60 - 27$	$90 - 74$
$33 - 14$	$63 - 56$	$92 - 89$
$36 - 27$	$63 - 19$	$92 - 69$

$40 - 19$	$70 - 61$	$100 - 97$
$45 - 19$	$70 - 34$	$100 - 89$
$42 - 23$	$74 - 49$	$100 - 49$
$42 - 34$	$74 - 36$	$100 - 24$

NUMBER TALKS GRADE

2

See Classroom Clip 3.3: Subtraction: 70 – 34.

149

For more on Removal, see page 66.

NUMBER TALKS
GRADE

2

Subtraction: Removal

Instructions

If students primarily view subtraction as taking away, they will gravitate toward this strategy. Starting with the whole, the subtrahend is removed in parts. The ability to decompose numbers into easy-to-remove parts gives students access to this strategy. Encouraging students to keep the whole (minuend) intact and remove the subtrahend in parts is important; otherwise, it is easy for them to lose sight of the whole and the part. The following number talk sequences help promote this idea.

Students may initially count back from the whole to solve subtraction problems. The key is to help them realize when this is and is not an efficient strategy. The closer the whole (minuend) and part (subtrahend) are, the more likely students are to use Counting Back as a strategy. At times this can be an efficient strategy as evidenced in the following problem, $21 - 19$. For this problem, using the standard U.S. subtraction algorithm would be an inefficient strategy; counting back or up would be much more efficient. However, if the numbers were farther apart as in $21 - 9$, counting back by 1s would become more cumbersome. Counting back by chunks is more efficient as the numbers get farther apart. For example, with the problem $21 - 9$, the 9 could be decomposed into $1 + 8$. The student could then remove 1 from the 21 with 20 as the answer, and then remove 8 from 20. Developing a sequence of problems to foster this strategy is not necessary. Instead look for appropriate times to discuss when this strategy is and is not appropriate.

The following number talks consist of three or more sequential problems. The sequence of problems within a given number talk allows students to apply strategies from previous

(continued)

problems to subsequent problems. These number talk problems may be used in two ways:

- selected at random from each category; or
- navigated in a systematic order by selecting problems with smaller numbers from a specific category, then building to larger numbers.

Category 1	152
Category 2	153
Category 3	154

NUMBER TALKS
GRADE

2

NUMBER TALKS
GRADE

2

Category 1: Removal

The following number talks use numbers that encourage removing the subtrahend in parts that are the same as the digit in the minuend.

$12 - 2$	$21 - 1$	$35 - 5$
$12 - 5$	$21 - 6$	$35 - 6$
$15 - 5$	$23 - 3$	$35 - 8$
$15 - 6$	$23 - 6$	$35 - 9$

$13 - 3$	$24 - 4$	$41 - 1$
$13 - 5$	$24 - 5$	$41 - 4$
$13 - 6$	$24 - 8$	$41 - 6$
$13 - 8$	$24 - 9$	$41 - 8$

$20 - 5$	$22 - 2$	$52 - 2$
$20 - 6$	$22 - 4$	$52 - 7$
$20 - 7$	$22 - 5$	$53 - 3$
$20 - 8$	$22 - 8$	$53 - 8$

Category 2: Removal

The following number talks use numbers that encourage removal in place-value chunks without regrouping.

$20 - 10$	$47 - 10$	$78 - 20$
$20 - 16$	$47 - 16$	$78 - 23$
$30 - 10$	$47 - 20$	$78 - 50$
$30 - 12$	$47 - 24$	$78 - 54$

$26 - 10$	$39 - 10$	$69 - 30$
$26 - 13$	$39 - 13$	$69 - 35$
$28 - 10$	$39 - 20$	$69 - 50$
$28 - 15$	$39 - 22$	$69 - 52$

$35 - 10$	$56 - 10$	$87 - 40$
$35 - 13$	$56 - 12$	$87 - 44$
$35 - 20$	$56 - 30$	$87 - 50$
$35 - 24$	$56 - 35$	$87 - 53$

NUMBER TALKS GRADE

2

Category 3: Removal

*The following number talks use numbers that encourage removal in place
-value chunks and decomposing a single-digit number to remove it in
parts.*

Category 3
provides
opportunities
for students
to use and
extend the tar-
geted strategy.

$25 - 10$
$25 - 16$
$35 - 10$
$35 - 16$

$23 - 10$
$23 - 15$
$36 - 10$
$36 - 19$

$54 - 10$
$54 - 18$
$52 - 30$
$52 - 34$

$32 - 10$
$32 - 13$
$32 - 20$
$32 - 13$

$41 - 20$
$41 - 23$
$45 - 20$
$45 - 28$

$58 - 20$
$58 - 29$
$51 - 30$
$51 - 35$

$37 - 20$
$37 - 28$
$42 - 20$
$42 - 23$

$52 - 20$
$52 - 25$
$38 - 10$
$38 - 19$

$63 - 40$
$63 - 44$
$66 - 30$
$66 - 38$

Section III

Student Thinking and Number Talks in the 3–5 Classroom

CHAPTER 5

How Do I Develop Specific Addition and Subtraction Strategies in the 3–5 Classroom?

Overarching Goals

During number talks, you are always urging students to be accurate, efficient, and flexible with their mathematical thinking. However, many other areas can and should be addressed: number sense, place value, fluency, properties, and connecting mathematical ideas. Unpacking each of these components and keeping them in the forefront during classroom strategy discussions will better prepare your students to be mathematically powerful and proficient.

Five Number Talks Goals for Grades 3–5

1. Number sense

2. Place value

3. Fluency

4. Properties

5. Connecting mathematical ideas

Classroom Link: Addition: 59 + 13
Classroom Clip 3.2

To view this video clip, scan the QR code or access via mathsolutions.com /NTWNC32

Before you watch the third-grade number talk for 59 +13, anticipate possible student strategies and how you might record them.

As you watch the third-grade number talk for 59 + 13, consider:

1. What evidence in the video supports student understanding of place value?

2. How do the students' strategies demonstrate number sense?

3. How does the teacher connect math ideas throughout the number talk?

4. How does the classroom community utilize student errors to build understanding?

5. What examples of properties can be observed in the strategies and discussion?

6. Which strategies were most accessible to you? More difficult to follow?

For commentary on the above, see Appendix A: Author's Video Reflections.

Number Sense

Number sense is often discussed in math education, but what is it? Fennell and Landis (1994) state, "[Number sense] is an awareness and understanding about what numbers are, their relationships, their magnitude, the relative effect of operating on numbers, including the use of mental mathematics and estimation" (187). Every time you elicit answers to a problem in a number talk and ask students to share whether the proposed solutions are reasonable, you are helping to build number sense. When you ask students to give an estimate before they begin thinking about a specific strategy, you are fostering number sense. As a math coach, I am frequently asked to assess struggling students. Time and time again I have found that the students I interview rarely can give an estimate to a problem. They may be able to apply a memorized procedure, but they cannot discern or justify whether their solution is reasonable. By asking students to estimate an answer before solving a problem and provide evidence that an answer is reasonable, we can help build this essential skill.

Place Value

Teaching *place value* is much more than requiring students to state how many hundreds, tens, and ones are in a number or having them write a number in expanded notation. The true test of whether students understand place value is if they can apply their understanding in computation. Number talks provide the opportunity to confront and use place-value understanding on a continual basis.

Fluency

Often fluency with numbers is compared to knowing basic facts; however, fluency is much more than fact recall. *Fluency* is knowing how a number can be composed and decomposed and using that information to be flexible and efficient with solving problems. Consider the string of numbers $5 + 7 + 8$. Knowing that 7 can be decomposed into $5 + 2$ in order to think about the problem as $5 + (5 + 2) + 8$ allows access to making quick tens. The problem can then be solved as $(5 + 5) + (2 + 8)$ through the associative property. Understanding that 100 can be decomposed to 90 and 10 or 93 and 7, to make subtracting 37 easier, is an example of fluency. Number talks provide opportunities to help students use and develop fluency.

Properties

In my own education, my experiences with the *properties* of mathematics consisted solely of memorizing definitions and matching terms to examples. I do not remember ever applying the commutative, associative, distributive, and identity properties. As students invent their own strategies, they create opportunities to link their thinking to mathematical properties and understand why they work.

Connecting Mathematical Ideas

One of the National Council of Teachers of Mathematics (NCTM) process standards is Connections. While this standard promotes connecting math to real-world applications, it strongly embraces making connecting links to big ideas in mathematics. Each time you compare student strategies, discuss how addition can be used to solve subtraction problems, and make links between arrays with multiplication and division, you are grounding your students in the idea that mathematical concepts are related and make sense. Helping students build on these connecting mathematical ideas is a critical component of number talks.

Using Models to Anchor Student Strategies with Addition and Subtraction

Two visual tools are especially helpful when discussing and modeling student strategies in addition and subtraction: the open number line and a part/whole box.

Open Number Line

The Open Number Line is similar to a regular number line with the exception that every quantity is not iterated. This allows the teacher and student to quickly capture the action happening in the strategy without making a mark for every number. Using the problem 50 – 26, we can use the open number line to model the Adding Up and Constant Difference strategies. (See Figures 5–1 and 5–2.)

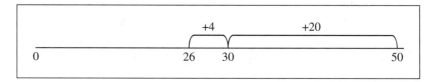

Figure 5–1   *Open Number Line for Adding Up Strategy for 50 – 26*

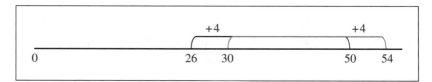

Figure 5–2   *Open Number Line for Constant Difference Strategy for 50 – 26*

Classroom Link: Subtraction: 70 – 59
Classroom Clip 3.3

Before you watch the third-grade number talk for 70 – 59, anticipate possible student strategies and how they might be recorded.

As you watch the third-grade number talk for 70 – 59, consider:

1. Which strategies seem most efficient to you? Why?

2. Would the student strategies work for larger numbers?

3. How is the open number line used to support the Constant Difference strategy?

4. How does the teacher use questions to support student thinking?

5. How are the goals for number talks supported throughout the number talk?

To view this video clip, scan the QR code or access via mathsolutions.com /NTWNC33

For commentary on the above, see Appendix A: Author's Video Reflections.

Mathematical Practice 3: Construct viable arguments and critique the reasoning of others.

This practice is a consistent theme running through every number talk. Social interaction— the exchanging of ideas and assimilating others' reasoning into our own understanding—is a core component of this classroom routine. With every number talk there is the expectation that students will communicate their reasoning and proof and offer justification for their strategies. Equally important is the expectation that students will listen to the reasoning of others and analyze classmates' strategies while looking for commonalities and differences from their own approaches.

Part/Whole Box

The Part/Whole Box is a visual model that helps students consider the relationship between the parts and the whole. It is especially useful in making connections between addition and subtraction:

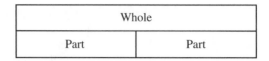

In addition, this model helps students visualize that the parts are known and the whole is the quantity to be found:

26 + 14

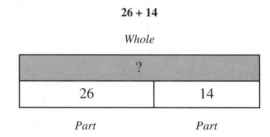

With subtraction, the Part/Whole Box helps identity that the whole and one of the parts are known and that the problem requires finding the unknown part:

50 – 26

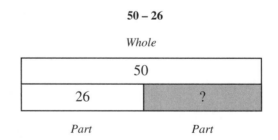

Using Real-Life Contexts

Once I began incorporating number talks as a regular component of my math instruction, I stopped showing students how to solve a computation problem. Instead, I provided story problems that

162

incorporated new operations and encouraged students to make sense of the problems and the numbers. Using a real-life context as a springboard for mathematical thinking serves to help students in three main ways.

> *Three Benefits of Using Real-Life Contexts*
>
> 1. A real-life context engages students in mathematics that is relevant to them.
>
> 2. A real-life context attaches meaning to the numbers.
>
> 3. A real-life context helps students access the mathematics.

1. A real-life context engages students in mathematics that is relative to them.

By crafting story problems that are intertwined in content that matters to students, you create a need for them to want to know. Designing problems around classroom parties, recess time, reading goals, games, or schoolwide projects naturally draws students into the mathematics.

2. A real-life context attaches meaning to the numbers.

A story-problem context allows students to envision a mental image of the mathematics. In contrast, problems that utilize only numbers require students to have a previous understanding of the operation and create their own mental images of the numerical actions.

3. A real-life context helps students access the mathematics.

A story-problem context provides multiple points of entry for students and allows them access to the math. A context also gives students a framework for deciding if an answer is reasonable. Real-world situations may also provide opportunities for students to notice commonalities between previously solved problems and a new problem.

Using a Real-Life Context with Addition

When embedded in the following story problem, 119 + 126 can be used to introduce third graders to addition with regrouping using three-digit numbers. Student representations using the specified contexts open the door for students to invent their own strategies for solving 119 + 126. Common first strategies are described in the following chart.

> *Mr. Novack's and Ms. Shelby's third-grade classrooms are raising money to buy equipment for the school science lab. Mr. Novack's students have earned $119 and Ms. Shelby's class has raised $126. How much money have the classes earned for their project?*

Three Different Strategies for Solving 119 + 126

① Student's Strategy: Breaking Each Number into Its Place Value	The Strategy as Recorded by the Teacher
Meg: I put the same numbers together. **Teacher:** Explain what you mean. **Meg:** I put all of the hundreds together, all of the tens together, and all of the ones together. So I got two hundred plus thirty plus fifteen. **Teacher:** How did you add those numbers? **Meg:** Thirty plus fifteen gave me forty-five, and two hundred plus forty-five made two hundred forty-five.	$119 + 126$ $(100 + 10 + 9) + (100 + 20 + 6)$ $100 + 100 = 200$ $10 + 20 = 30$ $9 + 6 = 15$ $30 + 15 = 45$ $200 + 45 = 245$
② Student's Strategy: Adding Up in Chunks	The Strategy as Recorded by the Teacher
Jim: I added up the numbers in a different way. **Teacher:** How did you add? **Jim:** I kept the one hundred nineteen together and added parts of the one hundred twenty-six. I	$119 + 126$ $119 + (100 + 20 + 1 + 5)$

thought about it on a number line. I first added one hundred nineteen plus one hundred, and got two hundred twenty-nine. Then I added two hundred nineteen plus twenty, and got two hundred thirty-nine. Next I added six to the two hundred thirty-nine.

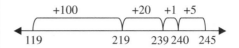

Teacher: How did you add the six onto the two hundred thirty-nine?

Jim: I knew if I added one from the six to two hundred thirty-nine, I would get two hundred forty. All I needed to do was add on five more.

③ Student's Strategy: Compensation	The Strategy as Recorded by the Teacher
Taylor: I made it into an easier problem. **Teacher:** How did you make this an easier problem? **Taylor:** I took one from the one hundred twenty-six and gave it to the one hundred nineteen to change it to one hundred twenty. **Teacher:** Why did you choose to do this? **Taylor:** Because one hundred twenty is easier to add than one hundred nineteen. I changed the problem to one hundred twenty plus one hundred twenty-five, and that made the answer two hundred forty-five.	119 + 126 119 + 126 + 1 − 1 120 + 125 = 245

Notice how the teacher uses the student-invented strategies to facilitate student thinking without telling them how to solve the problem. These initial strategies provide an opportunity for the teacher to build stepping stones to the mathematical ideas in this problem (decomposing or breaking apart numbers, place value, compensation, and associative property) and continue to help students attach meaning to the numbers.

Using a Real-Life Context with Subtraction

When embedded in the following story problem, 151 – 96 can be used to introduce third graders to subtraction with regrouping using three-digit numbers. Student representations using the specified context open the door for students to invent their own strategies for solving 151 – 96. Common first strategies are described in the chart below.

> *Ms. Melvin's and Mr. Tindle's third-grade classrooms are competing to raise money for a school garden. Ms. Melvin's class has raised $151, and Mr. Tindle's class has raised $96. How much more money does Mr. Tindle's class need to earn to catch up with Ms. Melvin's students?*

Three Different Strategies for Solving 151 – 96

① **Student's Strategy: Adding Up**	**The Strategy as Recorded by the Teacher**
Ashton: I started at ninety-six and counted up to one hundred fifty-one. **Teacher:** How did you count? **Ashton:** First I added four to ninety-six to get to one hundred. **Teacher:** Why did you choose to add four? **Ashton:** It would get me to an even hundred. Then I added fifty more to get to one hundred fifty and then one more to get to one hundred fifty-one. So Mr. Tindle's class needs fifty-five dollars.	151 – 96 +4 +50 +1 96 100 150 151

2 Student's Strategy: Adding Up	The Strategy as Recorded by the Teacher
Levi: I added up, too, but I did it a different way. **Teacher:** How did you add up? **Levi:** First I added four to get to one hundred, but then I jumped by tens to get to one hundred fifty. All I needed was one more to get to one hundred fifty-one.	$151 - 96$

3 Student's Strategy: Adjusting One Number to Create an Easier Problem	The Strategy as Recorded by the Teacher
Stephen: I made ninety-six a one hundred and changed the problem to one hundred fifty-one minus one hundred. **Teacher:** Why did you change ninety-six to one hundred? **Stephen:** It made it easier to take away. I did one hundred fifty-one minus one hundred equals fifty-one, but I took too much away, so I had to add four back. That gave me fifty-five.	$$\begin{array}{r} 151 - 96 \\ + 4 \\ \hline 100 \end{array}$$ $$\begin{array}{r} 151 - 100 = 51 \\ + 4 \\ \hline 55 \end{array}$$

Notice how the teacher uses the student-invented strategies to facilitate student thinking without telling them how to solve the problem. These initial strategies provide an opportunity for the teacher to build stepping stones to the mathematical ideas in this problem (relationship between addition and subtraction, subtraction as comparison, decomposing or breaking apart numbers, and part-to-whole relationships) and continue to help students attach meaning to the numbers. The teacher is thoughtfully structuring a foundation for students to build their understanding about subtraction and addition, and about the mathematical properties that undergird these relationships.

Discussing Efficiency

As students better understand the mathematics of an operation, number talks are used to investigate different strategies, test whether they will always work for any set of numbers, and discuss efficiency. By keeping each strategy posted for the duration of the number talk, students have an opportunity to discuss efficiency as well as the similarities and differences between strategies. If each strategy is labeled with a number (such as 1, 2, 3, 4), the teacher can ask students to use a hand signal to quietly indicate which strategy they consider to be the most efficient. This allows the teacher to glean information about which students are struggling to use tens and friendly numbers, break apart numbers, or manipulate numbers with ease.

Use the following narrative to consider how student strategies for the problem 119 + 126 can be used to explore the idea of efficiency.

Classroom Example: Discussing Efficiency with Addition Strategies

Teacher: I noticed there were a lot of signals for Strategy 3, Taylor's strategy. Could someone share why you thought this was the most efficient strategy?

Amy: He did it in two steps. That makes it quicker.

Micah: I think it was faster, too, but also confusing. I could follow Meg's strategy better.

Teacher: So even if a strategy is fast, it may not be an efficient one to use if we are unsure of why it works?

Shaun: Yes, but it makes me want to figure out how to use it.

Teacher: It looks like most of you think this is an efficient way, but you are not sure how it works. Let's try a smaller problem to test out Taylor's strategy.

Use the following narrative to consider how student strategies for the problem 151 – 96 can be used to explore the idea of efficiency.

Classroom Example: Discussing Efficiency with Subtraction Strategies

Teacher: I noticed there were a lot of signals for Strategy 1, Ashton's strategy. Could someone share why you thought this was the most efficient strategy?

Blakely: He counted up in easy chunks. That makes it quicker.

Jose: I think Ashton's and Levi's strategies are alike, but Ashton just used fewer jumps.

Teacher: So adding up to solve a subtraction problem can be efficient, especially if we make big jumps. What about Stephen's strategy?

Aaron: When he changed ninety-six to one hundred and then subtracted, it seemed really fast.

Willa: That part seemed fast, but I don't understand why he added four back. It seems like you would subtract it?

Teacher: It looks like most of you think this is an efficient way, but you are not sure how it works. Let's try a smaller problem to test out Stephen's strategy.

Anticipating Student Thinking

As we discussed in Chapter 2, do not be discouraged if you do not quickly access a student's thinking. It takes time to follow a strategy when you hear it for the first time. Students commonly use a limited number of strategies to solve different types of problems, and taking time to think through possible strategies for each problem beforehand will help you gain confidence in listening and following student thinking. As you become more accustomed to these strategies, you will find yourself anticipating your students' thinking and becoming more comfortable with understanding the approaches they have selected.

As you anticipate potential strategies for each problem, consider how you will capture each student's thinking so that the strategy may be accessible to others. Consider which mathematical ideas you want to highlight and how you might record the strategy to emphasize those specific concepts. For example, if making tens or utilizing place value is an important component in the strategy, make sure these ideas are prominent in your recording.

Many teachers and other adults are surprised that students can invent ways to solve a new problem. I have found, however, that by laying the foundation for making sense of number relationships, students are quite capable of inventing efficient strategies. Instructors can build a foundation of number sense and number relationships by asking students to: consider the reasonableness of their answers, provide mathematical proof and reasoning for their solutions, give an estimate before solving a problem, and represent quantities in multiple ways. For example, being able to represent 50 as 2 quarters, 5 tens, half of 100, 75 – 25, etc. demonstrates the ability to think about and reason with numbers in a variety of ways.

An Introduction to Common Addition Strategies

The following strategies represent a valued collection of mathematical ideas from third-, fourth-, and fifth-grade students. Do not be quick to discount them because the recording takes up written space; the students solved them very quickly using only mental math. Each strategy is labeled to help you better understand its foundation; however, in my classroom, strategies were often named for the students who invented them.

As numbers in addition problems become larger, strategies are often intertwined and interdependent. The focus should not be on attaching a specific label to each strategy, but on unpacking the mathematics for students. Keep this in mind as you look at the following strategies for solving 116 + 118.

Six Common Strategies for Addition

(A-1) Addition Strategy: Breaking Each Number into Its Place Value

Once students begin to understand place value, this is one of the first strategies they utilize. Each addend is broken into expanded form and like place-value amounts are combined. When combining quantities, children typically work left to right because it maintains the magnitude of the numbers.

$116 + 118$	
$(100 + 10 + 6) + (100 + 10 + 8)$	Each addend is broken into its place value.
$100 + 100 = 200$	100s are combined.
$10 + 10 = 20$	10s are combined.
$6 + 8 = 14$	1s are combined.
$200 + 20 + 14 = 234$	Totals are added from the previous sums.

(A-2) Addition Strategy: Making Landmark or Friendly Numbers

Landmark or friendly numbers are numbers that are easy to use in mental computation. Multiples of ten, one hundred, one thousand, and so on, as well as twenty-five and fifty, are examples of numbers that fall into this category. Students may adjust one or all addends by adding or subtracting amounts to make a friendly number.

$116 + 118$ $\underline{ + 2}$ $116 + 120 = 236$ $236 - 2 = 234$	In this example only the 118 is adjusted to make an easy landmark number. The extra 2 that was added on must be subtracted.

(continued)

171

(A-3) **Addition Strategy: Doubles/Near-Doubles**

Beginning as early as kindergarten, children are able to recall sums for many doubles. This strategy capitalizes on this strength by adjusting one or both numbers to make doubles or a near-doubles combination.

$116 + 118$ $\underline{-1 \quad\ -3}$ $115 + 115 = 230$ $\quad 230 + 4 = 234$	While these numbers could be adjusted to make doubles of $116 + 116$ or $118 + 118$, doubles with 5s tend to be easier. Since a total of 4 was removed from the initial addends, that quantity must be added back.

(A-4) **Addition Strategy: Making Tens**

Developing fluency with number combinations that make ten is an important focus in the primary grades. By the end of second grade, students should be able to break numbers apart quickly to make ten. The focus of this strategy is to be able to use fluency with ten to expedite adding.

A. $116 + 118$ $\quad (110 + 4 + 2) + (110 + 8)$ $\quad 110 + 110 + (2 + 8) + 4$ $\quad 110 + 110 + 10 + 4$ $\quad 230 + 4 = 234$	In Example A, the student decomposes the 6 into $4 + 2$ in order to add 2 more to the 8 for an easy 10.
B. $116 + 118$ $\quad (110 + 6) + (110 + 4 + 4)$ $\quad 110 + 110 + (6 + 4) + 4$ $\quad 110 + 110 + 10 + 4 = 234$	Example B demonstrates that it is also efficient to break the 8 into $4 + 4$ and combine one of the 4s with the 6 to make an easy 10.

(continued)

(A-5) **Addition Strategy: Compensation**

Similar to the Landmark or Friendly Numbers strategy, the goal of compensation is to manipulate the numbers into easier, friendlier numbers to add. The main difference between the two strategies is that when compensating, you remove a specific amount from one addend and give that exact amount to the other addend. This is a big idea in addition and one that students will need many experiences to investigate. As long as the quantities are kept the same, you can remove and add any amount; however, a big decision for students is choosing which amount will produce the most efficient addends with which to work.

A. $116 + 118$ $\quad -2 \quad +2$ $114 + 120 = 234$	In Example A, the student changes 118 to the friendly number of 120. Notice how 2 was subtracted from the 116 and then added to the 118.
B. $116 + 118$ $\quad +4 \quad -4$ $120 + 114 = 234$	Example B demonstrates that the student could have also subtracted 4 from 118 and added it to 116.

(A-6) **Addition Strategy: Adding Up in Chunks**

This strategy is similar to the Breaking Each Number into Its Place Value strategy except the focus is on keeping one addend whole and adding the second number in easy-to-use chunks. This strategy is slightly more efficient than the Breaking Each Number into Its Place Value strategy, since you are not breaking apart every number.

A. $116 + 118$ $116 + (100 + 10 + 4 + 4)$ $116 + 100 = 216$	In Example A, 116 is kept whole while 118 is broken into its place value and added in parts to the 116.

(continued)

$216 + 10 = 226$ $226 + 4 = 230$ $230 + 4 = 234$	Notice how 8 is decomposed into $4 + 4$ before adding to 226.
B. $116 + 118$ $(110 + 6) + 118$ $(118 + 110) + 6$ $228 + 6 = 234$	Example B demonstrates that either number can be kept whole. This time the 118 is kept intact, while 116 is broken into combinations that make the problem easier to solve.

Classroom Link: Addition: 38 + 37
Classroom Clip 3.1

To view this video clip, scan the QR code or access via mathsolutions.com /NTWNC31

Before you watch the third-grade number talk for 38 + 37, anticipate possible student strategies and how you might record them.

As you watch the third-grade number talk for 38 + 37, consider:

1. Which of the six common addition strategies are used by the students?

2. Are there some strategies that seem to be more efficient for this problem?

3. If you were to solve a similar problem, which strategy would you try?

4. What math foundations are necessary for students to successfully invent these strategies?

For commentary on the above, see Appendix A: Author's Video Reflections.

For CCSS insights on this clip, see page 24.

An Introduction to Common Subtraction Strategies

Many of us learned that subtraction was taking away an amount from a given quantity. While subtraction can involve removing an amount or taking it away, it also includes finding the difference between numbers, comparing numbers, and looking at part-to-whole relationships. By incorporating subtraction problems in a contextual situation, we can help students come to understand each type of subtraction as well as develop a toolbox of efficient strategies.

Five Common Strategies for Subtraction

We will use the problem $123 - 59$ to analyze common student subtraction strategies.

(S-1) Subtraction Strategy: Adding Up

This strategy allows students to build on their strength with addition by adding up from the subtrahend (the number being subtracted) to the minuend (the whole). When students begin to understand that subtraction is finding the difference between two quantities, they realize that they can add up to compute that distance. Even with large numbers the Adding Up strategy is effective and efficient. Some students will need to jump to every number. Help them think about jumps to get to the nearest ten or friendly number. The larger the jumps, the more efficient the strategy will be. Conversations that encourage students to focus on patterns with combinations that make ten, one hundred, one thousand, and so on, are important for navigating efficient jumps.

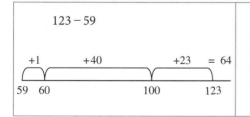

$123 - 59$

| +1 | +40 | +23 | = 64 |

59 60   100   123

As students begin to use this strategy, it is helpful to record their thinking on an open number line

(continued)

to show that they are tracking the distance between the subtrahend and minuend. Notice how the student first moves to the nearest 10 and then navigates from this point.

$123 - 59$

$59 + 1 = 60$

$60 + 40 = 100$

$100 + 23 = 123$

$1 + 40 + 23 = 64$

Eventually, students will be able to record their thinking without a physical number-line model.

(S-2) Subtraction Strategy: Removal or Counting Back

If students have primarily considered subtraction as taking away, they will gravitate toward this strategy. Starting with the whole or the minuend, the subtrahend is removed in parts that are easy for the student to navigate. The ability to decompose numbers into easy-to-remove parts gives students access to this strategy. Some students will need to take jumps of one all the way back to the subtrahend; others will remove numbers in pieces related to multiples of ten.

A. $123 - 59$

$123 - (10 + 10 + 10 + 10 + 10 + 3 + 6)$

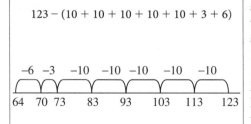

In Example A, the student has chosen to think about 59 as a combination of five 10s, three 1s, and six 1s. An open number line is used to show how each part of 59 was removed.

(continued)

B. $123 - 59$ $123 - (20 + 30 + 3 + 6)$ $123 - 20 = 103$ $103 - 30 = 73$ $73 - 3 = 70$ $70 - 6 = 64$	In this example, the student has broken 59 into larger chunks of 10 and has used a numerical representation to show her thinking.
C. $123 - 59$ $123 - (50 + 9)$ $123 - 50 = 73$ $73 - 9 = 64$	Example C demonstrates how the subtrahend can be decomposed into its place-value components and removed accordingly.

(S-3) Subtraction Strategy: Place Value and Negative Numbers

As students utilize this strategy, each number is broken apart into its respective place value. This can be represented by recording each number using expanded notation. Like place values are grouped and then subtracted. In problems where the standard U.S. regrouping algorithm could be used, negative values might result.

A. $123 - 59$ $(100 + 20 + 3) - (50 + 9)$ $\begin{array}{c c c} 100 & 20 & 3 \\ \hline - & 50 & 9 \\ \hline 100 & - 30 & - 6 \end{array}$ $100 - 30 = 70$ $70 - 6 = 64$	Even though the student approaches the problem as individual columns of numbers, the value of each number is kept intact and used in the computation.

(continued)

B. 123 − 59	Examples A and B demonstrate two different ways to record this strategy.
123	
$- 59$	
$100\;(100 - 0)$	
$- 30\;(20 - 50)$	
$- 6\;(3 - 9)$	
64	
C. 999	Example C models how this strategy would work if each part of the minuend (the whole) were a higher value than each part of the subtrahend (the parts being removed).
$- 345$	
$600\;(900 - 300)$	
$50\;(90 - 50)$	
$+\;\;4\;(9 - 5)$	
654	

(S-4) Subtraction Strategy: Keeping a Constant Difference

As students begin to understand subtraction as the difference between two quantities, they can investigate what occurs if both numbers are changed by the same amount. Allowing students to explore this relationship with smaller problems such as 5 − 3 is a way to help them build this understanding. If 5 and 3 are both changed by +2, the problem 7 – 5 will result. Notice that there is still a difference of 2. What if we removed 2 from each number in the problem 5 – 3? We would then create the problem 3 – 1, which still results in a difference of 2. Adding or subtracting the same quantity from both the subtrahend and minuend maintains the difference between the numbers. Manipulating the numbers in this way allows the student to create a friendlier problem without compromising the result.

(continued)

$123 - 59$ $123 + 1 = \quad 124$ $\underline{- 59 + 1 = - 60}$ $\qquad\qquad 64$	Both numbers have been adjusted by $+1$, which makes a problem with an easy 10. Deciding on the amount to subtract or add to adjust the problem is a big decision. For instance, would it have been helpful to adjust each number by -1? This would have created the problem $122 - 58$, which is not an easier problem to solve.

(S-5) Subtraction Strategy: Adjusting One Number to Create an Easier Problem

Sometimes it is efficient to adjust only one of the numbers in a subtraction problem. If this strategy is used, a couple of decisions must be made: 1) which number would be the most helpful to adjust and why, and 2) how does the final answer need to be adjusted to compensate for this? A student's understanding about part/whole relationships will help in reasoning through these decisions.

A. $123 - 59$ $\quad 123 \qquad\qquad 123$ $\underline{- 59 + 1 = - 60}$ $\qquad\qquad 63 + 1 = 64$	Example A adjusts the 59 to an easy multiple of 10. An important conversation to have with students is should this 1 be added back to the answer or subtracted and why? Again, a story context is helpful in thinking about this decision: *Joey has 123 marbles. He promised Zac 59 of the marbles. He accidentally gave Zac 60 instead of 59. What does Joey need to do?*

(continued)

179

Since Joey gave Zac "one too many" he needs to add the 1 back to the amount he has left, which is 63.

B. $123 - 59$

$$123 \qquad 123$$
$$\underline{-59} - 6 = \underline{-53}$$
$$70 - 6 = 64$$

What if the subtrahend had been adjusted by removing 6 so that the 1s in both numbers would be 3, as shown in Example B? How would the final answer need to be adjusted?

We would need to remove 6 more from Joey, because in this method Joey did not give Zac all of his 59.

C. $123 - 59$

$$123 + 6 = 129$$
$$\underline{-59} \qquad \underline{-59}$$
$$70 - 6 = 64$$

What happens when the minuend is adjusted by adding more? In Example C, the 123 was adjusted by $+6$ to make the 1s in both numbers the same.

We can use the marble problem to help decide how to adjust our final amount to account for this increase. Since Joey is now starting with 6 more than he really has, we will need to take the extra amount of 6 back.

D. $123 - 59$

$$123 - 4 = 119$$
$$\underline{-59} \qquad \underline{-59}$$
$$60 + 4 = 64$$

What if the minuend was decreased by 4 to make its 1s column match the 9 in the 59? How would the final answer need to be adjusted?

Again, we could use the marble problem to frame our thinking. If Joey did not start with enough marbles or 4 fewer, we would need to add 4 back to his amount.

Classroom Link: Subtraction: 1000 – 674
Classroom Clip 5.6

Before you watch the fifth-grade number talk for 1000 – 674, anticipate possible student strategies and how they might be recorded.

As you watch the fifth-grade number talk, consider:

1. What evidence in the video supports student understanding of place value?

2. How do the students' strategies exhibit number sense?

3. How does fluency with smaller numbers connect to the students' strategies?

4. Which strategies were most accessible to you? More challenging to follow?

5. How are accuracy, flexibility, and efficiency interwoven in the students' strategies?

To view this video clip, scan the QR code or access via mathsolutions.com /NTWNC56

For commentary on the above, see Appendix A: Author's Video Reflections.

Summary

In this chapter we have looked at the overarching goals during number talks, addition and subtraction student strategies, and tools and models to help support student mathematical understanding in 3–5 classrooms. In the following chapter we explore how to use number talks to develop specific addition and subtraction strategies in the 3–5 classroom.

CHAPTER 6

How Do I Design Purposeful Addition and Subtraction Number Talks in the 3–5 Classroom?

Overview

This chapter focuses on addition and subtraction number talks for third-, fourth-, and fifth-grade students. The number talks are organized by *operations* and *strategies*. Each strategy is divided into three categories that reflect the magnitude of the numbers used.

Teachers should use fluency number talks to build a strong foundation before moving into number talks that focus on computation with larger numbers.

CONTENTS

Third-, Fourth-, and Fifth-Grade Number Talks

The following number talks are designed to foster and elicit specific computation strategies. While each strategy possesses distinct characteristics, often similarities overlap. For example, many of the strategies build on changing numbers to landmark or friendly numbers; this is a similarity. The difference lies in *how* the landmark or friendly number is created. This subtle difference is the essence of the strategy.

As you begin to implement number talks in your classroom, start with small numbers that are age and grade-level appropriate. Using small numbers serves two purposes: 1) students can focus on the nuances of the strategy instead of the magnitude of the numbers, and 2) students are able to build confidence in their mathematical abilities. As their understanding of different strategies develops, you can gradually increase the size of the numbers. When the numbers become too large, students will rely on less efficient strategies, such as Counting All, or resort to paper and pencil, thereby losing the focus on developing mental strategies.

Each series of number talks is organized by specific strategies and categories. The categories are a suggested sequence to delineate beginning number talks to advanced number talks. They do not represent student math ability levels, but a scaffolding of problems from easier to more difficult problems.

NUMBER TALKS

3-5

Category Key

1. Category 1 represents introductory number talks that more readily encourage a specific strategy.

2. Category 2 number talks are crafted for students who are successfully using the selected strategy.

3. Category 3 provides opportunities for students to use and extend the targeted strategy.

Addition Number Talks

The following number talks are crafted to elicit specific addition strategies; students may also share other efficient methods to solve the problems. The overall purpose is to help students build a toolbox of efficient strategies based on numerical reasoning. The ultimate goal of number talks is for students to compute accurately, efficiently, and flexibly.

NUMBER TALKS

3–5

Addition: Making Tens

Instructions

One of the core foundations of our number system is the ability to recognize and use groups of ten. Looking for "quick tens" in computation is one of the first things you want to establish as a cornerstone strategy in computation. You want students to use this computation tool so that it becomes a default strategy. These are initial number talks for second- and possibly third-grade students, but if making tens is not a default strategy by the fourth and fifth grades, it would be appropriate to start with these problems.

The following number talks consist of three or more sequential problems. The sequence of problems within a given number talk allows students to apply strategies from previous problems to subsequent problems. These number talk problems may be used in two ways:

- selected at random from each category; or
- navigated in a systematic order by selecting problems with smaller numbers from a specific category, then building to larger numbers.

Category 1	186
Category 2	187
Category 3	188

For more on Making Tens, see page 172.

NUMBER TALKS

3–5

Category 1 represents introductory number talks that more readily encourage a specific strategy.

Category 1: Making Tens

The following number talks include two addends that make a quick ten.

$$7 + 3$$
$$7 + 5 + 3$$
$$3 + 6 + 7$$

$$5 + 5$$
$$5 + 6 + 5$$
$$5 + 9 + 5$$

$$9 + 5 + 1$$
$$8 + 9 + 1$$
$$1 + 4 + 9$$

$$8 + 2$$
$$2 + 4 + 8$$
$$8 + 3 + 2$$

$$9 + 1$$
$$9 + 7 + 1$$
$$1 + 6 + 9$$

$$2 + 5 + 8$$
$$4 + 7 + 6$$
$$5 + 5 + 8$$

$$6 + 4$$
$$4 + 9 + 6$$
$$6 + 8 + 4$$

$$3 + 5 + 7$$
$$6 + 5 + 4$$
$$2 + 9 + 8$$

$$3 + 8 + 7$$
$$9 + 1 + 2$$
$$4 + 9 + 6$$

Category 2: Making Tens

The following number talks consist of two pairs of numbers that make a quick ten.

$4 + 6 + 8 + 2$
$9 + 3 + 1 + 7$
$5 + 6 + 5 + 4$

$3 + 8 + 2 + 7$
$4 + 4 + 6 + 6$
$9 + 1 + 1 + 9$

$5 + 3 + 5 + 4 + 7$
$9 + 5 + 8 + 2 + 1$
$4 + 5 + 6 + 3 + 7$

$3 + 9 + 7 + 1$
$2 + 9 + 8 + 1$
$6 + 4 + 3 + 7$

$5 + 7 + 3 + 5$
$2 + 5 + 5 + 8$
$6 + 6 + 4 + 4$

$3 + 8 + 5 + 5 + 2$
$9 + 1 + 6 + 3 + 4$
$7 + 2 + 3 + 5 + 8$

NUMBER TALKS

3–5

$4 + 8 + 2 + 6$
$1 + 9 + 2 + 8$
$5 + 3 + 7 + 5$

$3 + 7 + 8 + 2$
$1 + 1 + 9 + 9$
$3 + 7 + 7 + 3$

$2 + 6 + 8 + 3 + 4$
$9 + 3 + 1 + 5 + 5$
$4 + 8 + 6 + 2 + 7$

Category 3: Making Tens

The following number talks encourage students to make a quick ten by decomposing at least one of the numbers.

9 + 1	8 + 2	7 + 3
9 + 1 + 4	8 + 2 + 3	7 + 3 + 2
9 + 5	8 + 5	7 + 5
9 + 8	8 + 4	7 + 6

10 + 5	10 + 5	10 + 6
9 + 5	8 + 5	7 + 6
10 + 7	10 + 7	10 + 4
9 + 7	8 + 7	7 + 4

9 + 3	8 + 2	7 + 3
9 + 5	8 + 5	7 + 6
9 + 8	8 + 4	7 + 4
9 + 9	8 + 7	7 + 5

10 + 14	10 + 12	10 + 13
9 + 14	8 + 12	7 + 13
10 + 23	10 + 23	10 + 25
9 + 23	8 + 23	7 + 25

Addition: Making Landmark or Friendly Numbers

Instructions

When students understand that you can compensate in addition (remove a specific quantity from one addend and add that same quantity to another addend) without altering the sum, they can begin to construct powerful mental computation strategies from this concept. Telling them that this will always work is not sufficient; they need to have opportunities to test and prove this idea. Initially you may want to have students use manipulatives to provide proof for their ideas. Numerical fluency (composing and decomposing numbers) is a key component of this strategy.

The following number talks consist of three or more sequential problems. The sequence of problems within a given number talk allows students to apply strategies from previous problems to subsequent problems. These number talk problems may be used in two ways:

- selected at random from each category; or
- navigated in a systematic order by selecting problems with smaller numbers from a specific category, then building to larger numbers.

Category 1	190
Category 2	191
Category 3	192

For more on Making Landmark or Friendly Numbers, see page 171.

NUMBER TALKS

3-5

Category 1: Making Landmark or Friendly Numbers

The following number talks are carefully designed to use numbers that are one away from a landmark or friendly number.

Category 1 represents introductory number talks that more readily encourage a specific strategy.

NUMBER TALKS

3–5

See Classroom Clip 3.2: Addition: 59 + 13.

19 + 2	39 + 16	46 + 59
19 + 5	28 + 39	33 + 69
19 + 8	59 + 13	58 + 39
19 + 12	23 + 49	76 + 24

9 + 8	25 + 25	37 + 69
19 + 5	25 + 26	79 + 26
9 + 26	24 + 26	89 + 28
16 + 19	26 + 49	99 + 19

7 + 19	49 + 8	99 + 5
16 + 29	49 + 23	99 + 15
19 + 18	49 + 37	99 + 26
29 + 33	49 + 51	99 + 51

Category 2: Making Landmark or Friendly Numbers

The following number talks consist of one addend that is two away from a multiple of ten or a landmark number.

Category 2 talks are crafted for students who are successfully using the selected strategy.

8 + 5
8 + 13
8 + 24
18 + 7

18 + 63
38 + 37
67 + 28
48 + 52

98 + 5
98 + 13
98 + 34
98 + 52

8 + 4
18 + 6
28 + 17
27 + 18

48 + 6
48 + 17
23 + 48
48 + 47

8 + 4 + 18
18 + 4 + 18
28 + 5 + 27
24 + 3 + 48

NUMBER TALKS

3-5

28 + 16
25 + 38
23 + 27
28 + 45

58 + 36
24 + 78
88 + 14
68 + 33

48 + 4 + 48
48 + 49 + 3
98 + 97 + 5
99 + 98 + 97 + 5

See Classroom Clip 3.1: Addition: 38 + 37.

Category 3: Making Landmark or Friendly Numbers

The following number talks consist of computation problems with two- and three-digit addends. The addends are one or more away from a multiple of ten or landmark number. The further the addends are from landmark numbers, the more challenging the strategy.

NUMBER TALKS

3–5

99 + 38	116 + 29	119 + 119
98 + 47	39 + 127	149 + 149
98 + 99	114 + 118	129 + 139
99 + 99 + 5	46 + 118	199 + 199

119 + 26	198 + 7	249 + 22
118 + 17	199 + 13	248 + 49
129 + 16	148 + 27	225 + 49
124 + 26	139 + 43	299 + 26

36 + 109	128 + 34	999 + 99
49 + 108	119 + 36	998 + 49
119 + 48	56 + 129	997 + 199
126 + 124	126 + 49	199 + 99 + 49

Addition: Doubles/Near-Doubles

Instructions

To foster the Doubles/Near-Doubles strategy, initially select numbers that are one away from doubles that students often use such as $5 + 5$, $25 + 25$, and $150 + 150$. If one addend is the targeted double and the other addend is just one away from that double, students will begin to notice this relationship. For example, $25 + 26$ lends itself to students thinking about 26 as $25 + 1$, so they will more readily think about $25 + 25$.

The following number talks consist of three or more sequential problems. The sequence of problems within a given number talk allows students to apply strategies from previous problems to subsequent problems. These number talk problems may be used in two ways:

• selected at random from each category; or
• navigated in a systematic order by selecting problems with smaller numbers from a specific category, then building to larger numbers.

Category 1	194
Category 2	195
Category 3	196

For more on Doubles/ Near-Doubles, see page 172.

NUMBER TALKS

3–5

Category 1: Doubles/Near-Doubles

The following number talks consist of doubles up to twenty.

NUMBER TALKS

3–5

5 + 5	8 + 8	16 + 16
5 + 6	8 + 7	17 + 17
5 + 7	8 + 9	17 + 18
5 + 8	8 + 6	16 + 17

6 + 6	9 + 9	18 + 18
5 + 6	8 + 9	18 + 19
6 + 7	8 + 8	18 + 17
6 + 8	8 + 7	19 + 19

7 + 7	15 + 15	20 + 20
6 + 7	15 + 16	19 + 19
7 + 8	17 + 15	18 + 18
7 + 9	15 + 18	19 + 18

Category 2: Doubles/Near-Doubles

The following number talks use doubles with two-digit numbers.

20 + 20
19 + 19
19 + 18
19 + 17

30 + 30
29 + 29
29 + 28
28 + 27

45 + 45
46 + 45
46 + 46
45 + 47

25 + 25
24 + 25
25 + 26
26 + 27

35 + 35
35 + 36
34 + 35
36 + 37

50 + 50
49 + 49
48 + 49
49 + 52

NUMBER TALKS

3–5

25 + 25
25 + 28
24 + 27
24 + 28

40 + 40
39 + 39
39 + 38
38 + 37

100 + 100
99 + 99
99 + 98
99 + 97

See Classroom Clips 2.3 and 3.1: Addition: 26 + 27 and Addition: 38 + 37.

Category 3: Doubles/Near-Doubles

The following number talks use doubles with two- and three-digit numbers.

100 + 100	200 + 200	400 + 400
99 + 99	199 + 199	399 + 399
98 + 99	198 + 199	398 + 399
97 + 99	198 + 198	398 + 398

125 + 125	250 + 250	500 + 500
124 + 126	249 + 249	499 + 499
126 + 127	249 + 248	498 + 499
124 + 128	248 + 248	498 + 497

150 + 150	300 + 300	1000 + 1000
149 + 149	299 + 299	999 + 999
148 + 149	298 + 299	998 + 999
148 + 148	298 + 297	998 + 998

Addition: Breaking Each Number into Its Place Value

Instructions

The key to crafting number talks to encourage students to break each number into its place value is to choose numbers that *do not* have an obvious relationship to each other. By selecting numbers with this characteristic, students are more likely to break numbers apart into their respective place values and work mentally from left to right. The categories in this strategy are based on the magnitude of the numbers.

The following number talks consist of three or more sequential problems. The sequence of problems within a given number talk allows students to apply strategies from previous problems to subsequent problems. These number talk problems may be used in two ways:

• selected at random from each category; or
• navigated in a systematic order by selecting problems with smaller numbers from a specific category, then building to larger numbers.

Category 1	198
Category 2	199
Category 3	200

For more on Breaking Each Number into Its Place Value, see page 171.

NUMBER TALKS

3–5

Category 1: Breaking Each Number into Its Place Value

The following number talks consist of smaller two-digit numbers. The first column on the left consists of problems that do not require regrouping. The two columns on the right include problems that encourage students to combine the ten from the ones column with the tens from the tens column.

NUMBER TALKS 3–5

28 + 11	15 + 27	25 + 35
14 + 35	23 + 18	32 + 28
22 + 15	17 + 25	36 + 27
18 + 31	16 + 27	26 + 24

36 + 22	22 + 18	17 + 33
12 + 37	15 + 26	24 + 38
13 + 14	17 + 28	16 + 38
24 + 32	16 + 26	37 + 18

18 + 31	26 + 28	27 + 15
23 + 14	23 + 27	35 + 26
37 + 12	27 + 25	17 + 33
32 + 25	28 + 24	25 + 38

Category 2: Breaking Each Number into Its Place Value

The following number talks consist of two- and three-digit numbers, some of which require regrouping.

> Category 2 talks are crafted for students who are successfully using the selected strategy.

74 + 18
58 + 28
37 + 26
46 + 38

77 + 36
58 + 65
46 + 88
74 + 47

354 + 111
267 + 232
215 + 136
342 + 64

26 + 45
38 + 17
28 + 42
53 + 38

113 + 56
122 + 37
114 + 44
121 + 48

216 + 137
285 + 127
156 + 85
274 + 57

NUMBER TALKS

3–5

37 + 38
28 + 47
66 + 28
45 + 47

158 + 221
136 + 113
205 + 134
262 + 35

135 + 219
315 + 192
167 + 173
115 + 293

> Category 3 provides opportunities for students to use and extend the targeted strategy.

Category 3: Breaking Each Number into Its Place Value

The following number talks consist of computation problems with three-digit numbers that require regrouping.

365 + 247	238 + 184	444 + 177
138 + 292	361 + 292	333 + 277
168 + 254	515 + 127	276 + 258
292 + 139	209 + 136	518 + 265

275 + 147	146 + 277	386 + 147
386 + 137	216 + 188	216 + 388
246 + 356	255 + 267	424 + 193
377 + 340	185 + 146	370 + 267

240 + 392	240 + 195	111 + 999
150 + 186	360 + 275	222 + 888
230 + 284	109 + 256	333 + 777
310 + 192	218 + 293	444 + 777

Addition: Adding Up in Chunks

Instructions

Beginning midyear in second grade, we want students to be able to add ten and then multiples of ten to any number with ease. Adding up numbers in chunks builds upon adding multiples of ten by encouraging students to keep one number whole while adding "chunks" of the second addend.

The following number talks consist of three or more sequential problems. The sequence of problems within a given number talk allows students to apply strategies from previous problems to subsequent problems. These number talk problems may be used in two ways:

- selected at random from each category; or
- navigated in a systematic order by selecting problems with smaller numbers from a specific category, then building to larger numbers.

For more on Adding Up in Chunks, see page 173.

NUMBER TALKS
3–5

Category 1	202
Category 2	203
Category 3	204

Category 1: Adding Up in Chunks

The following number talks build gradually from adding multiples of ten to a number to adding in chunks.

NUMBER TALKS

3–5

16 + 10	35 + 10	46 + 20
16 + 20	35 + 20	46 + 30
16 + 40	35 + 40	46 + 50
16 + 42	35 + 42	46 + 53

26 + 10	32 + 10	57 + 10
26 + 30	32 + 30	57 + 20
26 + 50	32 + 50	57 + 30
26 + 53	32 + 55	57 + 33

24 + 10	44 + 10	53 + 20
24 + 30	44 + 20	53 + 25
24 + 50	44 + 30	53 + 40
24 + 55	44 + 35	53 + 42

Category 2: Adding Up in Chunks

The following number talks consist of adding multiples of ten while keeping one number whole and then breaking apart the ones into friendly combinations. For example, 28 + 24 could be "chunked" as 28 + 20 = 48; the 48 + 4 could be added by breaking the 4 apart into 2 + 2. The problem could then be solved as (48 + 2) + 2 = 50 + 2 = 52.

> Category 2 talks are crafted for students who are successfully using the selected strategy.

18 + 10	29 + 10	57 + 10
18 + 13	29 + 15	57 + 14
18 + 20	29 + 20	57 + 30
18 + 23	29 + 24	57 + 36

16 + 20	38 + 20	65 + 30
16 + 25	38 + 26	65 + 36
16 + 30	38 + 30	65 + 50
16 + 36	38 + 33	65 + 57

> NUMBER TALKS
> **3–5**

17 + 10	45 + 30	73 + 30
17 + 14	45 + 38	73 + 38
17 + 30	45 + 40	73 + 50
17 + 35	45 + 46	73 + 58

NUMBER TALKS
3-5

> Category 3 provides opportunities for students to use and extend the targeted strategy.

Category 3: Adding Up in Chunks

The following number talks consist of adding multiples of ten and one hundred while keeping one number whole.

56 + 40	37 + 40	345 + 200
56 + 50	37 + 46	345 + 400
156 + 40	237 + 40	345 + 450
156 + 43	237 + 48	345 + 457

256 + 100	25 + 60	134 + 100
256 + 300	25 + 66	134 + 300
256 + 340	125 + 60	134 + 380
256 + 342	125 + 68	134 + 387

117 + 200	47 + 80	218 + 200
117 + 400	47 + 84	218 + 400
117 + 420	247 + 70	218 + 450
117 + 426	247 + 74	218 + 456

Subtraction Number Talks

The following number talks are crafted to elicit specific subtraction strategies; students may also share other efficient methods to solve the problems. The overall purpose is to help students build a toolbox of efficient strategies based on numerical reasoning. The ultimate goal of number talks is for students to compute accurately, efficiently, and flexibly.

NUMBER TALKS
3–5

Subtraction: Removal or Counting Back

For more on Removal or Counting Back, see page 176.

NUMBER TALKS

3–5

Instructions

Many students intuitively count back to solve subtraction problems. The key is to help them realize when this is and is not an efficient strategy. The closer the minuend and subtrahend are, the more likely students are to use Removal or Counting Back as a strategy. At times this can be an efficient strategy as evidenced by the following problem, 100 – 98. For this problem, using the standard U.S. subtraction algorithm would be an inefficient strategy; counting back or up would be much more efficient. However, if the numbers were farther apart as in 100 – 81, counting back by ones would become cumbersome. Counting back by chunks is more efficient as the numbers get farther apart.

It is not necessary to develop a sequence of problems to foster the Removal or Counting Back strategy. Instead, look for appropriate times to discuss when this strategy is and is not appropriate.

Subtraction: Adding Up

Instructions

Two ideas to consider when crafting number talks to encourage the Adding Up strategy for subtraction are: 1) keep the minuend and subtrahend far apart, and 2) frame the problem in a context that implies distance. Specific examples of using a context for subtraction can be found in Chapter 5.

The farther apart the subtrahend is from the minuend, the more likely it is that students will count or add up. The closer the two numbers are, the more the likelihood that students will count back. For example, if the problem is 50 – 47, it would be quite efficient and easy to count back; but if the problem is 50 – 17, it would be more cumbersome and tedious to count back.

Creating a word problem that implies distance also gives students a mental image and action of counting up or moving forward from the smaller number to the larger number. The following story problem is an example of a context that implies distance for 50 – 17:

> Martha's goal is to walk 50 laps on the school track. She has already walked 17 laps. How many more laps does Martha need to walk to reach her goal?

The scenario alone creates a mental picture and action of moving forward from seventeen to reach fifty and lends itself to the student solving the problem in this manner.

Other examples of contextual problems to promote Adding Up for subtraction are shown in the examples that follow. Notice how each problem uses numbers that are relatively far apart, and the context implies a distance to be bridged by starting with a part and working toward the whole.

(continued)

For more on Adding Up, see page 175.

NUMBER TALKS
3–5

Contextual Problems to Promote the Adding Up Strategy

Paul plans to read 90 pages each day. So far, he has read only 16 pages. How many more pages does Paul need to read to reach his goal?

Rebekah wants to buy an MP3 player that costs $182. She has saved $53 so far. How much more money does Rebekah need before she can buy the MP3 player?

If Green Acres School raises $5,000 for new books for the library, the students will receive a pizza party. So far the students have raised $1,238. How much more money do they need to reach their goal?

The following number talks consist of three or more sequential problems. The sequence of problems within a given number talk allows students to apply strategies from previous problems to subsequent problems. These number talk problems may be used in two ways:

• selected at random from each category; or

• navigated in a systematic order by selecting problems with smaller numbers from a specific category, then building to larger numbers.

To help your students be successful with this strategy, you may wish to introduce each of the problems embedded in a context similar to the situations discussed previously.

NUMBER TALKS
3-5

Category 1	209
Category 2	210
Category 3	211

Category 1: Adding Up

The following number talks include computation problems that foster the Adding Up strategy by incorporating two ideas: 1) the whole is a multiple of ten or one hundred, and 2) the subtrahend is close to a multiple of ten or a landmark number.

Category 1 represents introductory number talks that more readily encourage a specific strategy.

$20 - 15$	$50 - 44$	$80 - 69$
$20 - 14$	$50 - 39$	$80 - 59$
$20 - 9$	$50 - 29$	$80 - 49$
$20 - 8$	$50 - 24$	$80 - 39$

$30 - 24$	$60 - 54$	$90 - 79$
$30 - 19$	$60 - 49$	$90 - 74$
$30 - 15$	$60 - 39$	$90 - 49$
$30 - 12$	$60 - 29$	$90 - 44$

NUMBER TALKS

3–5

$40 - 34$	$70 - 59$	$100 - 89$
$40 - 29$	$70 - 49$	$100 - 74$
$40 - 24$	$70 - 39$	$100 - 49$
$40 - 19$	$70 - 34$	$100 - 44$

See Classroom Clips 3.3 and 3.4: Subtraction: $70 - 59$ and Subtraction: $70 - 34$.

Category 2 talks are crafted for students who are success- fully using the selected strategy.

Category 2: Adding Up

The following number talks include computation problems where the whole is a multiple of ten or one hundred, and the subtrahend is close to a multiple of ten or a landmark number.

NUMBER TALKS

3–5

$100 - 89$	$250 - 224$	$500 - 449$
$100 - 69$	$250 - 219$	$500 - 419$
$100 - 49$	$200 - 199$	$500 - 299$
$100 - 37$	$200 - 149$	$500 - 249$

$150 - 124$	$300 - 269$	$750 - 709$
$150 - 99$	$300 - 249$	$750 - 599$
$150 - 74$	$300 - 99$	$750 - 449$
$150 - 49$	$300 - 149$	$750 - 324$

$200 - 174$	$400 - 349$	$1000 - 899$
$200 - 149$	$400 - 299$	$1000 - 749$
$200 - 124$	$400 - 274$	$1000 - 624$
$200 - 99$	$200 - 199$	$1000 - 499$

Category 3: Adding Up

The following number talks consist of computation problems where the whole is no longer an exact multiple of ten or one hundred, and the subtrahend is a farther distance from the whole.

Category 3 provides opportunities for students to use and extend the targeted strategy.

$50 - 29$
$55 - 29$
$55 - 48$
$55 - 37$

$100 - 75$
$120 - 75$
$125 - 75$
$125 - 83$

$300 - 174$
$315 - 174$
$335 - 219$
$335 - 287$

$80 - 59$
$84 - 59$
$81 - 48$
$81 - 36$

$100 - 80$
$140 - 80$
$146 - 80$
$146 - 89$

$400 - 329$
$420 - 329$
$423 - 318$
$444 - 298$

NUMBER TALKS

3–5

$70 - 49$
$73 - 49$
$76 - 67$
$76 - 39$

$200 - 149$
$250 - 149$
$223 - 186$
$245 - 198$

$500 - 249$
$525 - 249$
$1000 - 499$
$1000 - 671$

For more on Removal, see page 176.

NUMBER TALKS

3–5

Subtraction: Removal

Instructions

A primary consideration in helping students think about the Removal strategy is to create a context that implies taking or removing an amount out of the whole. By structuring the following story problem for 50 – 17, we can create a removal action:

Bethany has 50 marbles. She decides to give her friend Marco 17 of her marbles. How many marbles will Bethany have left?

Notice how the following story problems also lend themselves to a Removal strategy by starting with the whole and taking out a part.

Contextual Problems to Promote a Removal Strategy

Richard has 90 paperback books. He plans to donate 16 of them to his neighborhood library. How many books will Richard have left?

Makalah saved $182. She bought a video game for $53. How much money does Makalah have left?

The students of Green Acres School raised $5,000 for new books for the school library. So far the librarian has purchased $1,238 in new books. How much money does the school have left to purchase books?

The following number talks consist of three or more sequential problems. The sequence of problems within a given number talk allows students to apply strategies from previous

(continued)

problems to subsequent problems. These number talk problems may be used in two ways:

- selected at random from each category; or
- navigated in a systematic order by selecting problems with smaller numbers from a specific category, then building to larger numbers.

To help your students be successful with this strategy, you may wish to introduce each of the problems embedded in a context similar to the situations discussed previously. It is also important to encourage students to keep the minuend intact and remove the subtrahend in parts; otherwise, it is easy for them to lose sight of the whole and the part. The following number talk sequences help promote this idea.

Category 1	214
Category 2	215
Category 3	216

NUMBER TALKS

3–5

Category 1: Removal

The following number talks consist of two-digit numbers that do not require regrouping or decomposing.

NUMBER TALKS

3-5

35 − 10	53 − 40	73 − 50
35 − 13	53 − 42	73 − 51
35 − 20	56 − 30	78 − 20
35 − 22	56 − 34	78 − 27

49 − 20	57 − 20	86 − 40
49 − 24	57 − 26	86 − 45
47 − 20	53 − 30	84 − 50
47 − 26	53 − 33	84 − 51

48 − 30	69 − 20	98 − 50
48 − 35	69 − 22	98 − 55
44 − 20	69 − 40	98 − 70
44 − 23	69 − 42	98 − 79

Category 2: Removal

The following number talks include computation problems with two-digit numbers that require regrouping or decomposing.

$23 - 10$
$23 - 14$
$23 - 18$
$23 - 15$

$42 - 30$
$42 - 33$
$43 - 10$
$43 - 14$

$72 - 50$
$72 - 54$
$72 - 30$
$72 - 36$

$33 - 10$
$33 - 14$
$33 - 20$
$33 - 25$

$51 - 30$
$51 - 35$
$55 - 20$
$55 - 26$

$81 - 50$
$81 - 55$
$83 - 70$
$83 - 74$

NUMBER TALKS

3–5

$45 - 20$
$45 - 26$
$45 - 10$
$45 - 16$

$64 - 40$
$64 - 45$
$64 - 20$
$64 - 28$

$91 - 60$
$91 - 63$
$94 - 50$
$94 - 56$

Category 3: Removal

The following number talks utilize two- and three-digit numbers; some require decomposing.

NUMBER TALKS

3–5

$100 - 50$	$150 - 20$	$150 - 15$
$100 - 52$	$150 - 28$	$150 - 100$
$100 - 60$	$155 - 20$	$150 - 115$
$100 - 64$	$155 - 28$	$153 - 115$

$100 - 80$	$200 - 100$	$345 - 200$
$100 - 86$	$200 - 150$	$345 - 220$
$100 - 30$	$200 - 153$	$345 - 222$
$100 - 37$	$210 - 153$	$345 - 234$

$100 - 50$	$200 - 60$	$543 - 20$
$120 - 50$	$270 - 60$	$543 - 100$
$126 - 50$	$270 - 65$	$543 - 120$
$126 - 55$	$276 - 65$	$543 - 240$

Subtraction: Place Value and Negative Numbers

Instructions

Many of us were told that in subtraction, "You can't take a bigger number from a smaller number, so you must go next door and borrow from your neighbor." Mathematically, this is an incorrect statement. You *can* subtract a larger number from a smaller number; you will be left with a negative amount. This idea, accompanied by an understanding of place value, is the core of the Place Value and Negative Numbers strategy.

My first experience with this strategy was in a second-grade classroom. The student had access to a posted number line that extended into negative numbers. The teacher presented the problem, 40 – 21. A student offered that 0 – 1 was –1 and 40 – 20 was 20; 20 and a –1 were 19. He showed on the number line that if he were at –1 and went up 20, he would be at 19. Since then I have continued to see second- through fifth-grade students successfully "invent" and use this strategy.

Initially start with problems that have a difference of –1 in the ones column until your students understand why you are "in the hole by 1."

The following number talks consist of three or more sequential problems. The sequence of problems within a given number talk allows students to apply strategies from previous problems to subsequent problems. These number talk problems may be used in two ways:

• selected at random from each category; or
• navigated in a systematic order by selecting problems with smaller numbers from a specific category, then building to larger numbers.

Category 1	218
Category 2	219
Category 3	220

For more on Place Value and Negative Numbers, see page 177.

NUMBER TALKS

3–5

NUMBER TALKS

3–5

Category 1 represents introductory number talks that more readily encourage a specific strategy.

Category 1: Place Value and Negative Numbers

The following number talks consist of computation problems that begin the discussion of what happens when you remove a larger number from a smaller quantity. The number line will be an important tool to use when reasoning with this strategy.

$5 - 5$	$4 - 4$	$20 - 10$
$5 - 6$	$4 - 5$	$2 - 4$
$5 - 7$	$4 - 6$	$22 - 14$
$5 - 8$	$4 - 7$	

$0 - 1$	$20 - 10$	$20 - 10$
$0 - 2$	$0 - 4$	$3 - 5$
$0 - 3$	$20 - 14$	$23 - 15$
$0 - 5$		

$6 - 6$	$20 - 10$	$20 - 10$
$6 - 7$	$1 - 3$	$5 - 6$
$6 - 8$	$21 - 13$	$25 - 16$
$6 - 9$		

Category 2: Place Value and Negative Numbers

The following number talks consist of two-digit computation problems to continue the work with this strategy. A deliberate sequence is used to support thinking for the initial problem in each section. The last problem in each section allows students to test their thinking with a similar problem.

Category 2 talks are crafted for students who are successfully using the selected strategy.

$20 - 10$	$40 - 20$	$70 - 40$
$4 - 6$	$8 - 9$	$2 - 5$
$24 - 16$	$48 - 29$	$72 - 45$
$23 - 15$	$44 - 26$	$77 - 28$

$30 - 10$	$50 - 10$	$80 - 30$
$2 - 5$	$3 - 7$	$1 - 8$
$32 - 15$	$53 - 17$	$81 - 38$
$35 - 17$	$54 - 26$	$83 - 44$

NUMBER TALKS

3-5

$30 - 10$	$60 - 30$	$90 - 50$
$6 - 9$	$6 - 8$	$6 - 7$
$36 - 19$	$66 - 38$	$96 - 57$
$33 - 16$	$64 - 29$	$93 - 68$

Category 3 provides opportunities for students to use and extend the targeted strategy.

Category 3: Place Value and Negative Numbers

The following number talks includes three-digit computation problems to continue the work with this strategy. A deliberate sequence is used to support thinking for the initial problem in each section. The last problem in each section allows students to test their thinking with a similar problem.

NUMBER TALKS
3–5

$0 - 6$	$300 - 100$	$600 - 300$
$100 - 40$	$50 - 80$	$50 - 60$
$100 - 46$	$7 - 8$	$0 - 5$
$100 - 19$	$357 - 188$	$650 - 365$
	$321 - 233$	$612 - 248$

$100 - 0$	$400 - 200$	$800 - 600$
$20 - 80$	$40 - 50$	$50 - 90$
$5 - 7$	$4 - 6$	$3 - 4$
$125 - 87$	$444 - 256$	$853 - 694$
$114 - 75$	$413 - 135$	$826 - 437$

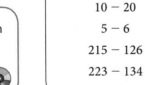
See Classroom Clip 5.6: Subtraction: 1000 – 674.

$200 - 100$	$500 - 300$	$1000 - 700$
$10 - 20$	$0 - 50$	$0 - 10$
$5 - 6$	$0 - 8$	$0 - 5$
$215 - 126$	$500 - 358$	$1000 - 715$
$223 - 134$	$500 - 263$	$1000 - 674$

Subtraction: Adjusting One Number to Create an Easier Problem

Instructions

If students do not have a strong understanding of the part–whole relationship in subtraction, they will be limited in the strategies they can use. When either the minuend or subtrahend is adjusted to make a friendlier number, the strategy will warrant that the remainder or answer also be adjusted. For the problem 50 – 24, some students change the problem to 49 – 24. Since the child changed the whole by removing 1, she has to add back 1 to the answer of 25 to get 26 (adjust the minuend):

$$
\begin{array}{ll}
50 - 1 & 49 \\
\underline{-\ 24} & \underline{-\ 24} \\
& 25 + 1 = 26
\end{array}
$$

For the same problem, other students might change the 24 to 25 to think about doubles or money. They have removed one too many and will need to add back one to the answer (adjust the subtrahend):

$$
\begin{array}{ll}
50 & 50 \\
\underline{-\ 24 + 1} & \underline{-\ 25} \\
& 25 + 1 = 26
\end{array}
$$

These are the types of discussions that will need to occur when using this strategy.

The following number talks consist of three or more sequential problems. The sequence of problems within a given number talk allows students to apply strategies from previous problems

(continued)

For more on Adjusting One Number to Create an Easier Problem, see page 179.

NUMBER TALKS

3–5

to subsequent problems. These number talk problems may be used in two ways:
- selected at random from each category; or
- navigated in a systematic order by selecting problems with smaller numbers from a specific category, then building to larger numbers.

Category 1	223
Category 2	224
Category 3	225

NUMBER TALKS
3–5

Category 1: Adjusting One Number to Create an Easier Problem

The following number talks consist of smaller quantities—even basic facts—to help students consider what happens when numbers are adjusted in a subtraction problem. The following problems focus on adjusting the whole or the minuend.

Category 1 represents introductory number talks that more readily encourage a specific strategy.

$9 - 4$	$31 - 15$	$30 - 19$
$10 - 4$	$30 - 15$	$29 - 19$
$19 - 14$	$29 - 15$	$40 - 19$
$20 - 14$	$32 - 15$	$39 - 19$

$15 - 5$	$51 - 25$	$37 - 18$
$14 - 5$	$50 - 25$	$38 - 18$
$10 - 5$	$49 - 25$	$44 - 25$
$11 - 5$	$52 - 25$	$45 - 25$

NUMBER TALKS

3–5

$20 - 15$	$50 - 28$	$99 - 73$
$21 - 15$	$49 - 28$	$100 - 73$
$19 - 15$	$60 - 28$	$100 - 64$
$22 - 15$	$59 - 28$	$100 - 82$

Category 2
talks are crafted
for students
who are suc-
cessfully using
the selected
strategy.

Category 2: Adjusting One Number to Create an Easier Problem

The following number talks include problems that focus on adjusting the subtrahend—the part being removed—to create an easier problem.

$20 - 10$	$30 - 15$	$70 - 30$
$20 - 9$	$30 - 16$	$70 - 31$
$20 - 11$	$30 - 14$	$70 - 29$
$21 - 9$	$30 - 19$	$70 - 49$

$25 - 15$	$50 - 25$	$80 - 40$
$25 - 16$	$50 - 24$	$80 - 39$
$25 - 18$	$50 - 26$	$80 - 41$
$25 - 19$	$50 - 19$	$80 - 49$

$40 - 20$	$60 - 30$	$100 - 50$
$40 - 19$	$60 - 29$	$100 - 51$
$40 - 21$	$60 - 31$	$100 - 49$
$40 - 18$	$60 - 39$	$100 - 52$

Category 3: Adjusting One Number to Create an Easier Problem

The following number talks require students to make decisions about which numbers might be adjusted to create an easier problem.

Category 3 provides opportunities for students to use and extend the targeted strategy.

$49 - 28$	$52 - 40$	$149 - 118$
$50 - 30$	$49 - 39$	$151 - 120$
$50 - 28$	$52 - 39$	$151 - 118$
$53 - 28$	$51 - 37$	$155 - 128$

$39 - 19$	$75 - 40$	$172 - 60$
$38 - 20$	$79 - 39$	$169 - 59$
$38 - 19$	$75 - 39$	$172 - 59$
$35 - 18$	$77 - 39$	$179 - 88$

NUMBER TALKS

3-5

$59 - 47$	$99 - 69$	$199 - 98$
$60 - 50$	$100 - 70$	$200 - 100$
$60 - 47$	$100 - 69$	$200 - 98$
$62 - 45$	$101 - 68$	$203 - 99$

For more on Keeping a Constant Difference, see page 178.

Subtraction: Keeping a Constant Difference

NUMBER TALKS

3–5

Instructions

With the Constant Difference strategy, both the minuend and subtrahend are adjusted by the same amounts. This maintains the distance or the space between the two quantities. This strategy can be efficient and beneficial because it allows the student to adjust the numbers to make a friendlier, easier problem.

An example of the effectiveness of this strategy can be seen with the problem 51 – 26. If both numbers are adjusted by subtracting 1, the problem is changed to 50 – 25, a common money problem. The answer of 25 is the same for either problem, because the numbers have both shifted by the same amount.

Number talks in Categories 1 and 2 provide a progression of problems designed to help the student notice the relationships between the problems. For example, in Category 1, the problem 14 – 10 is listed to help students notice that 13 – 9 could be solved by adjusting both numbers up by 1. Keep all problems in each sequence posted for the duration of the number talk. This will give your students the maximum opportunity to notice the relationships between the problems.

These number talk problems may be used in two ways:
- selected at random from each category; or
- navigated in a systematic order by selecting problems with smaller numbers from a specific category, then building to larger numbers.

Category 1	227
Category 2	228
Category 3	229

Category 1: Keeping a Constant Difference

The following number talks consist of computation problems that use numbers up to one hundred and are focused on adjusting both numbers by adding or subtracting one or two.

Category 1 represents introductory number talks that more readily encourage a specific strategy.

$14 - 10$	$42 - 20$	$61 - 29$
$13 - 9$	$39 - 17$	$62 - 30$
$14 - 7$	$41 - 19$	$59 - 27$
$15 - 6$	$51 - 19$	$49 - 17$

$20 - 15$	$50 - 25$	$90 - 45$
$19 - 14$	$49 - 24$	$89 - 44$
$21 - 16$	$51 - 26$	$91 - 46$
$41 - 16$	$71 - 36$	$98 - 52$

NUMBER TALKS

3–5

$30 - 15$	$35 - 20$	$100 - 51$
$29 - 14$	$30 - 15$	$99 - 50$
$31 - 16$	$34 - 19$	$100 - 36$
$51 - 16$	$44 - 29$	$100 - 48$

Category 2: Keeping a Constant Difference
The following number talks include computation problems with numbers above one hundred.

NUMBER TALKS
3–5

101 − 50
99 − 48
100 − 49
109 − 51

150 − 125
149 − 124
151 − 126
171 − 136

342 − 120
339 − 117
341 − 119
351 − 119

139 − 60
138 − 59
114 − 90
112 − 88

153 − 100
151 − 98
173 − 160
171 − 158

199 − 90
200 − 91
299 − 150
300 − 151

135 − 120
130 − 115
134 − 119
164 − 119

261 − 129
262 − 130
259 − 127
249 − 117

498 − 310
500 − 312
499 − 366
500 − 367

Category 3: Keeping a Constant Difference

The following number talks consist of computation problems that do not build one upon the other. Instead, each problem offers opportunities for students to choose the best method for keeping a constant difference. Many of the problems can be adjusted up or down to create easier problems.

Category 3 provides opportunities for students to use and extend the targeted strategy.

$32 - 19$	$111 - 56$	$234 - 119$
$48 - 29$	$134 - 68$	$271 - 158$
$35 - 18$	$127 - 88$	$251 - 126$
$41 - 13$	$122 - 77$	$209 - 151$

$35 - 17$	$133 - 95$	$391 - 146$
$53 - 29$	$114 - 89$	$359 - 127$
$62 - 37$	$123 - 105$	$251 - 116$
$44 - 26$	$100 - 34$	$315 - 106$

NUMBER TALKS
3-5

$86 - 47$	$236 - 119$	$300 - 214$
$90 - 36$	$200 - 137$	$500 - 289$
$78 - 59$	$287 - 118$	$700 - 477$
$52 - 35$	$151 - 98$	$1000 - 674$

CHAPTER 7

How Do I Develop Specific Multiplication and Division Strategies in the 3–5 Classroom?

Overarching Goals

During number talks, you are always urging students to be accurate, efficient, and flexible with their mathematical thinking. However, many other areas can and should be addressed: number sense, place value, fluency, properties, and connecting mathematical ideas. Unpacking each of these components and keeping them in the forefront during classroom strategy discussions will better prepare your students to be mathematically powerful and proficient.

Five Number Talks Goals for Grades 3–5

1. Number sense

2. Place value

3. Fluency

4. Properties

5. Connecting mathematical ideas

Number Sense

The term number sense is often discussed in math education, but what is it? Fennell and Landis (1994) state, "[Number sense] is an awareness and understanding about what numbers are, their relationships, their magnitude and the relative effect of operating on numbers, including

Classroom Link: Multiplication: 32 × 15
Classroom Clip 5.2

Before you watch the fifth-grade number talk for 32 × 15, anticipate possible student strategies and how they might be recorded.

As you watch the fifth-grade number talk for 32 × 15, consider:

1. What evidence in the video supports student understanding of place value?

2. How do the students' strategies exhibit number sense?

3. How does the teacher connect math ideas throughout the number talk?

4. What examples of properties can be observed in the strategies and discussion?

5. Which strategies were most accessible to you? Confusing?

6. How did the teacher and students' roles support learning?

For commentary on the above, see Appendix A: Author's Video Reflections.

To view this video clip, scan the QR code or access via mathsolutions.com /NTWNC52

CCSS

Number and Operations in Base Ten: Use place value understanding and properties of operations to perform multi-digit arithmetic.

4.NBT.B.5 Multiply a whole number of up to four digits by a one-digit whole number, and multiply two two-digit numbers, using strategies based on place value and the properties of operations. Illustrate and explain the calculation by using equations, rectangular arrays, and/or area models.

the use of mental mathematics and estimation" (187). Every time you elicit answers to a problem in a number talk and ask students to share whether the proposed solutions are reasonable, you are helping to build number sense. When you ask students to give an estimate before they begin thinking about a specific strategy, you are fostering number sense. As a math coach, I am frequently asked to assess struggling students. Time and time again I have found that the students I interview can rarely give an estimate to a problem. They may be able to apply a memorized procedure, but they cannot discern or justify whether their solution is reasonable. By asking students to estimate an answer before solving a problem and provide evidence that an answer is reasonable, we can help build this essential skill.

Place Value

Teaching place value is much more than requiring students to state how many hundreds, tens, and ones are in a number or to write a number in expanded notation. The true test of whether students understand place value is if they can apply their understanding in computation. Number talks provide the opportunity to confront and use place-value understanding on a continual basis.

Fluency

Often fluency with numbers is compared to knowing basic facts; however, fluency is more than fact recall. Fluency is knowing how a number can be composed and decomposed and using that information to be flexible and efficient with solving problems. Consider the string of numbers, $5 + 7 + 8$. Knowing 7 can be decomposed into $5 + 2$ in order to think about the problem as $5 + (5 + 2) + 8$ allows access to making quick tens. The problem can then be solved as $(5 + 5) + (2 + 8)$ through the associative property. Understanding that 100 can be decomposed into 90 and 10 or 93 and 7 to make subtracting 37 easier is an example of fluency. Number talks provide opportunities to help students use and develop fluency.

Properties

In my own education, my experiences with the *properties* of mathematics consisted solely of memorizing definitions and matching terms to examples. I do not remember ever applying the commutative, associative, distributive, and identity properties. As students invent their own strategies, there are opportunities to link their thinking to mathematical properties and understand why they work.

Connecting Mathematical Ideas

One of the National Council of Teachers of Mathematics (NCTM) process standards is Connections. While this standard promotes connecting math to real-world applications, it strongly embraces making connecting links to big ideas in mathematics. Each time you compare student strategies, discuss how addition can be used to solve subtraction problems, and make links between arrays with multiplication and division, you are grounding your students in the idea that mathematical concepts are related and make sense. Helping students build on these connecting mathematical ideas is a critical component of number talks.

Using Array Models to Anchor Student Strategies with Multiplication and Division

An array model is as important to multiplication and division as the number line model is to addition and subtraction. The visual representation of rows and columns helps students as they develop their proportional reasoning. Like the part/whole box model for addition and subtraction, the array identifies the parts (factors) and the whole (total area of product) and can be used to demonstrate and prove student strategies.

With the multiplication problem 8 × 25, students know the dimensions or factors of the array and are finding the area or product/whole. (See Figure 7–1.)

The array can be used to model and prove the Partial Products strategy for solving 8 × 25. Because 8 × 25 is represented as (8 × 20) + (8 × 5), the array can be partitioned accordingly. The area from the 8 × 20 array is combined with the area from the 8 × 5 array for a total area or product of 200. (See Figure 7–2 on the next page.)

As students become stronger with multiplicative reasoning and no longer need to have every square in the array confirmed, then the open-array model can be used. The open array maintains the dimensions as in a regular array, but does not include the interior squares. A benefit of using the open array is that it allows greater flexibility in representing student thinking—especially with larger numbers. (See Figure 7–3 on page 235.)

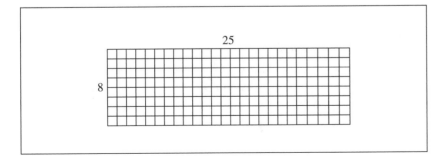

Figure 7–1   *Array for 8 × 25*

Classroom Link: Array Discussion: 8 × 25
Classroom Clip 3.7

To view this video clip, scan the QR code or access via mathsolutions.com /NTWNC37

As you watch the third-grade number talk in which an 8 × 25 array is used, consider:

1. How does the array model support the student strategies?

2. How does breaking the factors into friendly numbers promote the goals of efficiency and flexibility?

3. How do the teacher's questions foster an understanding of multiplication?

4. How could you represent other multiplication problems with an array?

5. How does the array help connect additive thinking with multiplicative reasoning?

6. What math understandings and misconceptions are addressed with this model?

For commentary on the above, see Appendix A: Author's Video Reflections.

Mathematical Practice 4: Model with mathematics.

When we think about modeling with mathematics, visual models such as arrays, number lines, ten-frames, hundreds charts, and so forth come readily to mind. As students share strategies during a number talk, teachers may choose to model their approaches using visual models.

Yet, modeling with mathematics also implies the ability to translate a situation or context into mathematics (mathematizing) as well as translate the mathematics into a situation. For example, the teacher may use a story problem to introduce a number talk on subtraction or present a picture of a collection of apples arranged in an array and ask students to figure out how many apples there are. Each of these situations describes opportunities for students to create a mathematical model from a context.

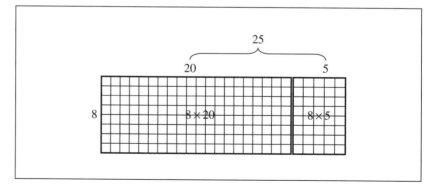

Figure 7–2   *Array Model with Partial Products for 8 × 25*

The array and open-array model is a valuable tool for division because it highlights that the whole (dividend) and one factor or dimension (divisor) are known, while the other factor or quotient is the unknown. The array for the problem 200 ÷ 8 can help us think about the known and unknown components in division. (See Figure 7–4.)

The array can be used to show how to build up to the dividend when solving a division problem with the Multiplying Up or Partial Quotients strategies. Using 200 ÷ 8, we can account for partial areas of (8 × 10) +(8 × 10) +(8 × 5), until we have a total area of 200. (See Figure 7–5 on the next page.)

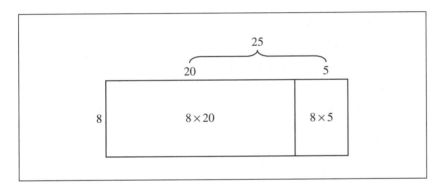

Figure 7–3   *The Open Array with Partial Products Strategy for 8 × 25*

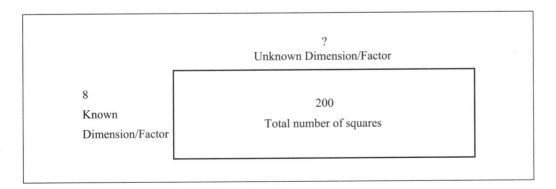

Figure 7–4   *Open Array for 200 ÷ 8*

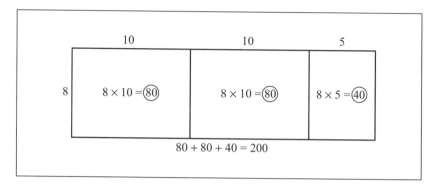

Figure 7–5   *One Multiplying Up Strategy for 200 ÷ 8*

Classroom Link: Array Discussion: 150 ÷ 15, 300 ÷ 15
Classroom Clip 5.4

To view this video clip, scan the QR code or access via mathsolutions.com /NTWNC54

CCSS connections to this clip are listed in the margin of the next page.

Before you watch the fifth-grade number talk for 150 ÷ 15 and 300 ÷ 15, anticipate possible student strategies and how they might be recorded.

As you watch the fifth-grade number talk for 150 ÷ 15 and 300 ÷ 15, consider:

1. How does the open array allow the students to make connections between multiplication and division?

2. What mathematical relationships are being built upon during the class discussion?

3. How does the teacher connect math ideas throughout the number talk?

4. What understandings and misconceptions does the array model help the students confront?

5. What examples of properties can be observed in the strategies and discussion?

For commentary on the above, see Appendix A: Author's Video Reflections.

Using Real-Life Contexts

Once I began incorporating number talks as a regular component of my math instruction, I stopped showing students how to solve a computation problem. Instead, I introduced new operations in a story-problem context and encouraged students to make sense of the problems and the numbers. Using a real-life context as a springboard for mathematical thinking serves to help students in three main ways.

> *Three Benefits of Using Real-Life Contexts*
>
> 1. A real-life context engages students in mathematics that is relevant to them.
>
> 2. A real-life context attaches meaning to the numbers.
>
> 3. A real-life context helps students access the mathematics.

1. A real-life context engages students in mathematics that is relative to them.

By crafting story problems that are intertwined in content that matters to students, you create a need for them to want to know. Designing problems around classroom parties, recess time, reading goals, or schoolwide projects naturally draws students into the mathematics.

2. A real-life context attaches meaning to the numbers.

A story-problem context allows the student to envision a mental image of the mathematics. In contrast, problems that utilize only bare numbers require the student to have a previous understanding of the operation and create their own mental image of the numerical actions.

3. A real-life context helps students access the mathematics.

A story-problem context provides multiple points of entry for students and allows them access to the math. A context also gives students a framework for deciding if an answer is reasonable. Real-world situations may also provide opportunities for students to notice commonalities between previously solved problems and a new problem.

CCSS Connections to Clip 5.4

Mathematical Practice 2: Reason abstractly and quantitatively.

The very essence of a number talk embraces this practice. Students engage in assessing entry points into problems, decide upon efficient strategies, and justify their reasoning to their peers. To reason in this manner requires understanding the relationships that are inherent in each problem and having the flexibility to look at multiple approaches simultaneously. Number talks provide a platform for students to bring meaning to the problem and to articulate the why and the how of their reasoning so it can be clearly represented using a community forum.

Number and Operations in Base Ten: Perform operations with multi-digit whole numbers and with decimals to hundredths.

5.NBT.B.6 Find whole-number quotients of whole numbers with up to four-digit dividends and two-digit divisors, using strategies based on place value, the properties of operations, and/or the relationship between multiplication and division. Illustrate and explain the calculation by using equations, rectangular arrays, and/or area models.

This classroom scenario provides an excellent example of students' place value understanding and the relationship between multiplication and division and proportional reasoning. Asking students to further explore these relationships through an array model allows them to continue to build a stronger foundation for their reasoning and clarify areas of confusion.

Using a Context with Multiplication

Consider the problem 3 × 12. When embedded in the following story problem, 3 × 12 can be used to introduce third graders to multiplication with larger numbers.

> *Michelle baked 3 pans of cookies. Each pan has 12 cookies. How many cookies did Michelle bake?*

Most children are familiar with baking cookies and would mentally picture or draw three pans with twelve cookies each:

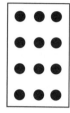

Student representations using the specified context open the door for students to invent their own strategies for solving 3 × 12. Common first strategies are described below.

Three Different Strategies for Solving 3 × 12

① **Student's Strategy: Repeated Addition**	**The Strategy as Recorded by the Teacher**
Balaz: I saw each pan had twelve cookies, so I did twelve plus twelve plus twelve. I knew twelve plus twelve was twenty-four, plus the other twelve was thirty-six.	12 + 12 + 12 12 + 12 = 24 24 + 12 = 36
Teacher: Mathematicians would use 3 × 12 to represent this problem because there are three groups of twelve cookies. You solved this problem by adding each group together, or Repeated Addition.	12 + 12 + 12 = 3 × 12 2 × 12 = 24 1 × 12 = 12 24 + 12 = 36

2 Student's Strategy: Repeated Addition	The Strategy as Recorded by the Teacher
McKenzie: I also added twelve plus twelve plus twelve, but I added all of the tens together first and then all of the twos together. That gave me thirty plus six, which was thirty-six.   	$12 + 12 + 12$ $10 + 10 + 10 = 30$ $2 + 2 + 2 = 6$ $30 + 6 = 36$
Teacher: Mathematicians would also represent your thinking with 3×12. Your $10 + 10 + 10$ is the same as 3×10, and your $2 + 2 + 2$ is the same as 3×2. Does 3×12 equal $(3 \times 10) + (3 \times 2)$? How can we find out?	$12 + 12 + 12 = 3 \times 12 = (3 \times 10) + (3 \times 2)^*$ $10 + 10 + 10 = 3 \times 10 = 30^*$ $2 + 2 + 2 = 3 \times 2 = 6^*$ $30 + 6 = 36$ *Note: This is not a violation of the equals sign since all quantities are equivalent.*

3 Student's Strategy: Skip Counting	The Strategy as Recorded by the Teacher
Stephen: I saw twelve threes and I knew how to count by threes, so I counted by three twelve times. 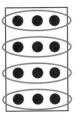 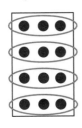 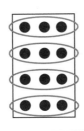	$3 + 3 + 3 + 3 + 3 + 3 + 3 + 3 + 3 + 3 + 3 + 3$ 3, 6, 9, 12, 15 , 18, 21, 24, 27, 30 , 33, 36

(continued)

Teacher: So you skip counted by threes. What if we had ninety-nine threes? That would be a lot of threes to count by! I wonder if there are any groups of threes we could quickly know? Does anyone instantly know how much five threes are? Could we use this to help us? What about ten threes?

$$\underbrace{3 + 3 + 3 + 3 + 3}_{3 \times 5 = 15} \underbrace{3 + 3 + 3 + 3 + 3}_{3 \times 5 = 15} \underbrace{3 + 3}_{2 \times 3 = 6}$$

These initial strategies provide an opportunity for the teacher to build stepping stones to the mathematical ideas in this problem (equal groups, relationship between addition and multiplication, and commutative property) and continue to help students attach meaning to the numbers as evidenced in the following narrative.

Notice how the teacher uses the student-invented strategies to facilitate students' thinking without telling them how to solve the problem. The initial recording of each strategy serves as an opportunity to tease out and scaffold important ideas. McKenzie's strategy is linked to preliminary discussions of the distributive property through the teacher's recording of 3×12 as $(3 \times 10) + (3 \times 2)$. As additional problems are posed, students will have the opportunity to further explore repeated addition, the relationship between addition and multiplication, properties, and breaking apart factors into addends. The teacher is thoughtfully structuring a foundation for students to build their understanding about addition, multiplication, and the mathematical properties that undergird these relationships.

Classroom Link: Doubling and Halving: 4 x 7, 2 x 14
Classroom Clip 3.6

As you watch the third-grade number talk for 4×7 and 2×14, consider:

1. How does using a context support student reasoning about the commutative property?

2. How is a context used to support student thinking about the doubling and halving strategy?

3. How does the context and the array bring student understandings and misconceptions to the forefront?

4. What questions does the teacher pose to help students confront their misconceptions?

For commentary on the above, see Appendix A: Author's Video Reflections.

To view this video clip, scan the QR code or access via mathsolutions.com /NTWNC36

Discussing Efficiency

As students better understand the mathematics of an operation, number talks are used to investigate different strategies, test whether they will always work for any set of numbers, and discuss efficiency. We will use the problem 9×15 (see the following pages) to consider the following student strategies and explore the idea of efficiency.

Three Different Strategies for Solving 9×15

① Student's Strategy: Skip Counting	The Strategy as Recorded by the Teacher
Anna: I counted by nines. **Teacher:** How did you count? **Anna:** I skip counted. **Teacher:** How did you know when to stop counting? **Anna:** I used my fingers to keep track of how many nines I had counted.	9, 18, 27, 36, 45, 54, 63, 72, 81, 90, 99, 108, 117, 126, 135

② Student's Strategy: Partial Products	The Strategy as Recorded by the Teacher
Jason: I broke the fifteen into a ten plus five, then I multiplied nine times ten and nine times five. This gave me ninety plus forty-five, which was one hundred and thirty-five.	$9 \times 15 = 9 \times (10 + 5)$ $9 \times 10 = 90$ $9 \times 5 = 45$ $90 + 45 = 135$

③ Student's Strategy: Making Landmark or Friendly Numbers	The Strategy as Recorded by the Teacher
Belinda: I changed the nine to a ten and then multiplied. **Teacher:** How did this help you solve the problem? **Belinda:** Well, multiplying by tens is easy for me. I knew that ten fifteens would be one hundred and fifty. Since I added on one to each nine, that gave me fifteen extra ones that I had to subtract.	9×15 $\underline{+1}$ $10 \times 15 = 150$ $150 - 15 = 135$

By keeping each strategy posted for the duration of the number talk, students have an opportunity to discuss efficiency as well as the similarities and differences between strategies. If each strategy is labeled with a number (such as 1, 2, 3), you can ask students to use a hand signal to quietly indicate which strategy they consider to be the most efficient. This allows the teacher to glean information about which students are struggling to use tens and friendly numbers, break apart numbers, or manipulate numbers with ease. A brief class discussion about efficiency can also be launched as indicated by the following classroom narrative.

Classroom Example: Discussing Efficiency for Multiplication Strategies

Teacher: I noticed there were a lot of signals for Strategy 3, Belinda's strategy. Could someone share why you thought this was an efficient strategy?

Meg: It's easy to multiply numbers by ten.

Taylor: It seems a little quicker. But I also think Jason's and Anna's strategies are kind of the same.

Teacher: Can someone share how they seem similar?

Lucinda: When Anna was keeping track with her fingers, she stopped at ten nines, which was just like Jason's. But then she added five more nines, which was also like Jason's. She just did it a little differently.

Teacher: So you're noticing a connection between skip counting and breaking one of the factors apart. Let's test out these strategies with a similar problem.

Anticipating Student Thinking

As discussed in Chapter 2, do not be discouraged if you do not access a student's thinking quickly. It takes time to follow a strategy when you hear it for the first time. Students commonly use a limited number of strategies to solve different types of problems, and taking time to think through possible strategies for each problem beforehand will help you gain confidence in listening and following student thinking. As you become more accustomed to these strategies, you will find yourself anticipating your students' thinking and becoming more comfortable with understanding the approaches they have selected.

As you anticipate potential strategies for each problem, also consider how you will capture each student's thinking so others may access the strategy. Consider which mathematical ideas you want to highlight and how you might record the strategy to emphasize those specific concepts. For example, if making tens or utilizing place value is an important component in the strategy, make sure these ideas stand out in your recording.

Many teachers and other adults are surprised that students can invent ways to solve a new problem. I have found, however, that by laying the foundation for making sense of number relationships, students are quite capable of inventing efficient strategies. The following strategies represent a valued collection of mathematical ideas from third-, fourth-, and fifth-grade students. Do not be quick to discount them because the recording takes up so much written space; the students solved them very quickly using only mental math. Each strategy is named to help you better understand its foundation; however, in my classroom strategies were often named for the students who invented them.

An Introduction to Common Multiplication Strategies

The ability to think flexibly about the factors in a multiplication problem is essential as students begin developing strategies for multiplicative thinking. Understanding that factors can be broken into different combinations of addends or smaller factors is an important idea as students begin to develop their own strategies for this operation. Building a conceptual understanding before procedural knowledge helps students navigate and explore different approaches to computation.

Classroom Link: Multiplication String: 7 × 7
Classroom Clip 3.5

Before you watch the third-grade number talk for 7 × 7, anticipate possible student strategies and how they might be recorded.

As you watch the third-grade number talk for 7 × 7, consider:

1. What evidence in the video supports student understanding of multiplication?

2. How do the students' strategies exhibit number sense?

3. How does the teacher connect math ideas throughout the number talk?

4. How does fluency with smaller multiplication problems support the students' strategies?

5. What examples of properties can be observed in the strategies and discussion?

6. Which strategies were most accessible to you? More challenging?

7. How could the strategies for 7 × 7 be connected using an array?

For commentary on the above, see Appendix A: Author's Video Reflections.

To view this video clip, scan the QR code or access via mathsolutions.com /NTWNC35

Operations and Algebraic Thinking: Understand properties of multiplication and the relationship between multiplication and division.

3.OA.B.5 Apply properties of operations as strategies to multiply and divide. *Examples: If 6 × 4 = 24 is known, then 4 × 6 = 24 is also known.*

Operations and Algebraic Thinking: Multiply and divide within 100.

3.OA.C.7 Fluently multiply and divide within 100, using strategies such as the relationship between multiplication and division (e.g., knowing that 8 × 5 = 40, one knows 40 ÷ 5 = 8) or properties of operations. By the end of Grade 3, know from memory all products of two one-digit numbers.

Five Common Strategies for Multiplication

(M-1) **Multiplication Strategy: Repeated Addition or Skip Counting**

These are often beginning strategies for students who are just learning multiplication. Help students build connections among these entry-level strategies and multiplication by making the links to multiplication explicit. Connecting

(continued)

A purposeful number talk string provides an introduction to the use of the distributive property as the foundation for an efficient strategy for multiplication. As the teacher selects accessible problems that build upon one another, she provides a scaffold for students to consider how factors can be decomposed into addends to make a more difficult problem accessible. Using 2×7 as the basis for the multiplication string, the teacher begins with a problem that is within reach of all students.

the student's strategy to an array model provides an essential visual model for multiplication.

6×15

$15 + 15 + 15 + 15 + 15 + 15$ $15 + 15 = 30$ $30 + 15 = 45$ $45 + 15 = 60$ $60 + 15 = 75$ $75 + 15 = 90$	Students will often think about the problem 6×15 as 6 groups of 15 and solve it by adding one number at a time. Record their thinking using the repeated addition, but extend this initial thinking by linking the addition to a multiplication representation with the following strategies.

6×15 Linked to Multiplication Expressions Using Known Facts

$\overline{(15 + 15)} + \overline{(15 + 15)} + \overline{(15 + 15)}$ $2 \times 15 = 30$ $2 \times 15 = 30 \ \big\}\ 90$ $2 \times 15 = 30$ or $15 + 15 + 15 + 15 + 15 + 15$ $6 \times 10 = 60$ $6 \times 5 \ = 30 \ \big\}\ 90$	Students are often comfortable using doubles and counting by fives and tens in addition. Help them connect this understanding by circling corresponding groups of numbers and recording a correlating multiplication sentence.

6×15 Linked to an Array Model

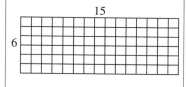	Every multiplication problem can be represented as a rectangle showing rows and columns. For example, 6×15 can be represented by an array with 6 rows and 15 columns.

(continued)

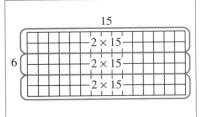

We can also show how thinking about 6 × 15 as repeated addition links to multiplicative reasoning with the array models for:

15 + 15 + 15 + 15 + 15 + 15 = (2 × 15) + (2 × 15) + (2 × 15)

or

15 + 15 + 15 + 15 + 15 + 15 = (6 × 10) + (6 × 5)

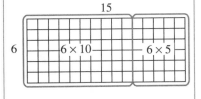

(M-2) Multiplication Strategy: Making Landmark or Friendly Numbers

Often a multiplication problem can be made easier by changing one of the factors to a friendly or landmark number. Students who are comfortable multiplying by multiples of ten will often adjust factors to allow them to take advantage of this strength.

9 × 15

9 × 15
+1 (group of 15)
10 × 15 = 150

With this strategy, notice that not just one, but one group of 15 was added. This is a very important distinction for students and one that comes as they develop multiplicative reasoning.

(continued)

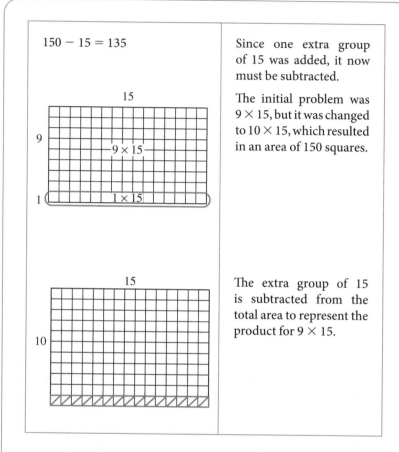

$150 - 15 = 135$

Since one extra group of 15 was added, it now must be subtracted.

The initial problem was 9×15, but it was changed to 10×15, which resulted in an area of 150 squares.

The extra group of 15 is subtracted from the total area to represent the product for 9×15.

(M-3) Multiplication Strategy: Partial Products

This strategy is based on the distributive property and is the precursor for our standard U.S. algorithm for multiplication—it just keeps the place value intact. The strategy more closely resembles the algorithm when written vertically. When students understand that the factors in a multiplication problem can be decomposed or broken apart into addends, this allows them to use smaller problems to solve more difficult ones. As students invent Partial Product strategies, they can break one or both factors apart.

(continued)

12 × 15

Horizontal	Vertical
12×15	15
$12 \times (10 + 5)$	$\times \ \underline{12}$
$12 \times 10 = 120$	$120 \ (12 \times 10)$
$12 \times 5 = 60$	$+ \ \underline{60} \ (12 \times 5)$
$120 + 60 = 180$	180

Whether the problem is written horizontally or vertically, the fidelity of place value is kept.

In this example, the 15 is thought about as $(10+5)$ while the 12 is kept whole.

12×15

$(4 + 4 + 4) \times 15$

$4 \times 15 = 60$

$4 \times 15 = 60$

$4 \times 15 = 60$

$60 + 60 + 60 = 180$

This time the 12 is broken apart into $(4 + 4 + 4)$ and the 25 is kept whole. The 12 could have been broken into $(10 + 2)$ or any other combination that would have made the problem accessible.

12×15

$(10 + 2) \times (10 + 5)$

$10 \times 10 = 100$

$10 \times 5 = 50$

$2 \times 10 = 20$

$2 \times 5 = 10$

$100 + 50 + 20 + 10 = 180$

Both factors can be broken apart, and as numbers become larger, students often use this method until they become more confident in multiplying with larger quantities. It is difficult for some students to keep up with all of the parts of the problem—especially when trying to use this strategy without paper and pencil.

(continued)

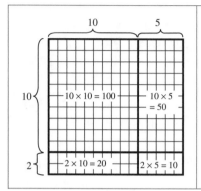

The array model is an excellent way to help students think about multiplying when breaking factors apart and providing proof for their reasoning. This example demonstrates how changing 12 × 15 to (10 + 2) × (10 + 5) works.

(M-4) **Multiplication Strategy: Doubling and Halving**

When students are provided opportunities to build arrays that have the same area and study the patterns of the dimensions, they often will notice a relationship that occurs between the factors or dimensions of the arrays. Consider the number 16. If we were to build all the possible arrays that would make 16 squares, we would have the following dimensions or factor pairs:

1 × 16

2 × 8

4 × 4

8 × 2

16 × 1

In every instance, we still have an area or product of 16, but our dimensions or factors have changed.

Did you notice how the factors on the left double every time, and the factors on the right halve each time? Let's look at the actual array models to see what happens physically.

(continued)

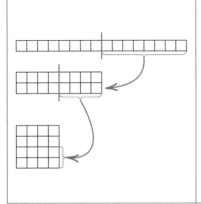

When the 1×16 is halved, the number of rows doubles and the number of columns halve, resulting in a 2×8.

When the 2×8 is halved, the number of rows doubles and the number of columns halve, resulting in a 4×4.

Doubling and halving can be continued until a 16×1 array is reached.

This strategy builds on the ease with which students double and halve numbers. We can apply this strategy to several problems.

$$8 \times 25$$
$$\div 2 \left(\right) \times 2$$
$$4 \times 50$$
$$\div 2 \left(\right) \times 2$$
$$2 \times 100 = 200$$

$$16 \times 16$$
$$\times 2 \left(\right) \div 2$$
$$32 \times 8$$
$$\times 2 \left(\right) \div 2$$
$$64 \times 4$$
$$\times 2 \left(\right) \div 2$$
$$128 \times 2 = 256$$

The intent of the strategy is to change the problem into a friendly problem to solve. Once the student reaches a point where the solution is easily obtained, then he or she would not continue doubling and halving.

Doubling and halving is especially beneficial when multiplying with double-digit problems. This can quickly turn the problem into a multiplication problem with a single-digit multiplier.

Note: Some problems do not lend themselves to doubling and halving. This would be an important area for students to investigate.

(continued)

(M-5) **Multiplication Strategy: Breaking Factors into Smaller Factors**

Breaking factors into smaller factors instead of addends can be a very efficient and effective strategy for multiplication. The associative property is at the core of this strategy. It is a powerful mental strategy—especially when problems become larger and one of the factors can be changed to a one-digit multiplier.

12×25 $(4 \times 25) + (4 \times 25) + (4 \times 25)$ $100 + 100 + 100 = 300$	Students will often approach a problem such as 12×25 by breaking the 12 into 3 groups of 4. They are comfortable with money amounts, and they will notice that four quarters equal one dollar.
$(4 \times 25) + (4 \times 25) + (4 \times 25)$ $= 3 \times (4 \times 25)$ $12 \times 25 = 3 \times (4 \times 25)$	Help them connect their thinking to the associative property by recording the problem as $3 \times (4 \times 25)$. Encourage them to discuss whether 12×25 is the same as $3 \times 4 \times 25$. This is one way to begin making a bridge into factors and using the associative property.
12×25 $12 \times (5 \times 5) = (12 \times 5) \times 5$ $60 \times 5 = 300$	We can also use the associative property and knowledge about factorization to think of 25 as 5×5.

The following array can help us think about how the associative property works with 12×25. This model shows how the problem can be represented as five groups of 12×5 or $(12 \times 5) \times 5$.

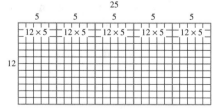

Classroom Link: Associative Property: 12 x 15
Classroom Clip 5.1

Before you watch the fifth-grade number talk string for 12 x 15, anticipate possible student strategies and how they might be recorded.

As you watch the fifth-grade number talk sequence for 12 x 15, consider:

1. What evidence supports student understanding of place value?

2. How do the students' strategies exhibit number sense?

3. How do the teacher and students connect math ideas throughout the number talk?

4. How do the students' strategies build upon smaller multiplication problems?

To view this video clip, scan the QR code or access via mathsolutions.com /NTWNC51

5. What questions does the teacher use to facilitate student thinking around the big ideas?

6. How is the associative property used throughout the number talk?

7. How could the strategies be modeled with an array?

For commentary on the above, see Appendix A: Author's Video Reflections.

Mathematical Practice 8: Look for and express regularity in repeated reasoning.

A number talk is purposefully designed to provide opportunities for students to look for and use number relationships to efficiently, flexibly, and accurately solve computation problems. By using a multiplication number talk string that always produces the same product, the teacher is creating a situation for students to consider how the problems are related and how this relationship can be consistently used as a strategy.

Noticing how quantities relate to multiples of ten, when it is efficient to compensate, and how to use smaller problems inside larger problems are examples of using regularity in repeated reasoning. Using the relationship between 199 and 200 to adjust the problem 199 + 153 to 200 + 153 demonstrates example of how students can look for and express regularity in reasoning. Making conjectures for approaches to new problems based on strategies used with previous problems or asking, "Will this always work?" encourages students to test and apply consistent patterns they notice during number talk discussions.

An Introduction to Common Division Strategies

Explicitly linking division to multiplication helps students use this relationship to invent flexible, efficient strategies. It is important for students to use what they know about multiplication to help them understand division. Presenting multiplication and division problems together can help students make this connection.

Introducing division in a story-problem context can help students make sense of this operation. Crafting contexts to include both partitive and quotative division situations will help students develop a better understanding of division and be able to move between both models with ease. As we look at common student strategies for division, we will initially link each to a context with a brief discussion about efficiency.

Four Common Strategies for Division

(D-1) Division Strategies: Repeated Subtraction or Sharing/Dealing Out

Repeated Subtraction and Sharing/Dealing Out are strategies students often use when they are in the process of developing multiplicative reasoning. Both of these early strategies present opportunities to make explicit connections to multiplication as the teacher records multiplication and division sentences to match student thinking.

Repeated Subtraction is one of the least efficient division strategies, especially as the magnitude of the numbers increases. Students may initially use this strategy if given a story-problem context that encourages quotative or measurement division such as:

> *Martha has 30 cookies. She plans to put 5 cookies in every container. How many containers will Martha need?*

In this problem the student knows the size of the group (five) and is trying to find how many groups of five can be made. This context lends itself to using repeated subtraction by removing five from thirty until all the cookies are gone. The following

(continued)

example demonstrates a way to connect this strategy to multiplicative thinking and efficiency.

Student's Strategy: Repeated Subtraction

$30 \div 5$ 30 $\underline{-\ 5}$ 25 $\underline{-\ 5}$ 20 $\underline{-\ 5}$ 15 $\underline{-\ 5}$ 10 $\underline{-\ 5}$ 5 $\underline{-\ 5}$ 0	**Teacher:** You kept removing groups of fives until the cookies were gone. How many groups of fives did you find? **Student:** Six. **Teacher:** So, six containers of five cookies, or six times five, could be found in thirty cookies. I wonder if there is a quicker way to use your strategy? Do you know how many two groups of five would be? **Student:** Ten. **Teacher:** Yes. So, two times five equals ten. Do we have enough cookies to do this again? **Student:** Yes. We can get two more fives, and then we can do that one more time. **Teacher:** [writes on the board] $2 \times 5 = 10$ $2 \times 5 = 10$ $2 \times 5 = 10$ Which gives us: $6 \times 5 = 30$ . . . the same as you got. Which way do you think is quicker and easier?

(continued)

The Sharing/Dealing Out strategy is also a beginning division strategy. The more fragile a child is with multiplication, the more likely the student will share or deal out amounts in small quantities. One of the goals in processing this strategy is to help make connections between multiplication and division and engage in discussions about efficiency.

In this strategy the student associates the divisor with the number of groups between which the whole is being shared. The following context for thirty divided by five can help us look at ways to move students toward a stronger understanding.

Martha has 30 cookies. She plans to share the cookies with 5 friends. How many cookies will each friend receive?

---

1 **Student's Stategy: Sharing/Dealing Out**

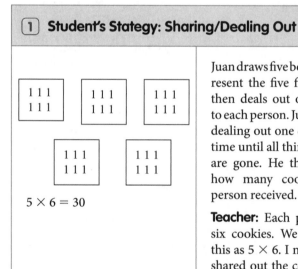

$5 \times 6 = 30$

Juan draws five boxes to represent the five friends. He then deals out one cookie to each person. Juan repeats dealing out one cookie at a time until all thirty cookies are gone. He then counts how many cookies each person received.

Teacher: Each person has six cookies. We can write this as 5×6. I noticed you shared out the cookies one at a time. Do you think there is another way we could have shared the cookies?

Juan: Maybe two at a time?

Teacher: Let's test that idea.

(continued)

2 Student's Strategy: Sharing/Dealing Out

2 2 2 2 2 2 2 2 2	Juan counts the first set of twos: 2, 4, 6, 8, 10.
2 2 2 2 2 2	**Teacher:** So, five twos, or fives times two, is ten. Do you think you have enough to give two to each person again?
	Juan: Yes. Twelve, fourteen, sixteen, eighteen, twenty. I only have ten more cookies to share.
	Teacher: How many do you think each person will get?
First deal: $5 \times 2 = 10$	**Juan:** Maybe two?
Second deal: $5 \times 2 = 10$ Third deal: $5 \times 2 = 10$	Notice that even though Juan previously dealt out one six times to each person, he is not confident that dealing out three twos to each person will work.

The teacher gradually forms a bridge between Juan's initial thinking to more efficient representations of the same strategy using multiplication.

(D-2) Division Strategy: Multiplying Up

Similar to the Adding Up strategy for subtraction, the Multiplying Up strategy provides access to division by building on the student's strength in multiplication. Students realize that they can also multiply up to reach the dividend. This is a natural progression as they become more confident in their use and understanding of multiplication and its relationship to division. Initially, students may rely on using smaller factors and multiples, which will result in more steps. This can provide an opportunity for discussions related to choosing efficient factors with which to multiply.

$384 \div 16$ $10 \times 16 = 160$ $10 \times 16 = 160$ $2 \times 16 = 32$ $2 \times 16 = 32$ $10 + 10 + 2 + 2 = 24$ $24 \times 16 = 384$	This strategy allows students to build on multiplication problems that are comfortable and easy to use such as multiplying by tens and twos.

The open array can be used to model the student's strategy and link the operations of multiplication and division.

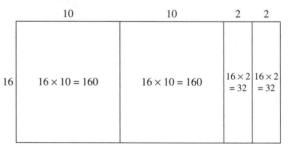

(D-3) Division Strategy: Partial Quotients

Like the Partial Products strategy for multiplication, this strategy maintains place value and mathematically correct information for students. It allows them to work their way toward

(continued)

the quotient by using friendly multipliers such as tens, fives, and twos without having to immediately find the largest quotient. As the student chooses larger multipliers, the strategy becomes more efficient.

384 ÷ 16
 	
A.   24
 	
16) 384
  − 160 |10
  224
  − 160 |10
  64   } 24
  − 32 |2
  32
  − 32 |2
  0
	When learning the procedure for the standard U.S. algorithm, students are often told that 16 cannot go into 3 (300), which is incorrect; 16 can divide into 3, but it would result in a fraction. With the Partial Quotients strategy, the "3" maintains its value of 300 and can certainly be divided by 16.
	
	As the student works, he keeps track of the partial quotients by writing them to the side of the problem. When the problem is solved, the partial quotients are totaled and the final answer is written over the dividend.

B.   24
 	
16) 384
  − 320 |20
  64   } 24
  − 64 |4
  0
	Example A demonstrates using friendly 10s and 2s to solve the problem. As the 10s and 2s are recorded to the side of the problem, they represent 10 × 16 and 2 × 16.
	
	Example B demonstrates a more efficient way to solve this problem.

(D-4) Division Strategy: Proportional Reasoning

As students become stronger with their understanding of factors, multiples, and fractional reasoning, they may look at

(continued)

division from a proportional reasoning perspective. If students have had experiences with doubling and halving to solve multiplication problems, they will often wonder if the same approach will work with division. This is an excellent way to launch an investigation to lead to the idea that you can divide the dividend and divisor by the same amount to create a simpler problem. If the dividend and divisor share common factors, then the problem can be simplified.

$384 \div 16$	Both 384 and 16 share the common factors of 2, 4, and 8. Let's simplify each number by dividing by 2.
$384 \div 16$ $\div 2 \quad \div 2$ $192 \div 8$	As we divide each number by 2, the problem becomes $192 \div 8$. While this is a simpler problem than the original, we can still simplify each number by 2 since they are both even numbers.
$192 \div 8$ $\div 2 \quad \div 2$ $96 \div 4$ $96 \div 4$ $\div 2 \quad \div 2$ $48 \div 2$	We can continue to divide by 2 to create an even smaller problem, or solve the problem whenever the numbers are easier to use.
$384 \div 16 = 24$ $192 \div 8 = 24$ $96 \div 4 = 24$ $48 \div 2 = 24$	We would have arrived at the correct answer of 24 with any of the problems.
$\dfrac{384}{16} = \dfrac{192}{8} = \dfrac{96}{4} = \dfrac{48}{2}$	It may be helpful to think of this sequence of division problems as equivalent fractions.

Classroom Link: Division String: 496 ÷ 8
Classroom Clip 5.5

Before you watch the fifth-grade number talk for 496 ÷ 8, anticipate possible student strategies and how they might be recorded.

As you watch the fifth-grade number talk for 496 ÷ 8, consider:

1. What evidence in the video demonstrates student understanding of place value?

2. How do students build upon their understanding of multiplication to divide?

3. How does the teacher connect math ideas throughout the number talk?

4. What examples of properties can be observed in the strategies and discussion?

5. Which strategies were most accessible to you? More challenging to follow?

To view this video clip, scan the QR code or access via mathsolutions.com /NTWNC55

For commentary on the above, see Appendix A: Author's Video Reflections.

Summary

In this chapter we have looked at the overarching goals during number talks, multiplication and division student strategies, and tools and models to help support student mathematical understanding in 3–5 classrooms. In the following chapter we explore how to use number talks to develop specific multiplication and division strategies in the 3–5 classroom.

Number and Operations in Base Ten: Perform operations with multi-digit whole numbers and with decimals to hundredths.

5.NBT.B.6 Find whole-number quotients of whole numbers with up to four-digit dividends and two-digit divisors, using strategies based on place value, the properties of operations, and/or the relationship between multiplication and division. Illustrate and explain the calculation by using equations, rectangular arrays, and/or area models.

CHAPTER 8

How Do I Design Purposeful Multiplication and Division Number Talks in the 3–5 Classroom?

Overview

This chapter focuses on multiplication and division number talks for third-, fourth-, and fifth-grade students. The number talks are organized by *operations* and *strategies*. Each strategy is divided into three categories that reflect the magnitude of the numbers used.

Teachers should use fluency number talks to build a strong foundation before moving into number talks that focus on computation with larger numbers.

CONTENTS

Third-, Fourth-, and Fifth-Grade Number Talks

The following number talks are designed to elicit and foster specific computation strategies. While each strategy possesses distinct characteristics, often similarities overlap. For example, many of the strategies build on changing numbers to landmark or friendly numbers; this is a similarity. The difference lies in *how* the landmark or friendly number is created. This subtle difference is the essence of the strategy.

As you begin to implement number talks in your classroom, start with small numbers that are age and grade-level appropriate. Using small numbers serves two purposes: 1) students can focus on the nuances of the strategy instead of the magnitude of the numbers, and 2) students build confidence in their mathematical abilities. As their understanding of different strategies develops, you can gradually increase the size of the numbers. When the numbers become too large, students will rely on less efficient strategies, such as Counting All, or resort to paper and pencil, thereby losing the focus on developing mental strategies.

Each series of number talks is organized by specific strategies and categories. The categories are a suggested sequence to delineate beginning number talks to advanced number talks. They do not represent student math ability levels, but a scaffolding of problems from easier to more difficult problems.

Category Key

1. Category 1 represents introductory number talks that more readily encourage a specific strategy.

2. Category 2 number talks are crafted for students who are successfully using the selected strategy.

3. Category 3 provides opportunities for students to use and extend the targeted strategy.

Multiplication Number Talks

The following number talks are crafted to elicit specific multiplication strategies; however, you may find that students also share other efficient methods. Keep in mind that the overall purpose is to help students build a toolbox of efficient strategies based on numerical reasoning. The ultimate goal of number talks is for students to compute accurately, efficiently, and flexibly.

NUMBER TALKS

3-5

Multiplication: Repeated Addition or Skip Counting

Instructions

Repeated Addition is an entry-level strategy for multiplication and will naturally occur when students are first presented with multiplication problems. Since we want to encourage students to move toward multiplicative thinking and away from an additive approach to multiplication, we do not present specific number talks to foster this strategy. If students share this method as their strategy, honor their thinking; however, always make connections to multiplication. Possible ways to make this explicit are shared using the problem 4×9.

For more on Repeated Addition or Skip Counting, see page 245.

NUMBER TALKS

3–5

If students share their strategy as $9 + 9 + 9 + 9$
$$18 \; + \; 18 = 36$$

Scaffold to multiplication with $(2 \times 9) + (2 \times 9)$
$$18 \; + \; 18 = 36$$

If students share their strategy as
$$9 \; + 9 \; + 9 \; + 9$$
$$+ 1 \; + 1 \; + 1 \; + 1$$
$$10 + 10 + 10 + 10 = 40$$
$$40 - 4 = 36$$

Scaffold to multiplication with $(4 \times 10) - 4 = 36$

If students share their strategy as $4 + 4 + 4 + 4 + 4$
$$+ 4 + 4 + 4 + 4$$

Scaffold to multiplication by looking at clusters of multiplication problems embedded in the problem, such as
$$(5 \times 4) + (2 \times 4) + (2 \times 4)$$
$$20 \; + \; 8 \; + \; 8 = 36$$

(continued)

Repeated Addition also affords an excellent vehicle for discussing efficiency: Is it more efficient to add four 9s or nine 4s? Is there a way we can build on something we know, such as 5×4, to make this problem more efficient? Which is more efficient, to add four 9s or four 10s? Each situation offers opportunities to help students think flexibly, fluently, and efficiently.

NUMBER TALKS

3–5

Multiplication: Making Landmark or Friendly Numbers

Instructions

A common error students make when changing one of the factors to a landmark number is to forget to adjust the number of groups. The problem 9×25 can help us consider the common errors children make when making this adjustment. If 9 had been changed to 10, then the product of 250 would need to be adjusted not just by 1 but by one group of 25.

For more on Making Landmark or Friendly Numbers, see page 247.

NUMBER TALKS

3–5

25 25 $\underline{\times\ 9} +1\ \underline{\times\ 10}$ $250 - 1 = 249$	This common error arises when children are applying what works with addition to multiplication. They do not consider that they have changed the problem by adding on one group of 25 instead of a 1.
25 25 $\underline{\times\ 9} +1\ \underline{\times\ 10}$ $250 - 25 = 225$	When students understand that one group of 25 has been added, they will adjust the answer accordingly.

The following number talks consist of three or more sequential problems. The sequence of problems within a given number talk allows students to apply strategies from previous problems to subsequent problems. These number talk problems may be used in two ways:

- selected at random from each category; or
- navigated in a systematic order by selecting problems with smaller numbers from a specific category, then building to larger numbers.

(continued)

Category 1	269
Category 2	270
Category 3	271

NUMBER TALKS

3–5

Category 1: Making Landmark or Friendly Numbers

The following number talks consist of 1 × 2-digit problems and have a connection to U.S. coin values. The problems in each section are purposefully ordered to help students build their knowledge from one problem to the next. This allows them to use the relationships from the initial problem in the final problem in the sequence. For example, 6 × 25 could be solved by using (2 × 25) + (2 × 25) + (2 × 25), by combining (2 × 25) + (4 × 25), or by using 4 × 25 twice and then removing 2 × 25 from that product.

> Category 1 represents introductory number talks that more readily encourage a specific strategy.

2×25	7×5	2×25
4×25	7×10	4×20
6×25	7×9	2×50
		4×50

NUMBER TALKS

3–5

2×50	5×5	5×5
4×50	5×10	5×10
8×50	5×20	5×30
	5×19	5×29

3×5	2×5	4×5
3×10	2×10	4×10
3×9	2×20	4×50
	2×19	4×49

Category 2: Making Landmark or Friendly Numbers

The following number talks are intentionally ordered to help students use relationships from the sequence to solve the final 1 × 3-digit problem.

NUMBER TALKS

3–5

4×25	3×10	3×100
4×200	3×50	3×200
4×250	3×100	3×199
4×249	3×149	

6×20	6×50	5×100
6×100	6×300	5×300
6×120	6×349	5×60
6×119		5×359

3×50	4×60	8×50
3×100	5×300	8×100
3×149	4×359	8×200
		8×199

Category 3: Making Landmark or Friendly Numbers

The following number talks consist of computation problems that are ordered to help students use relationships from the sequence to solve the final 2 × 2-digit and 2 × 3-digit problems.

Category 3 provides opportunities for students to use and extend the targeted strategy.

6 × 20
30 × 20
36 × 20
36 × 19

6 × 40
10 × 40
16 × 40
16 × 39

2 × 150
10 × 150
12 × 150
12 × 149

3 × 50
50 × 50
53 × 50
53 × 48

2 × 25
4 × 25
8 × 25
10 × 25
16 × 25

5 × 200
20 × 200
25 × 200
25 × 199

NUMBER TALKS

3–5

10 × 10
10 × 30
2 × 30
12 × 29

5 × 10
5 × 50
10 × 50
15 × 50
15 × 49

6 × 600
10 × 600
16 × 600
16 × 599

See Classroom Clip 3.7: Array Discussion: 8 × 25.

Multiplication: Partial Products

For more on Partial Products, see page 248.

NUMBER TALKS

3–5

Instructions

The Partial Products strategy can be used with any multiplication problem. This strategy is based on breaking one or both factors into addends through using expanded notation and the distributive property. While both factors can be represented with expanded notation, keeping one number whole is often more efficient. Several ways to solve the problem 8×25 using Partial Products follow:

Breaking 8 into Addends

$$(4 + 4) \times 25 = (4 \times 25) + (4 \times 25)$$
$$(2 + 2 + 4) \times 25 = (2 \times 25) + (2 \times 25) + (4 \times 25)$$

Breaking 25 into Addends

$$8 \times (20 + 5) = (8 \times 20) + (8 \times 5)$$
$$8 \times (10 + 10 + 5) = (8 \times 10) + (8 \times 10) + (8 \times 5)$$

Breaking Both Factors into Addends

$$(4 + 4) \times (20 + 5) = (4 \times 20) + (4 \times 5) + (4 \times 20) + (4 \times 5)$$

The following number talks consist of three or more sequential problems. The sequence of problems within a given number talk allows students to apply strategies from previous problems to subsequent problems. These number talk problems may be used in two ways:

• selected at random from each category; or
• navigated in a systematic order by selecting problems with smaller numbers from a specific category, then building to larger numbers.

Category 1	273
Category 2	274
Category 3	275

Category 1: Partial Products

The following number talks are ordered by section to help students use relationships from the sequence to solve the final 1 × 1-digit and 1 × 2-digit problems.

Category 1 represents introductory number talks that more readily encourage a specific strategy.

2×7
4×7
4×8
3×8
8×7

2×15
3×15
6×5
6×10
6×15

2×16
8×5
8×10
8×6
8×16

3×8
2×6
6×8

3×26
6×26
9×26

2×36
4×10
4×6
4×36

NUMBER TALKS

3–5

2×7
4×7
3×7
7×7

2×45
4×45
2×40
2×5
8×45

8×5
8×2
8×50
8×56

See Classroom Clip 3.5: Multiplication String: 7×7.

Category 2: Partial Products

The following number talks are ordered so that students can use the relationships from the sequence to solve the final 1 × 3-digit problems.

NUMBER TALKS
3–5

2×125	2×124	2×45
4×25	6×100	5×100
6×100	6×20	5×40
6×20	6×4	5×5
6×125	6×124	5×245

2×100	2×150	2×500
2×15	5×100	4×500
4×5	5×10	4×30
4×10	5×50	4×2
4×115	5×150	4×532

8×100	4×250	2×325
8×10	4×6	2×300
8×2	8×200	6×300
4×100	8×50	4×25
4×12	8×6	6×25
8×112	8×256	6×325

Category 3: Partial Products

The following number talks consist of multiplication problems designed to help students use the relationships from the sequence to solve the final 2 × 2-digit problems.

Category 3 provides opportunities for students to use and extend the targeted strategy.

3 × 15	2 × 16	5 × 30
10 × 15	10 × 16	10 × 30
13 × 10	10 × 14	3 × 15
13 × 5	2 × 14	10 × 15
13 × 15	14 × 16	15 × 33

15 × 10	25 × 10	35 × 10
15 × 1	25 × 4	35 × 2
10 × 11	14 × 10	35 × 20
5 × 11	14 × 5	35 × 24
15 × 11	25 × 14	

NUMBER TALKS

3-5

4 × 22	4 × 25	10 × 36
6 × 11	5 × 25	50 × 36
3 × 22	10 × 25	2 × 36
6 × 22	20 × 25	10 × 54
10 × 22	25 × 25	2 × 54
16 × 22		54 × 36

Multiplication: Doubling and Halving

For more on Doubling and Halving, see page 250.

NUMBER TALKS
3–5

Instructions

Halving and doubling is an excellent strategy to restructure a problem with multiple digits and make it easier to solve. Helping students notice the relationship between the two factors and the dimensions of the accompanying array is important to understanding this strategy. An equally important idea in this strategy is that the factors can adjust while the area of the array stays the same. Take, for instance, the problem 1×16. It can be represented with the following arrays:

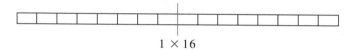

$$1 \times 16$$

But if we cut the length of the array in half and attach the second half below the first half, we have created a different array with the same area:

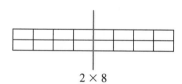

$$2 \times 8$$

We can repeat this process and half the length and double the width and still keep the same area:

$$4 \times 4$$

(continued)

As students begin their initial investigations of this strategy, choose small numbers that have a number of factors and have children build the arrays, list the accompanying multiplication sentences for each, and look for patterns that occur—just like we did for 16. As students become familiar with this strategy and when and how it works, they will look for opportunities to apply it.

The following number talks consist of three or more sequential problems. The sequence of problems within a given number talk allows students to apply strategies from previous problems to subsequent problems. These number talk problems may be used in two ways:

• selected at random from each category; or
• navigated in a systematic order by selecting problems with smaller numbers from a specific category, then building to larger numbers.

Category 1	278
Category 2	279
Category 3	280
Category 4	281

NUMBER TALKS

3–5

Category 1: Doubling and Halving

The following number talks investigate doubling and halving with basic facts.

NUMBER TALKS

3–5

1 × 16	1 × 24	1 × 12
2 × 8	2 × 12	2 × 6
4 × 4	4 × 6	4 × 3
8 × 2	8 × 3	
16 × 1		

1 × 36	1 × 48	1 × 32
2 × 18	2 × 24	2 × 16
4 × 9	4 × 12	4 × 8
	8 × 6	8 × 4
	16 × 3	16 × 2
		32 × 1

1 × 20	1 × 40	1 × 56
2 × 10	2 × 20	2 × 28
4 × 5	4 × 10	4 × 14
	8 × 5	8 × 7

Category 2: Doubling and Halving

The following number talks investigate doubling and halving with 1 × 2-digit and 1 × 3-digit numbers.

Category 2 talks are crafted for students who are successfully using the selected strategy.

8×16	8×125	125×8
4×32	4×250	250×4
2×64	2×500	500×2

8×32	84×5	345×8
4×64	42×10	690×4
2×128	21×20	1380×2

NUMBER TALKS

3–5

36×5	35×8	8×29
18×10	70×4	4×58
9×20	140×2	2×116

Category 3: Doubling and Halving

The following number talks investigate doubling and halving with 2 × 2-digit numbers.

3×60	104×3	112×2
6×30	52×6	56×4
12×15	26×12	28×8
		14×16

NUMBER TALKS

3–5

9×56	4×120	360×3
18×28	8×60	180×6
36×14	16×30	90×12
	32×15	45×24

See Classroom
Clips 5.2 and 5.3:
Multiplication:
32 × 15 and
Multiplication:
16 × 35.

		2×1440
2×280	100×4	4×720
4×140	50×8	8×360
8×70	25×16	16×180
16×35		32×90
		64×45

Category 4: Doubling and Halving

The following number talks are included for classes who may wish to investigate what happens when you third and triple or quarter and quadruple numbers. The problems also provide an opportunity to investigate whether halving and doubling will work with odd numbers. While these strategies are not common for children, they afford students an opportunity to investigate why this principle works.

9×12
3×36
1×108

15×16
60×4
240×1

18×12
9×24
4.5×48
2.25×96

27×15
9×45
3×135
1×405

25×48
100×12
400×3
1200×1

6×12
3×24
1.5×48

NUMBER TALKS

3–5

36×18
72×9
216×3
648×1

64×35
16×140
4×560
1×2240

6×24
3×48
1.5×96

Multiplication: Breaking Factors into Smaller Factors

For more on Breaking Factors into Smaller Factors, see page 252.

NUMBER TALKS

3–5

Instructions

Because of the focus on place value, students have many experiences breaking numbers into expanded form that lead to the Partial Products strategy. However, they tend to have limited experiences breaking factors into smaller factors and applying the associative property. Providing number talk opportunities for students to grapple with equivalence with problems such as $8 \times 25 = 2 \times 4 \times 25$ or $8 \times 25 = 8 \times 5 \times 5$ or $8 \times 5 = 2 \times 4 \times 5 \times 5$ are critical to building understanding of the associative property and its real-life applications with multiplication.

The following number talks consist of three or more sequential problems. The sequence of problems within a given number talk allows students to apply strategies from previous problems to subsequent problems. These number talk problems may be used in two ways:

- selected at random from each category; or
- navigated in a systematic order by selecting problems with smaller numbers from a specific category, then building to larger numbers.

Category 1	283
Category 2	284
Category 3	285

Category 1: Breaking Factors into Smaller Factors

The following number talks consist of problems that focus on breaking basic facts into smaller factors.

Category 1 represents introductory number talks that more readily encourage a specific strategy.

$2 \times 3 \times 4$
$4 \times 3 \times 2$
6×4

$2 \times 3 \times 8$
$4 \times 2 \times 6$
6×8

$4 \times 3 \times 4$
$2 \times 2 \times 12$
$8 \times 3 \times 2$
$2 \times 2 \times 3 \times 4$
12×4

$3 \times 2 \times 6$
$3 \times 3 \times 2 \times 2$
$2 \times 2 \times 9$
6×6

$2 \times 3 \times 2 \times 3$
$3 \times 3 \times 4$
$9 \times 2 \times 2$
9×4

$5 \times 2 \times 6$
$5 \times 4 \times 3$
$2 \times 2 \times 3 \times 5$
5×12

NUMBER TALKS

3–5

$2 \times 3 \times 3 \times 3$
$3 \times 6 \times 3$
$9 \times 3 \times 2$
6×9

$4 \times 4 \times 2$
$2 \times 8 \times 2$
$2 \times 2 \times 2 \times 2 \times 2$
4×8

$5 \times 2 \times 4$
$4 \times 5 \times 2$
$2 \times 2 \times 5 \times 2$
8×5

Category 2: Breaking Factors into Smaller Factors

The following number talks use the associative property to solve 1 × 2-digit multiplication problems.

$3 \times 5 \times 4$
$2 \times 15 \times 2$
15×4

$5 \times 5 \times 8$
$2 \times 4 \times 25$
$2 \times 25 \times 4$
25×8

$2 \times 4 \times 35$
$8 \times 5 \times 7$
8×35

$2 \times 10 \times 5$
$4 \times 5 \times 5$
20×5

$8 \times 9 \times 3$
$3 \times 24 \times 3$
$9 \times 12 \times 2$
24×9

$8 \times 10 \times 5$
$50 \times 2 \times 4$
$25 \times 4 \times 4$
50×8

$4 \times 2 \times 16$
$4 \times 4 \times 8$
$2 \times 4 \times 8 \times 2$
$8 \times 8 \times 2$
16×8

$32 \times 4 \times 2$
$16 \times 4 \times 4$
32×8

$9 \times 10 \times 3$
$5 \times 6 \times 3 \times 3$
$15 \times 2 \times 9$
30×9

Category 3: Breaking Factors into Smaller Factors

The following number talks use the associative property to solve 2 × 2-digit multiplication problems.

$3 \times 4 \times 25$
$5 \times 12 \times 5$
$5 \times 2 \times 25$
12×25

$2 \times 45 \times 8$
$5 \times 16 \times 9$
$4 \times 5 \times 4 \times 9$
16×45

$2 \times 15 \times 4 \times 3 \times 3$
$8 \times 5 \times 9 \times 3 \times 9$
$24 \times 5 \times 9$
72×15

$2 \times 15 \times 6$
$5 \times 12 \times 3$
$4 \times 5 \times 3 \times 3$
$4 \times 5 \times 9$
12×15

$6 \times 6 \times 3 \times 5$
$6 \times 5 \times 3 \times 6$
$4 \times 15 \times 9$
36×15

$6 \times 5 \times 7 \times 3$
$9 \times 5 \times 2 \times 7$
$7 \times 5 \times 2 \times 9$
18×35

NUMBER TALKS

3–5

$4 \times 4 \times 25$
$8 \times 2 \times 25$
$16 \times 5 \times 5$
16×25

$2 \times 12 \times 3 \times 5$
$4 \times 15 \times 6$
$24 \times 5 \times 3$
24×15

$2 \times 35 \times 6$
$12 \times 5 \times 7$
$3 \times 4 \times 5 \times 7$
12×35

See Classroom Clip 5.1: Associative Property: 12×15.

Division Number Talks

The following number talks are crafted to elicit specific division strategies; however, you may find that students also share other efficient methods. Keep in mind that the overall purpose is to help students build a toolbox of efficient strategies based on numerical reasoning. The ultimate goal of number talks is for students to compute accurately, efficiently, and flexibly.

NUMBER TALKS

3–5

Division: Repeated Subtraction or Sharing/Dealing Out

Instructions

Repeated Subtraction is an entry-level strategy for division and will naturally occur when students are presented with initial division problems. Since we want to encourage students to move toward multiplicative thinking and away from a removal approach to division, specific number talks are not presented to foster this strategy. If students share this method as their strategy, honor their thinking; however, always make connections to multiplication. Possible ways to make this explicit are suggested in the example that follows using the problem $12 \div 2$:

For more on Repeated Subtraction or Sharing/ Dealing Out, see page 254.

If students share their strategy as $\quad 12 - 2, \quad -2, \quad -2,$
$$-2, \quad -2, \quad -2$$

Scaffold to multiplication with $\quad 3 \times 2 = 6, \; 3 \times 2 = 6$

$$So \ldots 6 \times 2 = 12$$

$$So \ldots 12 \div 2 = 6$$

NUMBER TALKS

3–5

Repeated Subtraction also affords an excellent vehicle for discussing efficiency: Is it more efficient to subtract 2s or to multiply groups of 2? Is there a way we can build on something we know, such as 3×2, to make this problem more efficient? Each situation offers opportunities to help students think flexibly, fluently, and efficiently.

For more on Partial Quotients, see page 258.

NUMBER TALKS

3–5

Division: Partial Quotients

Instructions

The Partial Quotients strategy maintains the integrity of place value and allows the students to approach the problem by building on multiplication problems with friendly multipliers such as 2, 5, 10, powers of 10, and so on. This strategy allows the student to navigate through the problem by building on what they know, understand, and can implement with ease.

As we look at the problem $550 \div 15$, we can see how students could approach this problem using the Partial Quotients strategy. (See Figure 8–1.)

While we might say that the third example is more efficient than the other two, it is important to note that regardless of how the student scaffolds her thinking, access and opportunities are there to build on individual understanding. Whether the student multiplies 2×15 over and over again or uses higher multiples of ten efficiently, she can reach a correct solution. For this

(continued)

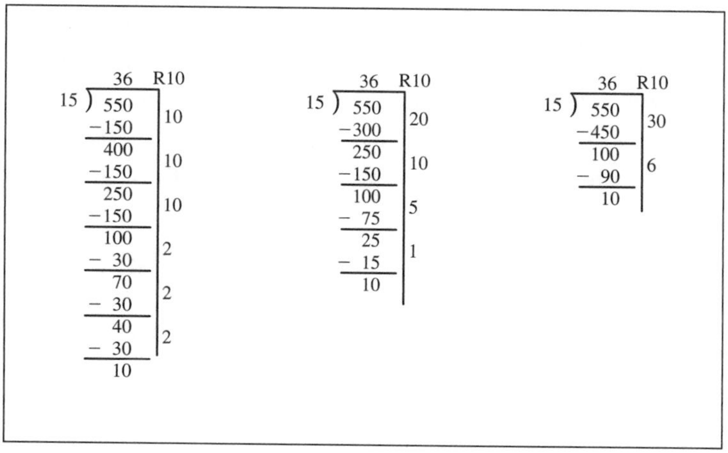

Figure 8–1   *Three Examples of a Student's Approach to Solving 550 ÷ 15 Using the Partial Quotients Strategy*

reason, the Partial Quotient strategy will work with any division problem.

When comparing this strategy to the standard U.S. long division algorithm, note that the place value of the numbers remains intact. When using this algorithm, students are taught to test if the divisor will divide into the first digit of the dividend. For the problem 550 ÷ 15, students would be asked to consider whether 15 could "go into" 5, and they would be prompted to respond that it could not. When the 500 is treated as five 1s, teachers are in essence asking students to ignore place value. This is mathematically incorrect information since groups of 15 can be found in 500.

The following number talks consist of three or more sequential problems. The sequence of problems within a given number talk allows students to apply strategies from previous problems to subsequent problems. These number talk problems may be used in two ways:

- selected at random from each category; or
- navigated in a systematic order by selecting problems with smaller numbers from a specific category, then building to larger numbers.

Category 1	290
Category 2	291
Category 3	292

NUMBER TALKS

3–5

Category 1: Partial Quotients

The following number talks consist of computation problems that help students to build on multiples of ten and find easy multiples of the divisor within the dividend. The following problems focus on double-digit numbers with a single-digit divisor.

Category 1 represents introductory number talks that more readily encourage a specific strategy.

NUMBER TALKS

3–5

40 ÷ 4	
16 ÷ 4	
56 ÷ 4	

40 ÷ 4
24 ÷ 4
67 ÷ 4

30 ÷ 3
18 ÷ 3
48 ÷ 3

30 ÷ 3
24 ÷ 3
54 ÷ 3

40 ÷ 4
80 ÷ 4
4 ÷ 4
88 ÷ 4

30 ÷ 3
90 ÷ 3
92 ÷ 3

50 ÷ 5
30 ÷ 5
80 ÷ 5

40 ÷ 4
80 ÷ 4
16 ÷ 4
96 ÷ 4

5 ÷ 5
10 ÷ 5
25 ÷ 5
50 ÷ 5
77 ÷ 5

Category 2: Partial Quotients

The following number talks include problems that encourage students to build on multiples of ten and one hundred and find easy multiples of the divisor within the dividend. The problems that follow focus on three-digit numbers with a single-digit divisor.

Category 2 talks are crafted for students who are successfully using the selected strategy.

$300 \div 3$
$120 \div 3$
$420 \div 3$

$400 \div 4$
$80 \div 4$
$16 \div 4$
$496 \div 4$

$120 \div 6$
$18 \div 6$
$60 \div 6$
$300 \div 6$
$180 \div 6$
$500 \div 6$

$30 \div 6$
$18 \div 6$
$300 \div 6$
$348 \div 6$

$100 \div 4$
$40 \div 4$
$24 \div 4$
$4 \div 4$
$124 \div 4$

$100 \div 5$
$200 \div 5$
$30 \div 5$
$5 \div 5$
$235 \div 5$

NUMBER TALKS

3–5

$100 \div 4$
$200 \div 4$
$40 \div 4$
$16 \div 4$
$256 \div 4$

$160 \div 8$
$16 \div 8$
$400 \div 8$
$80 \div 8$
$496 \div 8$

$900 \div 3$
$300 \div 3$
$240 \div 3$
$12 \div 3$
$852 \div 3$

See Classroom Clip 5.5: Division String: $496 \div 8$.

Category 3: Partial Quotients

The following number talks include computation problems that help students build on multiples of ten and one hundred to find easy multiples of the divisor within the dividend. These problems focus on three-digit numbers with a two-digit divisor.

NUMBER TALKS

3–5

$100 \div 25$
$250 \div 25$
$500 \div 25$

$120 \div 12$
$240 \div 12$
$368 \div 12$

$70 \div 35$
$105 \div 35$
$350 \div 35$
$525 \div 35$

$150 \div 15$
$300 \div 15$
$600 \div 15$

$130 \div 13$
$26 \div 13$
$52 \div 13$
$195 \div 13$

$100 \div 25$
$200 \div 25$
$500 \div 25$
$75 \div 25$
$675 \div 25$

$120 \div 12$
$240 \div 12$
$360 \div 12$
$36 \div 12$
$396 \div 12$

$100 \div 20$
$200 \div 20$
$400 \div 20$
$500 \div 20$

$30 \div 15$
$90 \div 15$
$300 \div 15$
$150 \div 15$
$540 \div 15$

Division: Multiplying Up

Instructions

Following the same principle as Adding Up to Subtract, Multiplying Up is an accessible division strategy that capitalizes on the relationship between multiplication and division. Similar to Partial Quotients, this strategy provides an opportunity for students to gradually build on multiplication problems they know until they reach the dividend. A subtle distinction between the two strategies can be seen with the problem $550 \div 15$. (See Figure 8–2.)

For more on Multiplying Up, see page 258.

$$15 \times \boxed{10} = 150 \;\rbrace$$
$$15 \times \boxed{10} = 150 \;\rbrace \; 450$$
$$15 \times \boxed{10} = 150 \;\rbrace$$

$$15 \times \boxed{2} = 30 \;) \; 480$$
$$15 \times \boxed{2} = 30 \;) \; 510$$
$$15 \times \boxed{2} = 30 \;) \; 540$$

$$15 \times \circled{36} = 540$$
$$\underline{+10}$$
$$550$$

$$550 \div 15 = 36 \, R10$$

$$15 \times \boxed{20} = 300$$
$$15 \times \boxed{10} = 150$$
$$15 \times \boxed{5} = 75$$
$$15 \times \boxed{1} = \underline{15}$$
$$15 \times 36 = 540$$

$$550 \div 15 = 36 \, R10$$

$$15 \times \boxed{30} = 450$$
$$15 \times \boxed{6} = \underline{90}$$
$$15 \times 36 = 540$$

$$550 \div 15 = 36 \, R10$$

NUMBER TALKS

3-5

Figure 8–2   *Three Examples Showing the Differences Between the Multiplying Up and Partial Quotients Strategies*

Notice how the student is building up to the dividend through multiplication in each example. While the third example is much more efficient, the other examples allow students to build on their understanding of the relationship between multiplication and division and scaffold this understanding to reach an accurate solution.

(continued)

The following number talks consist of three or more sequential problems. The sequence of problems within a given number talk allows students to apply strategies from previous problems to subsequent problems. These number talk problems may be used in two ways:

• selected at random from each category; or
• navigated in a systematic order by selecting problems with smaller numbers from a specific category, then building to larger numbers.

Category 1	295
Category 2	296
Category 3	297

NUMBER TALKS

3–5

Category 1: Multiplying Up

The following number talks consist of computation problems that build on using multiples of ten with two-digit numbers with single-digit divisors.

Category 1 represents introductory number talks that more readily encourage a specific strategy.

4×10
4×5
4×4
$56 \div 4$

5×5
5×10
5×2
$79 \div 5$

3×10
3×20
3×3
3×2
$68 \div 3$

3×10
3×20
3×30
3×1
$96 \div 3$

2×10
2×5
2×2
$38 \div 2$

5×5
5×10
5×2
$85 \div 5$

NUMBER TALKS

3-5

4×10
4×5
4×2
$48 \div 4$

4×10
4×5
4×8
4×4
$72 \div 4$

6×10
6×5
6×6
6×2
$99 \div 6$

Category 2: Multiplying Up

The following number talks include three-digit numbers with single-digit divisors that encourage students build on multiples of ten and one hundred.

NUMBER TALKS

3–5

3×100
3×50
3×1
$453 \div 3$

4×25
4×100
4×20
$999 \div 4$

4×25
4×50
4×100
$500 \div 4$

4×25
4×50
4×3
$215 \div 4$

3×100
3×20
3×30
$960 \div 3$

8×100
8×50
8×10
$792 \div 8$

6×100
6×50
6×60
6×5
$536 \div 6$

4×25
4×100
4×10
4×20
$484 \div 4$

7×100
7×10
7×5
7×2
$836 \div 7$

Category 3: Multiplying Up

The following number talks consist of three digit numbers with two-digit divisors that build on using multiples of ten and one hundred.

Category 3 provides opportunities for students to use and extend the targeted strategy.

50×2
50×5
50×10
$900 \div 50$

35×2
35×10
35×20
$755 \div 35$

25×10
25×4
25×2
$840 \div 25$

15×10
15×20
5×40
15×2
$658 \div 15$

24×5
24×10
24×20
$756 \div 24$

10×15
20×15
2×15
1×15
$498 \div 15$

NUMBER TALKS

3-5

10×17
20×17
40×17
2×17
$699 \div 17$

5×21
10×21
2×21
$321 \div 21$

10×27
20×27
30×27
$825 \div 17$

For more on Making Tens, see page 172.

NUMBER TALKS

3–5

Division: Proportional Reasoning

Instructions

Division of whole numbers can also be represented as a fraction with the whole divided into a specific number of parts. For example, if I have 16 candies to be shared among 8 children, *16* would be my whole (numerator) and *8* would be the number of parts the whole will be divided into, or the denominator. Sixteen divided by 8 can be symbolically written as $16 \div 8$, $8)\overline{\,16}$, or $\frac{16}{8}$.

When division is considered from a fractional perspective, this provides opportunities for students to explore the relationship of the part to the whole through proportional reasoning using equivalent fractions. Knowing that the divisor and dividend in $\frac{16}{8}$ share common factors, students can simplify the quantity to any of the following equivalent fractions: $\frac{8}{4}$, $\frac{4}{2}$, or $\frac{2}{1}$.

The following number talks are included for classes who may wish to investigate what occurs when you halve and halve or third and third with division instead of doubling and halving as in multiplication. While these strategies are not common for children, they afford students an opportunity to investigate why this principle works.

The following number talks consist of three or more sequential problems. The sequence of problems within a given number talk allows students to apply strategies from previous problems to subsequent problems. These number talk problems may be used in two ways:

• selected at random from each category; or
• navigated in a systematic order by selecting problems with smaller numbers from a specific category, then building to larger numbers.

Division: Proportional Reasoning   299

Division: Proportional Reasoning

The following number talks consist of division problems that can be solved using proportional reasoning.

$100 \div 4$
$200 \div 8$
$400 \div 16$

$720 \div 36$
$360 \div 18$
$60 \div 3$

$800 \div 40$
$80 \div 4$
$40 \div 2$

$100 \div 4$
$200 \div 8$
$400 \div 16$

$250 \div 2$
$500 \div 4$
$1000 \div 8$

$384 \div 16$
$96 \div 4$
$48 \div 2$

NUMBER TALKS

3–5

$172 \div 3$
$144 \div 6$
$288 \div 12$

$46 \div 2$
$92 \div 4$
$184 \div 8$

$308 \div 7$
$308 \div 14$
$308 \div 28$

Section IV

The Facilitator's Guide

CHAPTER 9

What Does a Number Talk Look Like at My Grade Level?

CONTENTS

Talking About Number Talks
Using Number Talks for Professional Learning
Author Clip A.2

In an interview with the author, Sherry Parrish shares how bringing a common number talk focus to teacher conversations can impact professional learning.

To view this video clip, scan the QR code or access via mathsolutions.com/NTWNCA2

Introduction

A Closer Look at Number Talks by Grade Level

Chapter 9 serves as a facilitator's guide by providing readers with an opportunity to immerse themselves more deeply in number talks through viewing the DVD segments by grade level. Each grade-level section features a classroom overview, a typical math time structure, an interview with the featured classroom teacher, and video clips from a specific classroom. Each video clip includes a set of discussion questions (note that these sets are different from and can be used in addition to the Classroom Links questions throughout the other chapters). The questions are designed either to be used individually, in grade-level teams, or in other learning-group settings. While this organization allows for immersion in a specific grade level, it also provides the reader with an opportunity to consider how number talks build and evolve from kindergarten through fifth grade. The chapter concludes with questions structured to prompt readers to take a closer look at their current practice in light of the newly formed understandings.

A Closer Look at South Shades Crest Elementary School

The classroom video clips were filmed in early October of 2009 at South Shades Crest Elementary School in Hoover, Alabama. The students had been in school for approximately two months at the time of filming.

South Shades Crest Elementary School opened in August 1995 and is one of ten elementary schools in the Hoover City Schools District. During the 2009–10 school year, the K–5 school served more than 715 students. Throughout the past several years, the student population has gradually transitioned from a predominantly Caucasian clientele to a more diverse population. Its current demographic composition is as follows: Asian (8 percent), African American (20 percent), Hispanic (4 percent), and Caucasian (68 percent). Approximately 10 percent of the student population receives special education services, and around 18 percent participate in the free and reduced lunch program.

Since its inception, South Shades Crest Elementary has served as a forerunner for math education in its school district by being one of the first schools to implement number talks on a regular basis in its classrooms. The school gradually transitioned from a teaching-by-telling approach using a traditional math basal to a teaching-by-questioning method using an inquiry-based resource. The Investigations in Number, Data, and Space series (Pearson Scott Foresman TERC 2006) has served as the primary math resource for the school and the district for the past six years. The district recently elected to continue with this math approach by adopting the second edition (2008) of the same series. The teachers and administration have invested time and effort in educating parents about teaching mathematics for understanding. They host schoolwide and grade-level math nights to help parents deepen their own understanding of mathematics and equip them with ways to have math conversations at home. Teachers invite parents to observe and participate in grade-level number talks with their children.

South Shades Crest's math mission statement captures the essence of its belief regarding teaching and learning mathematics:

> Our goal as educators in Hoover City Schools is to help students become confident and competent in mathematics. We strive to create a classroom environment that encourages students to think critically about math in a variety of situations. As students explain their thinking to others, they self-correct and clarify their ideas leading to a deeper understanding of underlying mathematical concepts. Accuracy and the development of efficient problem-solving strategies are essential to student's learning. The ability to solve problems many different ways and to understand

the connections between mathematical ideas is equally important. As children learn to question, reconsider and justify solutions they become more confident in their own abilities as mathematicians.

Kindergarten Classroom
A Closer Look at Erin Keenan's Kindergarten Classroom

Erin Keenan's kindergarten class is a diverse group of seventeen students who can easily be classified as young mathematicians. Ms. Keenan is masterful at laying the foundation for students to make sense of mathematics, articulate their thinking, and build fluency with smaller numbers. She introduces the students to hand signals to use during number talks to help them learn the importance of communication in mathematics. Two frequently used communication signals are a thumbs-up to indicate they have an answer and a "me too" sign to indicate they agree with the person sharing.

Talking About Number Talks: Kindergarten
Erin Keenan • Teacher Clip T.K

All of the components of the kindergarten sixty-minute math block work in tandem to lay a beginning foundation for students who can reason accurately, flexibly, and fluently with numbers. Each of these classroom structures is essential in developing early number sense; however, number talks are viewed as a critical element as evidenced by Erin Keenan's commentary.

To view this video clip, scan the QR code or access via mathsolutions.com /NTWNCTK

Math Time Structure

The students are accustomed to reasoning with numbers through games, literature, classroom investigations, menu tasks, and number talks. A typical math block is sixty minutes and is structured to include the following components:

Calendar (ten minutes)

During calendar time students engage in discussions that focus on one-to-one correspondence, counting one- and two-digit numbers, calendar vocabulary and application, as well as patterns and graphing. They keep track of the number of days in school using dots posted on five- and ten-frames. This activity allows students to begin building an understanding of five and ten as important units for counting.

Number Talk (five to fifteen minutes)

As discussed in Chapters 3 and 4, kindergarten number talks are designed to focus on the big ideas in number, with special emphasis on building number fluency with small numbers. A kindergarten number talk might include dot images, five- and ten-frames, or a context such as literature or games.

Refer to Chapters 3 and 4 for specific kindergarten number talks and ways to implement them.

Math Investigation or Math Menu (twenty-five minutes)

Students work independently, with a partner, or in a small group during this block that incorporates either a classroom investigation or a math menu. A *classroom investigation* can be an authentic class problem the students are trying to solve such as how they can organize the classroom's math manipulatives into easier-to-count groups of twos, fives, or tens, or how a classroom snack may be fairly shared. A *math menu* is a collection of math tasks such as games, fluency tasks, or counting opportunities designed to allow the students to engage

(continued)

in mathematics. A math menu can also be crafted around a specific concept, such as fluency, to provide opportunities for students to immerse themselves and build understanding in this area. Resources for creating math menus and classroom math investigations can be found in Appendix C.

Whole-Group Processing (ten minutes)

The whole-group processing time provides an opportunity for the teacher to elicit from the students the ideas they have been immersed in during an investigation or menu. This brings the ideas to the forefront for the class and provides an anchor for student thinking. For example, if students have been working on ways to make five during a math menu, the teacher could use this time to craft a chart with ways to make five based on combinations shared by students. This processing time is essential and helps to delineate a standard center time from a math menu or investigation.

A Second Look at Kindergarten Number Talks

The kindergarten classroom video clips are referenced throughout the book; in this chapter they are grouped together to provide an opportunity for analysis, discussion, and reflection on teacher and student roles, the purpose of number talks, and student thinking about math content. Each video clip is accompanied by discussion questions designed to help readers immerse themselves more deeply in the pedagogy and content of the number talk. An author commentary for each segment is located in Appendix A, "Author's Video Reflections."

Kindergarten: Ten-Frames and Dot Cards
Classroom Clip K.1

Discussion Questions

1. Observe the students' responses to the ten-frame with five dots. Which students are able to subitize and unitize five and which ones are not? What evidence supports your conclusions?

2. How does the teacher help students learn to articulate their thinking?

3. How does the ten-frame with seven dots provide opportunities for the students to use five as a unit?

4. Notice that the teacher does not tell the students how to figure out that there are seven dots on the ten-frame. How does she elicit and support their use of different strategies?

5. The teacher requires students to share their reasoning and proof to convince the class that there are ten dots on the dot cards. What are some of the strategies the students share?

For commentary on the above, see Appendix A: Author's Video Reflections.

To view this video clip, scan the QR code or access via mathsolutions.com /NTWNCK1

Kindergarten: Rekenreks
Classroom Clip K.2

To view this video clip, scan the QR code or access via mathsolutions.com /NTWNCK2

Discussion Questions

1. How does the rekenrek warm-up with four and six provide the teacher with information to guide her instructional decisions?

2. When does the teacher tell or show information to the students during the number talk, and when does she provide opportunities for them to make sense of the mathematics? How is this similar or different from your math instruction?

3. What examples of one-to-one correspondence and conservation of number surface in the lesson?

4. Are there specific number combinations that seem more accessible to the students? How does the teacher build on this foundation?

For commentary on the above, see Appendix A: Author's Video Reflections.

Kindergarten: Counting Book
Classroom Clip K.3

To view this video clip, scan the QR code or access via mathsolutions.com /NTWNCK3

Discussion Questions

1. How does using a context provide support for student thinking?

2. Which numbers appear to be easier for the children? More difficult? Why do you think this is so?

3. What can the teacher learn about her students' understandings from this number talk?

4. What is the role of mistakes in this classroom?

For commentary on the above, see Appendix A: Author's Video Reflections.

Second-Grade Classroom

A Closer Look at Galey Thomas's Second-Grade Classroom

Galey Thomas's class consists of a multicultural group of fifteen second-grade students. The majority of the students have been at South Shades Crest Elementary School since kindergarten and are accustomed to reasoning with numbers and sharing their thinking. Ms. Thomas incorporates games, literature, classroom investigations, menu tasks, and number talks into her mathematics block and encourages her students to defend their reasoning and ask questions to clarify understanding.

Talking About Number Talks: Second Grade
Galey Thomas ● Teacher Clip T.2

Galey Thomas believes strongly in the importance of number talks and their ability to build mathematically powerful students and teachers. Listen as she shares how her teaching practice changed as she learned to value her students' reasoning about numbers.

To view this video clip, scan the QR code or access via mathsolutions.com /NTWNCT2

Math Time Structure

A typical math block is sixty minutes and is structured to include the following components.

Calendar Time (ten minutes)

A daily conversation using the calendar provides students with opportunities to learn and apply vocabulary and concepts related to measurement, number, algebraic reasoning, and data. Discussions revolve around representing the day of the week in multiple ways, looking for numerical patterns, recording and analyzing weather trends, and keeping track of the number of days in school using ten-frames.

Number Talk (five to fifteen minutes)

Second-grade number talks initially focus on building fluency with composing and decomposing numbers up to ten and developing strategies for basic facts using dot cards, ten-frames, and rekenreks. A natural progression is to incorporate operations with single-digit and two-digit numbers with a gradual move to two-digit computation.

Refer to Chapters 3 and 4 for specific second-grade number talks and ways to implement them.

Math Games, Math Menu, or Math Investigation (twenty-five minutes)

The core component of the math time structure is focused on providing opportunities for students to investigate and explore conceptual ideas through purposeful investigations or math menus. An example of a *math investigation* at the second-grade level is to have students use manipulatives to prove what makes a number even or odd and to search for patterns to help with identification. A *math menu* at this level might be composed

(continued)

of choices of games to promote fact knowledge or strategic thinking, tasks to explore addition properties or patterns, or a series of activities to delve deeper into the underlying principles of addition and subtraction. Resources for creating math menus and classroom math investigations can be found in Appendix C.

Whole-Class Processing (ten minutes)

At the conclusion of a menu or investigation, students need an opportunity to share their findings and wonderings and form generalizations and new questions to investigate. This processing time allows the teacher to create a forum to help students build understandings of the big mathematical ideas in which they have been immersed. For example, if students have been investigating why a number is odd or even, they might conclude that an even number is any number that can be divided fairly into two parts and determine that any number ending in 0, 2, 4, 6, or 8 is an even number because it fits this generalization.

A Second Look at Second-Grade Number Talks

The second-grade classroom video clips are referenced throughout the book; in this chapter they are grouped together to provide an opportunity for analysis, discussion, and reflection on teacher and student roles, the purpose of number talks, and student thinking about math content. Each video clip is accompanied by discussion questions designed to help readers immerse themselves more deeply in the pedagogy and content of the number talk. An author commentary for each segment is located in Appendix A, "Author's Video Reflections."

Grade 2: Ten-Frames: 8 + 6
Classroom Clip 2.1

To view this video clip, scan the QR code or access via mathsolutions.com /NTWNC21

Discussion Questions

1. What are examples of how the ten-frame model supports student strategies for 8 + 6?

2. How does the ten-frame encourage students' understanding of 10 as an important number in computation?

3. What seems to be a core strategy throughout this number talk?

4. 8 + 6 is considered to be a basic addition fact. What role can number talks play in helping students build basic fact knowledge?

For commentary on the above, see Appendix A: Author's Video Reflections.

Grade 2: Addition: 16 + 15
Classroom Clip 2.2

To view this video clip, scan the QR code or access via mathsolutions.com /NTWNC22

Discussion Questions

1. How does the teacher use the hundred chart to help students think about efficiency with addition strategies?

2. What examples of composing and decomposing numbers do you notice in the students' strategies?

3. Madeline uses a doubles + 1 strategy to solve the problem. What math understandings must be in place for her to approach the problem in this way?

4. What evidence indicates that the students understand and can apply place value?

For commentary on the above, see Appendix A: Author's Video Reflections.

Grade 2: Addition: 26 + 27
Classroom Clip 2.3

Discussion Questions

1. How do the strategies demonstrate that children have built an understanding of place value?

2. In each strategy the students start from the left and work to the right. How does this help build number sense and a sense of reasonableness for the answer?

3. What role does the hundred chart play in helping children understand place value?

4. How are students using their understanding of number relationships in their strategies?

5. A major focus of kindergarten number talks is to build fluency with small numbers. How is this idea incorporated in the students' strategies?

6. What underlying math concepts are embedded in each of the addition strategies?

For commentary on the above, see Appendix A: Author's Video Reflections.

To view this video clip, scan the QR code or access via mathsolutions.com/NTWNC23

3

Third-Grade Classroom

A Closer Look at Jann Montgomery's Third-Grade Classroom

The majority of Jann Montgomery's eighteen third-grade students have been actively involved in number talks since they were kindergartners. They expect math to make sense and readily invest in building computation strategies based on number relationships. By third grade, students are accustomed to sharing their thinking, considering the reasonableness of an answer, and engaging in discussions to debate an idea.

Talking About Number Talks: Third Grade
Jann Montgomery ● Teacher Clip T.3

Jann Mongomery is a known leader in the area of number talks in her school district and a source of expertise for other teachers. She is passionate about students learning for understanding as evidenced by the video clip.

To view this video clip, scan the QR code or access via mathsolutions.com/NTWNCT3

Math Time Structure

Ms. Montgomery's math time is a minimum of sixty minutes with time allotted to include the following components:

Number Talk (five to fifteen minutes)

As a daily part of math, number talks are used to investigate computation strategies, build fluency with larger numbers, test and apply properties of whole numbers, and provide an opportunity for students to build an understanding of number relationships.

(continued)

Refer to Chapters 5, 6, 7, and 8 for specific third-grade number talks and ways to implement them.

Math Investigation or Math Menu (twenty-five minutes)

Students move from the number talk into a math investigation or menu where they work either individually, with a partner, or in a small group. A math investigation might be designed around a discussion that surfaced during the number talks. Some sample investigations could be the following: will a specific strategy always work, can a number always be broken into addends for easier multiplication, or can you double and halve to solve any multiplication problem? A math menu may be focused on a particular concept, operation, or a strand of mathematics, and students make choices about which tasks they select and the order in which they work on them. One of the benefits of using either of these investigative approaches is that students are given an opportunity to immerse themselves in a big idea and access it at their own level and pace. By organizing a math block in this manner, teachers create a time to pull out small groups for additional support as the other students focus on the tasks they have selected. A list of resources for creating math menus and investigations can be found in Appendix C.

Whole-Class Processing (ten minutes)

After students have formulated their ideas and drawn conclusions from the menu tasks and investigations, it is essential that they come back together to process their ideas. This provides an opportunity for the class to share important conceptual ideas and make generalizations to apply to future tasks. For example, if the students were investigating patterns that occur with factors of numbers, the agreed-upon ideas could be posted on a chart and referenced during future computation tasks, number talks, or investigations.

(continued)

Math Games or Computation Practice (ten minutes)

While number talks provide an opportunity for students to reason with numbers and invent efficient computation strategies, students need opportunities to practice applying their ideas. Requiring students on a daily basis to solve five computation problems that mirror the number talk focus provides this practice opportunity and also gives the teacher a way to formatively assess student understanding and make instructional decisions for the next day. Some teachers elect to have students solve one problem two ways before they transition into math investigations or menus. This allows the teacher to instantly know who needs additional support so they can attend a small-group session during menu time. Often teachers alternate between computation practice and math fact games to provide support in both areas.

A Second Look at Third-Grade Number Talks

The third-grade classroom video clips are referenced throughout the book; in this chapter they are grouped together to provide an opportunity for analysis, discussion, and reflection on teacher and student roles, the purpose of number talks, and student thinking about a math content. Each video clip is accompanied by discussion questions designed to help readers immerse themselves more deeply in the pedagogy and content of the number talk. An author commentary for each segment is located in Appendix A, "Author's Video Reflections."

Grade 3: Addition: 38 + 37
Classroom Clip 3.1

Discussion Questions

1. The teacher asks students to think about previous strategies they have used before solving the current problem. Why would it be important for the teacher to encourage the students to consider previous strategies they have discussed?

2. The teacher chooses momentarily to leave Arzoo's strategy and then return to it. What purpose does this serve?

3. How is place value emphasized during the number talk?

4. How does each strategy foster number sense and the use of number relationships?

For commentary on the above, see Appendix A: Author's Video Reflections.

To view this video clip, scan the QR code or access via mathsolutions.com /NTWNC31

Grade 3: Addition: 59 + 13
Classroom Clip 3.2

Discussion Questions

1. How is place value maintained in the strategies that are shared?

2. How does each strategy foster number sense and the use of number relationships?

3. How does the teacher's role encourage student reasoning?

4. Choose one of the strategies to model with the open number line. How could this be an effective tool for your students?

For commentary on the above, see Appendix A: Author's Video Reflections.

To view this video clip, scan the QR code or access via mathsolutions.com /NTWNC32

Grade 3: Subtraction: 70 – 59
Classroom Clip 3.3

To view this video clip, scan the QR code or access via mathsolutions.com /NTWNC33

Discussion Questions

1. How does the number line provide support for understanding Grant's Constant Difference strategy? In what other ways could you model this strategy to help students understand why it works?

2. The students share several subtraction strategies: Constant Difference, Adding Up, Removing in Chunks, and Adjusting One of the Numbers. Discuss how these strategies are similar and different.

3. When Andrew shared his strategy, students were unsure whether 1 should be added or subtracted. Share your observations about the student and teacher roles during the class discussion. How could you help students understand his thinking?

For commentary on the above, see Appendix A: Author's Video Reflections.

Grade 3: Subtraction: 70 – 34
Classroom Clip 3.4

Discussion Questions

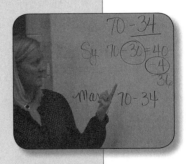

1. What structures are present in the classroom community that allow:

   - Mary to be comfortable thinking about her errors with the class,

   - incorrect answers to be posted, or

   - students to change their answers when presented with other students' reasoning?

2. How is the relationship between addition and subtraction used to build efficient strategies?

3. Why did Grant choose to increase both numbers by 6? Are there other ways he could have altered the problem to make friendly numbers?

To view this video clip, scan the QR code or access via mathsolutions.com /NTWNC34

For commentary on the above, see Appendix A: Author's Video Reflections.

Grade 3: Multiplication String: 7 × 7
Classroom Clip 3.5

Discussion Questions

1. How does this sequence of multiplication problems help students understand how the distributive property can be applied in multiplication?

2. How does the teacher help connect Je'Nya's Repeated Addition strategy to Grant's Partial Products strategy?

(continued)

3. What are some other ways students could have used the smaller multiplication problems to efficiently solve 7×7?

4. The teacher accepted correct and incorrect answers for 7×7. How does this help promote an environment of sensemaking in mathematics?

For commentary on the above, see Appendix A: Author's Video Reflections.

To view this video clip, scan the QR code or access via mathsolutions.com /NTWNC35

Grade 3: Doubling and Halving: 4×7, 2×14
Classroom Clip 3.6

Discussion Questions

1. The teacher chooses to use a context as students consider the relationship between 4×7 and 2×14. How does this context help support student thinking?

2. How is the commutative property addressed in the discussion?

3. How do the teacher's questions help students begin to build an understanding of doubling and halving?

4. The teacher is continually assessing her students during the number talk. What student understandings and misconceptions will she use to guide her next instructional steps?

For commentary on the above, see Appendix A: Author's Video Reflections.

To view this video clip, scan the QR code or access via mathsolutions.com /NTWNC36

Grade 3: Array Discussion: 8 × 25
Classroom Clip 3.7

Discussion Questions

1. The class had shared strategies for solving 8 × 25 before the teacher introduced the array model. Why do you think this instructional decision was made? How did she link previous strategies to the array?

2. Noel incorrectly refers to columns as rows in the array. The teacher does not correct her. Why do you think she chose to ignore this error?

3. How does the teacher connect the students' additive thinking to multiplication?

4. How does the array support student understanding of multiplication? the commutative property? the distributive property? the associative property?

For commentary on the above, see Appendix A: Author's Video Reflections.

To view this video clip, scan the QR code or access via mathsolutions.com /NTWNC37

5

Fifth-Grade Classroom

A Closer Look at Lee Ann Davidson's Fifth-Grade Classroom

Lee Ann Davidson's fifth-grade classroom is composed of a diverse group of twenty-one students, one-fourth of whom transferred to the school within the past year. The majority of the students in this class have attended this school since kindergarten and have been immersed in inquiry-based mathematics. They are accustomed to reasoning with numbers, providing proofs for their strategies, and making sense of mathematics. The consistency in math instruction and expectations has been instrumental in developing this group of mathematically powerful students.

Talking About Number Talks: Fifth Grade
Lee Ann Davidson ● Teacher Clip T.5

Lee Ann Davidson firmly believes that number talks provide a strong foundation for students to approach computation from a sensemaking perspective. Her experiences in primary and intermediate grades have helped to solidify the idea that students become mathematically powerful when given opportunities to reason with numbers.

To view this video clip, scan the QR code or access via mathsolutions.com/NTWNCT5

Math Time Structure

A typical math period is between sixty and seventy-five minutes and consists of the following components:

Number Talk (five to fifteen minutes)

A typical math lesson begins with a number talk that is purposefully designed to address the areas in which the students

(continued)

Refer to Chapters 5, 6, 7, and 8 for specific fifth-grade number talks and ways to implement them.

need to focus. Often the number talk is crafted to correlate to the upcoming math investigation or menu.

Math Investigation or Math Menu (thirty minutes)

Students move from the number talk into either a math investigation or a menu where they work individually, with a partner, or in a small group. A *math investigation* might be designed around a discussion that surfaced during the number talks. Sample investigations could include: will a specific strategy always work, can a number always be broken into factors for easier multiplication, or can you make a division problem easier by dividing the divisor and dividend by a common factor. A *math menu* can be focused on a particular concept, an operation, or a strand of mathematics. One of the benefits of using either of these investigative approaches is that students are given an opportunity to immerse themselves in a big idea and access it at their own level and pace. By organizing a math block in this manner, teachers create time to pull out small groups for additional support. A list of resources for creating math menus and investigations can be found in Appendix C.

Whole-Class Processing (ten to fifteen minutes)

After students have formulated their ideas and drawn conclusions from the menu tasks and investigations, it is essential that the teacher reserve some time to process these ideas. This provides an opportunity for the class to share important conceptual ideas and make generalizations to apply in future tasks. For example, if the students were investigating patterns that occur with factors of numbers, the agreed-upon ideas could be posted on a chart and referenced during future computation tasks, number talks, or investigations.

Computation Practice or Math Games (ten to fifteen minutes)

While number talks provide an opportunity for students to reason with numbers and invent efficient computation

(continued)

strategies, students need opportunities to practice applying their ideas. Requiring students to solve five computation problems daily that mirror the number talk focus provides this practice opportunity and also gives the teacher a way to formatively assess student understanding and make instructional decisions for the next day. Some teachers elect to have students solve one problem two ways before they transition into math investigations or menus. This allows the teacher to instantly know who needs additional support so those students can be pulled out for a small-group session during the menus. Often teachers alternate between computation practice and math fact games to provide support in both areas.

A Second Look at Fifth-Grade Number Talks

The fifth-grade classroom video clips are referenced throughout the book; in this chapter they are grouped together to provide an opportunity for analysis, discussion, and reflection on teacher and student roles, the purpose of number talks, and student thinking about a math content. Each video clip is accompanied by discussion questions designed to help readers immerse themselves more deeply in the pedagogy and content of the number talk. An author commentary for each segment is located in Appendix A, "Author's Video Reflections."

Grade 5: Associative Property: 12 × 15
Classroom Clip 5.1

Discussion Questions

1. How do the hand signals used by the students help the teacher assess student access and understanding?

2. What evidence indicates that the students' thinking is grounded in understanding versus the memorization of rules?

3. Jilian's strategy for 2 × 15 × 6 breaks the 6 into a 3 + 3. Why did she multiply by 3 and then double her answer?

(continued)

4. How do the teacher's questions keep the purpose of the number talk in the forefront of the class discussion?

5. How did this series of problems help students develop a working understanding of the associative property?

To view this video clip, scan the QR code or access via mathsolutions.com /NTWNC51

For commentary on the above, see Appendix A: Author's Video Reflections.

Grade 5: Multiplication: 32 × 15
Classroom Clip 5.2

Discussion Questions

1. What examples support the strong learning community that exists in this classroom?

2. Which student strategy closely resembles the standard U.S. algorithm for double-digit multiplication? How are they similar? Different?

3. The distributive property is interwoven in most of the students' strategies. What examples do you notice of this property being used?

4. The topic of efficiency surfaces in this discussion. Which strategies would you deem to be most efficient and why?

5. Choose one of the strategies to model with the open array. Share your thinking with someone.

To view this video clip, scan the QR code or access via mathsolutions.com /NTWNC52

For commentary on the above, see Appendix A: Author's Video Reflections.

Grade 5: Multiplication: 16 × 35
Classroom Clip 5.3

To view this video clip, scan the QR code or access via mathsolutions.com /NTWNC53

Discussion Questions

1. Omar chooses to distribute all of the numbers by breaking them apart into addends; in doing so he makes a careless error. As he shares his thinking, he finds his error. What is the value of students thinking about their reasoning to uncover their errors versus the teacher telling them their answer is wrong?

2. Why did Sarah Grace subtract 140 in her strategy? What would the array look like for this strategy?

3. Jarvis has continued to ponder the idea of breaking factors into prime factors as shared by another student during the associative property string (Classroom Clip 5.1). Ms. Davidson refers to this moment in "Talking About Number Talks" (Teacher Clip T.5). How does shifting the source of knowledge from the teacher to the student affect learning in the classroom?

For commentary on the above, see Appendix A: Author's Video Reflections.

Grade 5: Array Discussion: 150 ÷ 15, 300 ÷ 15
Classroom Clip 5.4

Discussion Questions

1. How did this particular sequence of problems help students use number relationships to solve the problem?

2. What student confusions and misunderstandings surfaced with the array model?

3. How did the teacher navigate the discussion to build understanding about multiplication, division, and the array model?

(continued)

4. What evidence exists to indicate that the students understand the relationship between multiplication and division?

5. The next problem in the series is 600 ÷ 15. How does this problem relate to the previous two division problems? How would the array change?

For commentary on the above, see Appendix A: Author's Video Reflections.

To view this video clip, scan the QR code or access via mathsolutions.com /NTWNC54

Grade 5: Division String: 496 ÷ 8
Classroom Clip 5.5

Discussion Questions

1. How does the succession of problems provide a scaffold for students to solve 496 ÷ 8?

2. How does this sequence provide multiple ways for students to access the problem?

3. In what other ways could 496 ÷ 8 be solved using the prior problems?

4. Jillian had a lovely strategy for solving this problem; however, she struggled to state what her answer was. Where is Jillian's answer in the recording on the board? What mathematical concepts are embraced in her reasoning?

5. Students struggle to follow Jackson's strategy for 496 ÷ 8. What components of division and multiplication does Jackson understand?

6. The teacher repeatedly asks students to explain where their answer is in their strategy. Why is this an important focal point throughout the discussion?

For commentary on the above, see Appendix A: Author's Video Reflections.

To view this video clip, scan the QR code or access via mathsolutions.com /NTWNC55

Grade 5: Subtraction: 1000 – 674
Classroom Clip 5.6

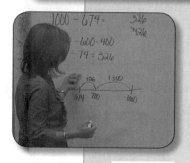

To view this video clip, scan the QR code or access via mathsolutions.com /NTWNC56

Discussion Questions

1. How is number sense used to determine whether an answer is reasonable or not?

2. What purpose is served by the teacher accepting both correct and incorrect answers for the problem?

3. How is the student's role different from typical classrooms?

4. Often subtraction is explained as "taking away." Cole's strategy does not remove or take away an amount; instead, he adds to solve the problem. Why does this work?

For commentary on the above, see Appendix A: Author's Video Reflections.

Schoolwide Perspective

A Closer Look at Number Talks from a Schoolwide Perspective

The previous primary and intermediate video clips represent students' number talk journeys from kindergarten through fifth grade. While teacher personalities and physical environments may change as students transition from classroom to classroom, essential number talk content and characteristics remain consistent from year to year. This consistency in teaching the mathematically big ideas, instruction rooted in asking rather than telling, developing a safe learning community, and an unwavering quest for making sense are essential in building mathematically powerful students. The consistency from grade level to grade level does not occur by coincidence; it is purposefully orchestrated by the school learning community.

The following discussion questions are designed to help individual teachers, faculties, administrators, and staff developers analyze K–5 number talks from a collective perspective instead of by individual grade levels. Taking the time to view the talks collectively instead of individually will allow you to have a global perspective for your school community and make changes accordingly.

Schoolwide Perspective
All Video Clips

Discussion Questions

1. View each of the grade-level video clips in the table below and discuss how the following areas are exhibited in each grade.

Grade	Classroom Clip	Area
Kindergarten	K.1	Classroom Community
Grade 2	2.1	Teacher's Role
Grade 3	3.1	Student's Role
Grade 5	5.2	Communication

What similarities do you notice between the grades in regard to these areas?
What differences do you notice?

2. Use the same video clips as in Question 1 and discuss how the content changes from grade to grade.

3. One focus of kindergarten number talks is composing and decomposing small numbers. How is this idea built upon and used in the other grade levels? Use the following clips to find evidence for your statements:

Grade	Classroom Clip
Grade 2	2.2
Grade 3	3.2

4. Students typically begin learning about multiplication in third grade. Use the following video clips to consider how

(continued)

students' initial reasoning with multiplication strategies enables them to easily assess 16 × 35.

Grade	Classroom Clip
Grade 3	3.5
Grade 5	5.3

5. View each of the following grade-level clips and discuss how the following areas are exhibited in each grade:

Grade	Classroom Clip	Area
Kindergarten	K.2	Commutative Property
Grade 2	2.2	Models/Tools
Grade 3	3.3	Student Strategies
Grade 5	5.4	Place Value

What similarities do you notice between the grades in regard to these areas?

What differences do you notice? How do the strategies build?

6. Write an addition number talk problem for each grade level from kindergarten through fifth grade. Solve each problem using two strategies students might commonly use. How do the strategies build from grade level to grade level? What math concepts need to be developed at each grade level to allow students to be mathematically powerful? How does this affect student understanding in future grade levels?

Your Practice: A Closer Look

The mark of a master teacher is the ability to reflect on his practice. Using the following reflection questions, consider your current practice. What changes might you make make from your experiences with this book and the DVD?

By three methods we may learn wisdom: First, by reflection, which is noblest; second, by imitation, which is easiest; and third, by experience, which is the bitterest. (Confucius, philosopher and teacher [c. 551–478 BCE])

Questions for Personal Reflection

1. How are the student and teacher roles in your classroom similar to or different from the featured teachers and classrooms?

2. Think about a recent math lesson you have taught. What role does a learning community play in your lesson? What opportunities exist for students to learn through inquiry-based tasks? How does your lesson build number sense?

3. Throughout the book and the DVD, students are engaged in applying conceptual ideas such as place value, properties, and number relationships. How are these concepts addressed in your classroom? How is this similar to or different from the classrooms you have encountered in your readings and viewings?

4. Consider the types of questions asked by teachers and students in the DVD segments. How are questions in your classroom used to help students build conceptual ideas?

5. Think about how student errors are addressed in your classroom. How does this compare with examples you have seen on the classroom number talks DVD?

6. How are you currently using models and tools to support student thinking about numbers and operations?

7. How can you incorporate a context in a future math lesson to help support student thinking and understanding?

8. Remember to start small in making shifts in your classroom practice related to number talks. Write down one change you will make.

Appendices

Appendix A: Author's Video Reflections

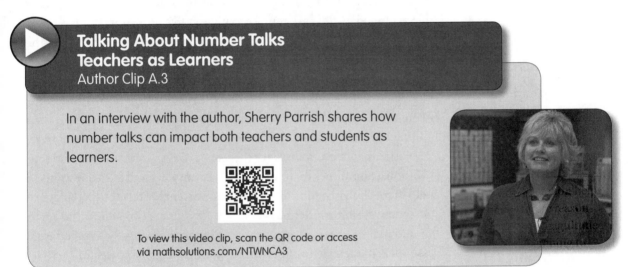

Talking About Number Talks
Teachers as Learners
Author Clip A.3

In an interview with the author, Sherry Parrish shares how number talks can impact both teachers and students as learners.

To view this video clip, scan the QR code or access via mathsolutions.com/NTWNCA3

Kindergarten

Classroom Clip K.1: Ten-Frames and Dot Cards

See pages 36, 309

The choice to begin with five dots in the ten-frame allows students the opportunity to establish five as a unit while simultaneously considering the whole frame as one unit of ten. It is important too for the teacher to establish this unit before showing students the next card with 7 dots. By observing the students, the teacher can quickly assess who is able to sub-itize five and use it as a foundation for the upcoming problem.

The students still need help articulating their thinking, so the teacher readily probes their responses and helps supply words to match their reasoning. As they process seven, she is trying to find out if they used one of the following strategies to solve this problem: adding two to five, counting on from five, counting all, or using reasoning from the whole of ten. Each response helps her to formatively assess her students' understanding.

Moving from one model to the next is not problematic to adults, but young children must adjust their thinking. Even though the students readily articulated the relationship between five and ten with the ten-frames, their understanding is fragile when viewing the dot card with two sets of five. Students who only moments before knew that ten dots on the ten-frame made ten are now uncertain whether two sets of five arranged as dice are ten. Recognizing five as a subset of the ten is important for solving the dot card and in providing a framework for the following problem of four and one.

As students solve the dot card with four and one, we can see various strategies surface: counting all, using the relationship of six minus one, using the relationship between five and seven, subitizing four and then adding one, and moving the dots around to make a dice image of five.

Notice that in every instance the teacher never confirms the students' solutions. She allows them to prove their answers and asks questions to help them clarify their thinking. It is important to start this pedagogical perspective with kindergartners. Developing a disposition that math should make sense and answers must be mathematically justified is an essential characteristic of becoming mathematically powerful.

▶ Classroom Clip K.2: Rekenreks

See pages 42, 310

The warm-up period with the number four serves two purposes. It establishes how to use the rekenrek and allows the teacher to see who is fluent with combinations to four. Having the students build four in a different way provides an opportunity for the teacher to bring the commutative property to the forefront of the discussion. By contrasting two similar bead arrangements for four (one bead on the top and three beads on the bottom with three beads on the top and one bead on the bottom), the teacher is introducing the commutative property to the kindergartners. Introducing this idea with a number that is accessible to the students allows the students to focus on this new concept.

Once the procedures are established for using the rekenrek, the teacher quickly moves to the number six. Before moving on to the game *Can You Guess My Way?*, the teacher provides an open exploration of six that allows her to assess the children's understanding of composing and decomposing six. This preteaching moment provides support for those who are not yet fluent with the number six and gives them a preview of possible combinations to use during the game.

Structuring the game so that all students are responding simultaneously ensures engagement and access. The game provides an opportunity for students to think through all of the possible ways to make six, which keeps them engaged in productive mathematics. This is a much richer math task than having students supply rote answers on a worksheet.

The lesson is grounded in differentiation, because students are accessing the combinations that they know while being exposed to less familiar ones. By observing how the students count the beads, the teacher can see who has mastered one-to-one correspondence and who is able to conserve number without having to recount. This will guide her next steps.

When students have incorrect responses, the teacher prompts them to check if their beads total 6. The teacher's role is not to tell the students whether they are right or wrong; instead, she supplies a question to direct them to revisit their thinking. This simple action places the responsibility for verification on the students and requires them to adjust or maintain their answers.

Opportunities to link the commutative property arise throughout the number talk as the teacher shares with the class that her way is the "opposite" of a student's. This helps students begin to understand that the addends of a number can be represented in any order. The identity property is also addressed as students build a number using the number on one row and zero on the other row. Notice how the teacher uses the language of zero instead of none.

▶ Classroom Clip K.3: Counting Book

See pages 49, 310

From the initial discussion of types of counting books, we can tell that this classroom has had numerous experiences using literature as a context for mathematics. Providing a context for thinking about mathematics helps students connect math to real-life experiences. The teacher immediately involves them in the story *Ten in the Bed* by Penny Dale by singing and having them build the numbers with their personal manipulatives, their fingers. She moves quickly through the higher numbers and allows the class more time to immerse themselves in numbers that they are building fluency with such as seven, six, and five.

Throughout the contextual number talk, the teacher has multiple opportunities to observe who can build each of the numbers and whether they use the same strategy for every number. Many students use doubles or a number plus one. Few children utilize combinations that are two or three plus a number. The teacher also gathers information about who counts all, counts on, adjusts from a previous combination, or is already fluent with a number.

Children make mistakes throughout the number talk, but these are treated as opportunities to learn. The teacher often asks students to recount their ways of solving the problems; others adjust their thinking by observing their peers. Her questions encourage the children to stretch their thinking. By asking who can make five with two hands, students must shift from their initial responses of one hand of five to combinations with two addends. She also encourages them to think flexibly and fluently when they are asked, "Is there another way to make _____?"

This simple lesson builds on many math ideas: magnitude of numbers, one-to-one correspondence, one less, counting backward, fluency, subitizing, and conserving number.

Second Grade

Classroom Clip 2.1: Ten-Frames: 8 + 6

See pages 43, 314

Learning basic addition facts is a core component of the second-grade curriculum. Number talks with double ten-frames help students develop strategies to build fact fluency. The ten-frames serve as a visual model for decomposing and composing numbers and as an anchor for using ten to build numbers in the teens and higher. Throughout the video clip we can see evidence of students mentally moving parts of the numbers to create easier problems. As the teacher physically moves the dots on the ten-frames, she links students' oral explanations to a concrete model. When the teacher asks, "Where is the four? Where is the six?" she is helping students connect the strategy to the visual.

Second graders are more adept at explaining their thinking, but it is still important to help anchor the strategies for the class. By taking a moment at the end of the talk to highlight the strategies used, the teacher helps students build a repertoire of efficient strategies to use for future problems. We will use the table that follows to help us explore accurate, efficient, and flexible strategies for the basic fact 8 + 6.

Strategies for Ten-Frames: 8 + 6

Strategy: Doubles/Near-Doubles	Observations
8 + 6 (6 + 2) + 6 (6 + 6) + 2 6 + 6 = 12 12 + 2 = 14	In this student's strategy, the ten-frame is not used to think about a group of five or ten; instead, the student views sixes in both frames and builds on this understanding of doubles. Knowing you can break numbers apart and move the parts into different groupings is a big idea to develop. While the teacher does not formally address the use of the associative property, this is the basis for this strategy. A formal label for this property will be introduced at a later time.
Strategy: Making Tens	**Observations**
8 + 6 (5 + 3) + (5 + 1) (5 + 5) + (3 + 1) 5 + 5 = 10 3 + 1 = 4 10 + 4 = 14	While the previous student strategy viewed eight and six through the lens of sixes, this student sees fives as a part of both numbers. The ten-frame helps foster this thinking. The teacher does not assume everyone follows this strategy. By asking the class where parts of the numbers are, the teacher helps other students access how the strategy works. Even with the teacher's questions and emphasis on approaching this problem as 10 + 4, not all students grasp this idea as evidenced by Cameron. After other strategies are shared, Cameron comes back to this idea of making a ten with two fives. However, he cannot visualize this arrangement; he needs to physically group the fives together and the 3 + 1 together. This is important because we often assume a child understands something once it has been taught or shared. This example shows that children must build their understanding at their own pace.

(continued)

Strategy: Building on Known Facts	Observations
$6 + 7 = 13$ $13 + 1 = 14$	Building from what you already know is often an efficient strategy.

Strategy: Compensation	Observations
A. $\quad 8 \quad + \quad 6$ $\quad \dfrac{-1 \quad +1}{7 \quad + \quad 7 = 14}$ B. $\quad 8 \quad + \quad 6$ $\quad \dfrac{+2 \quad -2}{10 \quad + \quad 4 = 14}$	Both of these strategies are grounded in compensation; however, their purposes are different. Compensation is used in Strategy A to create doubles and in Strategy B to make a ten.

▶ **Classroom Clips 2.2 and 2.3:**
Addition: 16 + 15 and Addition: 26 + 27

See pages 58, 59, 314, 315

Second-grade students are building an intimate knowledge of place value, and for many this is still fragile. They are using place value in a more simplistic way than what you would find in third grade. For example, in the strategies for both of the problems, students tend to cluster like place values; they put all of the tens together and all of the ones together. As they become more solid in their understanding, you will begin to see them chunking a number. They will keep one addend whole and break the second number into its place values before adding.

Each of the strategies in the following table relies heavily on this level of place-value understanding as well as decomposing and composing numbers and the associative property. A more detailed recording of the problem is shown in the following table so that the use of the associative property is more prominent. Using the term *associative property* is not essential at this point; however, it is important for students to understand that numbers may be grouped and added in any order in addition.

Strategies for 16 + 15 and 26 + 27

Strategy: Doubles/Near-Doubles	Observations

A. 16 + 15
 	
  (1 + 15) + 15
 	
  1 + (15 + 15)
 	
  1 + 30 = 31
 	
B. 26 + 27
  $\underline{-1}$ $\underline{-2}$
  25 + 25 = 50
 	
  50 + 3 = 53
	Both of these Doubles strategies require students to decompose one or more numbers to make a double.
	
	In Strategy A the teacher asks the student to prove how she knows that 15 + 15 makes thirty. This question is intended more for the other students instead of the author of the strategy. The teacher knows that many of the students would benefit from hearing how numbers can be broken into their place values to add.
	
	Linking Strategy B to money (quarters) helps provide access to students and demonstrates the number relationships between twenty-six, twenty-seven, and twenty-five.

Strategy: Making Tens	**Observations**
16 + 15 (1 + 15) + 15 1 + 10 + 5 + 10 + 5 10 + 10 + 10 = 30 30 + 1	While this strategy initially takes the same approach as Strategy A in the Doubles +1 section, the student has a completely different reason for decomposing 16 into 15 + 1. She knows 10 can be represented by 5 + 5, and she uses this knowledge to develop an efficient Making Tens strategy.
Strategy: Breaking Each Number into Its Place Value	**Observations**
	Maintaining place value during computation helps students know whether their answers are reasonable, and it also provides a sense of the magnitude of the number. Second graders are beginning to

(continued)

A. 16 + 15

10 + 10 = 20

6 + 5 = 11

20 + 11 = 31

build an understanding of place value, so it is important for this concept to remain intact as they solve problems.

In Strategy A, the student does not explain how he knows that 20 + 11 is 31, but by having him model his thinking on the hundred chart, we see that he probably counted on by ones from twenty. The hundred chart discussion is important. It helps students think about twenty as two groups of ten, and it models adding by tens as more efficient than counting up by ones.

B. 26 + 27

20 + 20 = 40

6 + 7 = 13

13 + 40 = 53

As the same student shares Strategy B and is asked to model his thinking on the hundred chart, there is evidence that he is thinking about the ideas from the Strategy A discussion as he makes four jumps of ten from thirteen.

Strategy: Adding Up in Chunks	Observations
16 + 15 (11 + 5) + 15 11 + (5 + 15) 11 + 20 = 31	Decomposing 16 into 11 + 5 is key to this strategy because it allows the student to make an easy twenty. An important question to ask would be, "Why did you choose to break sixteen into eleven and five? Are there other numbers that would also work?"
Strategy: Breaking Each Number into Its Place Value and Making Tens Combined	Observations
26 + 27 (20 + 3 + 3) + (20 + 7) (20 + 20) + (3 + 7) + 3 40 + 10 + 3 = 53	As discussed in Chapter 3, strategies are often combined as shown by this example. The student has purposefully chosen to decompose twenty-six to find a three to go with the seven. Could he have decomposed the seven from twenty-seven into three and four, and placed the four with the six in twenty-six? Absolutely. However, students at this grade level use doubles, and 6 could easily be broken into a double.

Third Grade

Classroom Clips 3.1 and 3.2:
Addition: 38 + 37 and Addition: 59 + 13

See pages 24, 158, 174, 319

Between introducing the problem and accepting answers, the teacher is able to informally assess which students respond quickly, rely on their fingers for basic facts, struggle to access the problem, and have more than one strategy. This information helps the teacher anticipate adjustments that she might need to make as the class shares strategies. Possible changes that she could make in the number talk are adjusting the magnitude of the numbers, choosing to process strategies for basic facts, or even shifting to a different operation. Since several students struggle with basic recall of 8 + 7, the teacher makes an instructional decision to process efficient ways to solve this fact. One student builds on earlier experiences with decomposing numbers and changes the problem to 7 + 7 + 1 (a Doubles + 1 strategy).

Three primary strategies surface during the addition number talks for 38 + 37 and 59 + 1: Adding Up in Chunks, Breaking Each Number into Its Place Value, and using Landmark or Friendly Numbers. Notice how number sense and place value are maintained in each approach. The following table outlines how the strategies are used and offers insight into content and pedagogical observations.

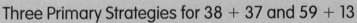

Three Primary Strategies for 38 + 37 and 59 + 13

Strategy: Adding Up in Chunks	Observations

A. 38 + 37
 	
  38 + 30 = 68
 	
  68 + 7 = 75
	Does it matter in which order the addends are used? This is an important idea for students to construct. The students seem to understand that this works, but why? The associative property helps to explain it.

(continued)

B. 38 + 37 38 + 7 = 45 45 + 30 = 75	The original problem can be represented as follows: 38 + 30 + 7. The associative property proves that the order in which the addends are grouped does not affect the sum: $(38 + 30) + 7 = (38 + 7) + 30$
C. 59 + 13 59 + 3 = 62 62 + 10 = 72	Likewise, 59 + 13 can be represented with the associative property as follows: $59 + (10 + 3) = (59 + 3) = 10$
Strategy: Breaking Each Number into Its Place Value	**Observations**
A. 38 + 37 30 + 30 = 60 8 + 7 = 15 60 + 15 = 75	While place value initially remains intact with this strategy, note that the student seems to resort to single-digit thinking when combining 60 + 15. Instead of being able to automatically add fifteen, the student must literally add zero and five, then six and one. The teacher's question regarding six and one is timely and helps the student consider the value of the digits.
B. 59 + 13 50 + 10 = 60 60 + 9 = 69 69 + 3 = 72	With 59 + 13 the teacher again questions the student to maintain the place value of fifty and ten.
Strategy: Making Landmark or Friendly Numbers	**Observations**
A. 38 + 37 40 + 40 = 80 80 − 5 = 75	This strategy exhibits an understanding of number relationships, the importance of tens, and the magnitude of number. As the teacher questions why five is subtracted, she is helping other students better understand these relationships.
B. 59 + 13 60 + 13 = 73 73 − 1 = 72	A critical component of this strategy is being able to choose a friendly number to use. The teacher helps bring this idea to the forefront for the class when she asks the student why he chose sixty.

<table>
<tr><td></td><td>"When do I stop eliciting student strategies?" is a common question with number talks. A good rule of thumb to follow is to stop when you have unearthed the big ideas you are trying to address. We can see an example of this with 36 + 37 when the teacher asks if anyone used the Sharing strategy (Landmark or Friendly Numbers). She wanted this strategy to be brought to the forefront.</td></tr>
</table>

Classroom Clips 3.3 and 3.4: Subtraction: 70 − 59 and Subtraction: 70 − 34

See pages 6, 161, 320, 321

The subtraction video clips offer an insight into this third-grade learning community. They show a mutual respect between teacher and student as well as among students. Incorrect responses are offered without negative reactions, students such as Mary are allowed to change their minds and revisit their thinking with support, and students welcome questions from peers and teacher alike. Even in the think-pair-share opportunity in Clip 3.3, students exhibit a willingness to approach learning as a group with a common goal of understanding.

Four overarching goals of the number talks for grades 3 to 5 are addressed and supported throughout the subtraction number talks: number sense, place value, fluency, and connecting mathematical ideas (refer to Chapter 5 for a complete discussion of each goal).

- *Number sense.* Grant's Constant Difference strategy demonstrates understanding the power of friendly numbers in computation and that subtraction can be viewed as finding the distance between two numbers. Using the open number line helps to keep the magnitude of the numbers in perspective as well as the relationship between a number and the next ten.

- *Place value.* Students can be observed keeping the tens as whole quantities instead of using them as single digits. The use of the open number line model helps to support this idea as students make jumps of tens.

- *Fluency.* We often think of number fluency as the ability to break smaller numbers apart, but fluency can also be the ability to compose and decompose larger numbers. We see students exhibit fluency with larger numbers as they break numbers into smaller "chunks" to remove.

- *Connecting mathematical ideas.* The third-grade subtraction number talks make a number of important connections between mathematical ideas:

  linking the Constant Difference strategy to the Adding Up strategy for 70 − 50;

  broadening the perspective of subtraction to finding the difference between two numbers; and

  testing the relationship between addition and subtraction.

We will discuss how to address these opportunities as we look at the following strategy tables for 70 − 59 and 70 − 34.

Strategies for 70 − 59

Strategy: Keeping a Constant Difference	Observations
70 − 59 + 1 + 1 ——— 71 − 60 60 + 11 = 71	Determining how to adjust the numbers to create an easier problem is an important decision with the Constant Difference strategy. The teacher's questions about why the student chose to change the problem to 71 − 60 raise a necessary point for discussion. As adults, we may see how this makes the problem easier, but it is not so obvious to the students. As the student explains why subtracting tens is simple, this helps other students consider this method as an option. Using this "think-aloud" moment provides a stepping stone to understanding for the class. The open number line is a critical tool for helping the class access this strategy. It provides a visual model of what is occurring in the strategy itself and also helps students understand why adjusting fifty-nine to sixty makes use of a close ten.

	After renaming 70 − 59 to 71 − 60, Grant uses the Adding Up strategy to find the solution of eleven. The open number line again helps students consider how jumps of ten are efficient and effective. This connection to the Adding Up strategy with the new problem provides a bridge for students.
Strategy: Adding Up	**Observations**
70 − 59 59 + 1 = 60 60 + 10 = 70 10 + 1 = 11	Modeling both the Constant Difference and Adding Up strategies on the same open number line is an important instructional decision. It allows students to consider how the problems are similar and how the distance between the numbers remains the same.
Strategy: Removal	**Observations**
70 − 59 70 − 50 = 20 20 − 9 = 11	To successfully use this strategy, students need to have a strong understanding of place value as well as the relationship between the part and the whole.
Strategy: Adjusting One Number to Create an Easier Problem	**Observations**
$\begin{array}{r} 70 - 59 \\ +\ 1 \\ \hline 60 \end{array}$ 70 − 60 = 10 10 + 1 = 11	Because students are more comfortable with addition, they tend to overgeneralize what works with addition and extend it to their thinking about subtraction. For instance, in addition if you add one too many, you would remove the extra one from the sum. This is not true in subtraction. Discussing whether to add or subtract one from the difference is an important conversation. It helps students to confront their overgeneralizations and make sense of the relationships of the numbers. Using an open number line to model what occurs in this relationship helps children visualize and better understand the strategy.

Strategies for 70 − 34

Strategy: Removal	Observations
70 − 34 70 − 30 = 40 40 − 4 = 36	Notice how all answers—correct or incorrect—are accepted. The teacher does not react to any of the solutions, even though she knows only one correct answer is exhibited. She is giving ownership of the solution to the students, and it is up to them to provide proof for their answers. We can see evidence of student ownership as students remove answers when they have been convinced by their peers that their answers are incorrect. The students are vested in understanding why a strategy does or does not work. An excellent example of this can be seen when Mary asks for help in thinking about her original reasoning.
Strategy: Adding Up	**Observations**
70 − 34 34 + 6 = 40 40 + 30 = 70	The Adding Up strategy does not always need to be accompanied by a number line model as shown in this example. The student seems to have a strong understanding of place value, landmark numbers, and adding by multiples of ten.
Strategy: Keeping a Constant Difference	**Observations**
$\begin{array}{rr} 70 & - \quad 34 \\ +\,6 & +\,6 \\ \hline 76 & - \quad 40 = 36 \end{array}$	While the Constant Difference strategy is efficiently used for this problem, it is not necessarily accessible to all of the students. The teacher knows that students need to be presented with information regarding why specific numbers were chosen to adjust. By asking the student to justify his rationale for renaming the problem to 76 − 40, students have an opportunity to think about how this makes the problem easier to solve.

▶ Classroom Clip 3.5: Multiplication String: 7 × 7

See pages 245, 321

The students in this classroom are still in the early stages of learning about multiplication, and most of the children think about this operation as repeated addition. Their strategies primarily consist of visualizing circles for groups of objects and adding the quantities; however, several are beginning to make stronger connections to multiplicative thinking as they realize that smaller multiplication problems exist inside larger problems. Note that even in the initial phases of learning about multiplication, students are already at different levels of conceptual understanding and application.

This series of multiplication problems is carefully crafted to provide several points of access for all students. By starting with 2 × 7, the teacher is providing an opportunity for all students to enter the conversation. Notice that there is little need for discussion or to explore several strategies for this beginning problem. Students quickly agree that fourteen is the correct solution. By confirming what they do know, the students can begin to apply this information to more complex problems.

The table below offers a look at the different strategies used and important observations.

Strategies for 2 × 7

Strategy: Repeated Addition	Observations
2 × 7 = 14 7 + 7 = 14	While some of the students could have quickly shared fourteen as the answer, many of them needed to actually visualize two circles with seven objects to access this problem.

Strategies for 4 × 7

Strategy: Repeated Addition	Observations
4 × 7 7 + 7 + 7 + 7 (7 + 7) + (7 + 7) 14 + 14 = 28	The patterns in the incorrect answers (24, 28, 36) indicate that students were either skip counting or using repeated addition to solve the problem. Notice how the teacher and students accept all answers without judgment, and students remove answers as reasoning and proof is offered. Students still need to visualize (and have the teacher draw) four circles to represent four cookies. Even though the student shares that she imagined seven chocolate chips in each "cookie," the teacher encourages the child to use the number representation for seven instead of seven individual dots. This will help the students think of the seven as a unit when adding the numbers.
Strategy: Partial Products	**Observations**
4 × 7 (2 × 7) + (2 × 7) 2 × 7 = 14 2 × 7 = 14 14 + 14 = 28	It is with this strategy that we see the first benefit of starting with 2 × 7. Students begin to notice the relationship between two sevens and four sevens and apply this in their strategies. This is where we also see the use of the distributive property. The focus is on the conceptual understanding of this property and not the vocabulary term. One student comments that the original 2 × 7 was doubled. The teacher chooses to acknowledge that the product is doubled, but does not elect to explore the associative property connected with this idea. She is staying with her main purpose related to the distributive property. If the teacher had elected to follow the reasoning using the associative property, the strategy could have been recorded as 2 × (2 × 7).

Strategies for 3 × 7

Strategy: Repeated Addition	Observations
3 × 7 7 + 7 + 7 14 + 7 = 21	Again, we see the need for a concrete model to bridge multiplication to repeated addition.
Strategy: Partial Products	**Observations**
3 × 7 (2 × 7) + (1 × 7) 2 × 7 = 14 1 × 7 = 7 14 + 7 = 21	Several students are able to use an earlier problem to help them solve 3 × 7. The teacher helps all of the students follow this strategy by explicitly discussing where the three sevens are in this approach. This use of the distributive property will be a building block for the final problem.

Strategies for 7 × 7

Strategy: Repeated Addition	Observations
7 × 7 7 + 7 + 7 + 7 + 7 + 7 + 7 (7 + 7) + (7 + 7) + (7 + 7) + 7 14 + 14 + 14 + 7 (14 + 14) + (14 + 7) 28 + 21 = 49	Keeping all of the previous problems and their answers posted encourages the students to use what they know to figure out an unknown. This is an important disposition in mathematics. By observing which students do and do not have a thumb up for an answer to this problem, the teacher sees that some are struggling to find a solution or even a strategy. Challenging them to be diligent during the processing discussion is important. It tells them they are accountable for their learning and need to take ownership of finding a strategy that makes sense to them.

(continued)

Strategy: Partial Products	Observations
7×7 $(3 \times 7) + (4 \times 7)$ $21 + 28 = 49$	Whenever possible it is important to connect a less efficient strategy to a more efficient strategy. The Repeated Addition and Breaking into Addends strategies provided a natural connection since they both produced the same addends of twenty-eight and twenty-one. Helping children to explicitly connect strategies is necessary to help them become cognizant of opportunities to use number relationships and efficiency. While no one shared how they used 2×7 to solve this problem, this could have occurred in a number of ways. The previously shared Repeated Addition strategy could be used as a possible springboard by linking the groupings of sevens to multiplication. The recording would resemble the following: $(7 + 7) + (7 + 7) + (7 + 7) + 7$ $(2 \times 7) + (2 \times 7) + (2 \times 7) + (1 \times 7)$

▶ **Classroom Clip 3.6: Doubling and Halving: $4 \times 7, 2 \times 14$**

See pages 241, 322

How important is it to be purposeful when recording student thinking? In this class discussion the initial recording of 4×7 and 2×14 help set the stage for students to begin noticing a relationship between factors that produce the same product. By purposefully recording the sets of problems with factors above factors, students are able to notice the doubling pattern that occurs.

$$4 \times 7$$

$$2 \times 14$$

Even though students initially view the factors as both doubling instead of one doubling and the other halving, this will serve as a precursor to doubling and halving. Transitioning to a familiar context helps provide a much-needed visual representation for the students' exploration of this idea.

Is the student's drawing of a 7 × 4 crate of apples the same as four rows of seven apples? In regard to the commutative property, yes, but contextually you could argue that they are not the same. Instructionally, the teacher chooses not to elicit a debate about this idea, but stays focused on her purpose of investigating the relationships involved in doubling and halving. This is a strong example of the importance of knowing the objective of your number talk.

Several important ideas surface throughout the discussion: commutative property, the whole can remain the same even when multiplying by different factors, the benefit of a context to support thinking, and the importance of student representations. The teacher's questions help the children focus on each of these ideas. Through her questions and the class discussion, she assesses her students' understandings and misconceptions. As a group, the students are applying the commutative property in multiplication, and they are noticing that the product can be arranged using different factors. Only a few students are beginning to make sense of the relationships involved in doubling and halving. The teacher will need to provide many more experiences with this idea.

Classroom Clip 3.7: Array Discussion: 8 × 25

See pages 234, 323

Before introducing the array model, the teacher presented a number talk using the following sequence of problems: 2 × 25, 4 × 25, and 8 × 25. The numbers were specifically chosen because of their doubling pattern and accessible number relationships. Having the students construct strategies for 8 × 25 before introducing the array model allows them to make stronger connections to the array.

Focusing on how many squares or "apples" are inside the box instantly creates an interesting problem that students are eager to consider. Just as important as the quality of problem is that this task is accessible to all students, whether counting by ones or multiplying by twenty-fives. Students initially begin with a lower level of reasoning—counting by ones. Because of the sheer number of squares inside the array, they readily move toward more efficient ways of approaching the problem.

Efficiency conversations can be overheard as students discuss whether two twenty-fives or twenty-five twos would be faster to compute. This topic is important for students to consider from both a commutative property standpoint and an efficiency perspective.

While a minor goal is for the students to figure out how many squares are in the rectangle, a more important goal is for students to visualize efficient ways to solve the problem. The teacher's question, "Who sees it another way?" lays the path to connecting their original strategies to an array model. It also helps students consider the relationships between smaller and larger multiplication problems. The model helps students visualize that 8 × 25 can be broken into numerous smaller problems and provides a foundation for understanding the distributive and associative properties.

Note how the teacher approaches the vocabulary associated with the array. The children often use rows and columns interchangeably, and the teacher does not correct them. Instead she incorporates the correct vocabulary as she responds or asks questions. Her focus continues to target students' understanding of the power of the array model; the vocabulary will come.

Fifth Grade

Classroom Clip 5.1: Associative Property: 12 × 15

See pages 253, 326

The series of problems leading to 12 × 15 provides a catalyst for students to question why every problem produces the same product. Initially, the focus is on solving the problem in an efficient manner, but it gradually shifts to looking at what relationship the problems have in common. Recognizing that three or more factors can be multiplied in any order to obtain a product is one step. Knowing that a factor can be broken into smaller factors to make multiplication of a larger problem easier is a new idea.

Let's use the following table to more closely view the students' thinking for this sequence of problems.

Strategies for the 12 × 15 Number String

Strategies for 2 × 15 × 6	Observations
A. $2 \times 15 \times 6$ $(2 \times 15) \times 6$ 30×6 $3 \times 6 \times 10$ $18 \times 10 = 180$	The student strategies for $2 \times 15 \times 6$ are an excellent example of honoring multiple ways for students to solve a problem. As we look at Strategies A, B, and C we can see how each student has crafted a strategy that was most accessible to himself. Even though one of the main goals of the number talk is to use the associative property to make larger problems easier, the teacher takes the opportunity to help the students understand why 30×6 is not the same as 3×6 with a zero added at the end when discussing Strategy A. Understanding that it is eighteen multiplied by ten is critical to maintaining place value.
B. $2 \times 15 \times 6$ $(2 \times 15) \times 6$ $2 \times 15 = 30$ $30 \times 3 = 90$ $90 \times 2 = 180$	Strategy B is an excellent example of flexibility with numbers and shows how the student changes the problem from $2 \times 15 \times 6$ to $2 \times 15 \times 3 \times 2$ by factoring the six.
C. $2 \times 15 \times 6$ $2 \times (15 \times 6)$ $15 \times 6 = 90$ $90 \times 2 = 180$	Strategy C demonstrates how this problem can be turned into a double by choosing to multiply 15×6 first.

(continued)

Strategy for 5 × 12 × 3	Observations
$(5 \times 12) \times 3$ $5 \times 12 = 60$ $60 \times 3 = 180$	When students are beginning to notice a relationship between numbers and problems, it is often useful for them to articulate their thinking. This can help them clarify what they do and do not understand, but it can be a messy process and sometimes difficult to follow. As the teacher was faced with this situation during Omar's sharing, notice how she allowed clarification to come from another student instead of herself. This example beautifully exhibits the power of the classroom community.
Strategies for 4 × 5 × 3 × 3	**Observations**

A. $4 \times 5 \times 3 \times 3$
 	
    $(4 \times 5) \times 3 \times 3$
 	
    $4 \times 5 = 20$
 	
    $20 \times 3 = 60$
 	
    $60 \times 3 = 180$
 	
B. $4 \times 5 \times 3 \times 3$
 	
    $(4 \times 3) \times 5 \times 3$
 	
    $4 \times 3 = 12$
 	
    $12 \times 5 = 60$
 	
    $60 \times 3 = 180$
 	
C. $4 \times 5 \times 3 \times 3$
 	
    $(4 \times 5) \times (3 \times 3)$
 	
    $3 \times 3 = 9$
 	
    $4 \times 5 = 20$
 	
    $9 \times 20 = 180$
	While the students have several strategies for approaching this problem, the focus begins to shift from finding an answer to noticing patterns in number relationships between the first three problems in the number talk string. The teacher's question, "How do these problems relate?" is used to help focus the students on the primary purpose of the number talk: breaking factors into smaller factors to create easier multiplication problems.

Strategy for 12 × 15	Observations
12×15 $12 \times 10 = 120$ $12 \times 5 = 60$ $120 + 60 = 180$	Note that even with a number talk that elicits student responses and discussions that meet the teacher's goals, not every student will be convinced or ready to use the ideas that have been unearthed. Most of the students immediately knew that 12×15 was 180 because of their earlier number talk work. Others needed to use strategies that were more comfortable for them; they were not ready to apply the ideas that had surfaced.

▶ **Classroom Clips 5.2 and 5.3:**
Multiplication: 32 × 15 and Multiplication: 16 × 35

See pages 17, 231, 327, 328

Both of the multiplication clips provide strong examples of class discussions focused on making sense of the mathematics in the problems. Students can be seen questioning other students' strategies, offering support as individuals reflect upon their thinking, and testing out new ideas. The resulting strategies are accurate, flexible, and efficient. Strategies used for both problems are further explored in the following tables.

Strategies for 32 × 15

Strategy: Partial Products	Observations
A. 32×15 $(30 + 2) \times 15$ $30 \times 15 = 450$ $2 \times 15 = 30$ $450 + 30 = 480$	Both of these approaches are grounded in the distributive property and are closely linked. The first approach is more efficient because it does not require the problem to be broken into as many steps. As one student points out, "It is a lot of numbers to keep in your head." This is a great opportunity to help students think about efficiency and keeping numbers intact.

(continued)

B. 32×15

$(30 + 2) \times (10 + 5)$

$30 \times 10 = 300$

$2 \times 10 = 20$

$5 \times 30 = 150$

$2 \times 5 = 10$

$300 + 20 + 150 + 10 = 480$

Strategy: Making Landmark or Friendly Numbers	Observations
32×15 $\underline{+\ 4}$ 36×15 $(3 \times 12) \times 15$ $3 \times (12 \times 15)$ $3 \times 180 = 540$ $540 - (4 \times 15)$ $540 - 60 = 480$	Even though thirty-six would not typically be considered a friendly number, the student views it as friendly since she can decompose it to link to the previous problem of 12×15. The strategy exhibits strong number sense, use of number relationships, and flexibility with numbers. By asking students why sixty is subtracted from five-hundred forty, the teacher is providing support to those who are unclear about the mathematics of the strategy. This opportunity for students to sift through the math and voice their understandings helps clarify any confusion.

Strategy: Doubling and Halving	Observations
32×15 16×30 8×60 4×120 2×240 $1 \times 480 = 480$	Two questions come to mind with the doubling and halving strategy: 1) When do you stop doubling and halving, and 2) Is this always an efficient strategy? When a student chooses to stop doubling and halving will depend upon the student. Some students will need to continue to double and halve until they have reached a number multiplied by one; others will be able to stop as soon as they recognize an easier problem such as 8×60. Helping students think about the efficiency in this area is important. The class discussion about whether this strategy will always work is one that requires testing numerous problems and forming generalizations.

Strategies for 16 × 35

Strategy: Partial Products	Observations
16×35 $(10 + 6) \times (30 + 5)$ $10 \times 30 = 300$ $6 \times 5 = 30$ $30 \times 6 = 180$ $5 \times 10 = 50$ $(300 + 180) + (30 + 50)$ $480 + 80 = 560$	Accepting and recording all answers without judgment provides an opportunity for students to revisit their thinking and question whether their answers are reasonable. Sometimes, as is the case with the answer 480, a student will change or remove his answer and offer a rationale for why it is not a feasible response. Other times, students will choose to keep their answers posted to elicit help in looking at their thinking. Talking through a strategy with support from the class can be very valuable and insightful. Being able to identify your own error, instead of having a teacher show you where it is wrong, builds

(continued)

	mathematical confidence and a productive disposition toward solving problems.
	The strategy being analyzed is based on the distributive property, as is the standard U.S. algorithm for multiplication. However, in this case, it is not the most efficient mental strategy.
Strategy: Making Landmark or Friendly Numbers	**Observations**
16×35 $20 \times 35 = 700$ $35 \times 4 = 140$ $700 - 140 = 560$	Adjusting the problem to use a friendly or landmark number is much more efficient than the previous strategy and demonstrates a strong sense of flexibility with numbers.
Strategy: Doubling and Halving	**Observations**
16×35 $8 \times 70 = 560$	While the doubling and halving strategy could have continued, the student's purpose was to simplify the problem to the point where she could quickly solve it.
Strategy: Breaking Factors into Smaller Factors	**Observations**
16×35 $8 \times 2 \times 7 \times 5$ $4 \times 2 \times 2 \times 7 \times 5$ $2 \times 2 \times 2 \times 2 \times 7 \times 5$	Breaking a problem into its prime factors isn't necessarily the most efficient strategy for this specific problem; however, it is important to note that the student author of this strategy had been germinating this idea from an earlier number talk. He had been considering how factoring numbers into prime numbers could be useful in solving multiplication problems. This is an excellent example of why student conversations are essential in math. This student continued to ponder a small idea, and the class celebrated his thinking by testing it out.

Classroom Clip 5.4: Array Discussion: 150 ÷ 15, 300 ÷ 15

See pages 236, 328

By starting with two division problems that are closely related, the teacher purposefully crafts a situation for students to consider two relationships: 1) how number relationships can be used in computation, and 2) the relationship between multiplication and division. The array model provides a vehicle for students to grapple with both of these ideas.

The students use multiplication to solve both division problems. We can represent their thinking as follows:

$150 \div 15$	$300 \div 15$
$15 \times 10 = 150$	*Strategy 1:* $(15 \times 10) \times 2 = 300$
	Strategy 2: $15 \times 20 = 300$

Even though the students use 15×10 as a foundation for solving $300 \div 15$ and would lead us to assume they understand the relationship between the two problems, the teacher asks them to use an array to show how the two problems are related. This question is an important one, because it will highlight any misconceptions that exist and any understandings that are fragile.

Note that the teacher does not tell the students how to approach the array. She depends upon the class to ask questions and lead the discussion. The students grapple with the following ideas:

- Which problem needs to be represented: $150 \div 15$ or $300 \div 15$?

- What factors or dimensions are needed to represent $300 \div 15$?

- Where is 150 represented in the array for $300 \div 15$?

- Where is 15×10 and 15×20? Which factor is halved?

The students arrive at several conclusions through this discussion using the array model. They understand that with division you know the whole and with multiplication you are searching for the whole. An array can be a powerful tool for looking at number relationships in multiplication and division.

Classroom Clip 5.5: Division String: 496 ÷ 8

See pages 261, 329

The sequence of division problems leading to 496 ÷ 8 is designed to help students consider options for breaking the dividend into smaller problems while maintaining number sense and place value. While the list of problems is not exhaustive, it does provide a starting point for students to build on problems they know and understand and apply these to new situations. In essence this is another form of fluency or composing and decomposing numbers.

In many instances, the students focus on making sure they have the whole in the division problem and lose sight of solving for the answer. The teacher uses these opportunities to help them keep this idea in the forefront of their thinking.

We can look more closely at the sequence of problems and the students' approaches by using the table below.

Strategies for 496 ÷ 8 Number String

Strategies for 160 ÷ 8	Observations
160 ÷ 8 8 × 2 = 16 8 × 20 = 160 160 ÷ 8 80 × 2 = 160 8 × 20 = 160	Even though the associative property is not the teacher's main focus, she takes the time to extract this important idea by asking if 8 × 20 is the same as 80 × 2 and if so, why. Helping students to understand what occurs when multiplying by ten and powers of ten is a foundational anchor that should be highlighted. As Reagen begins to explain why these two problems are equivalent, the teacher's recording helps students make the connection that both problems can be represented by 8 × 2 × 10.
Strategy for 16 ÷ 8	**Observations**
16 ÷ 8 8 × 2 = 16	When you are first using number talks, you may be tempted to belabor every problem. Notice that the teacher does not elicit multiple strategies for this

	problem, because it will detract from her ultimate goal. Knowing when to immerse the class and when to continue can be achieved by asking yourself, "Will processing this help me reach my goal?"
Strategy for 400 ÷ 8	**Observations**
400 ÷ 8 8 × 5 = 40 40 × 10 = 400	This Multiplying Up strategy efficiently navigates the students to the whole of four hundred, but the students lose sight of the answer. Asking the class to focus on where the answer is located helps students think about what is happening in the problem. While one student shares that since the answer (forty) was multiplied by ten, one of the factors or forty must also be multiplied by ten, the students are still confused about this. Recording the response as 8 × 5 × 10 and then using the associative property to group the factors as 8 × (5 × 10) may help make this thinking clearer.
Strategy for 80 ÷ 8	**Observations**
80 ÷ 8 8 × 10 = 80	Again, the teacher chooses not to process multiple ways to solve this problem. She expects the students to know this answer.
Strategies for 496 ÷ 8	**Observations**
A. 496 ÷ 8 496 ÷ 8 = 10 80 ÷ 8 = 10	This sequence of strategies demonstrates that the previous problems provided a foundation for students to decompose four-hundred ninety six into smaller problems to be divided by 8. Each of the students' approaches

(continued)

$16 \div 8 = 2$ $50 + 10 + 2 = 62$ B. $496 \div 8$ $12 \times 8 = 96$ $400 \div 8 = 50$ $50 + 12 = 62$ C. $496 \div 8$ $8 \times 50 = 400$ $8 \times 8 = 64$ $4 \times 8 = 32$ $50 + 8 + 4 = 62$	exhibit accuracy, efficiency, and flexibility with numbers and achieve the teacher's goal. Students are comfortable moving between multiplication and division and use the relationship between these two operations. Even with this ease in navigating between operations, students often lose sight of their answer. This leads the teacher to ask the students to discuss where the answers are located in each strategy. She rephrases the question multiple times, "How many eights are in four hundred?"

▶ **Classroom Clip 5.6: Subtraction: 1000 − 674**

See pages 181, 330

In the following strategies, we see a nice contrast between subtraction being viewed as removal or taking away and subtraction as the difference between two quantities. Regardless of the approach, number sense is always present. One way number sense is held intact is by thinking about numbers in regard to their place value and not as single digits. Maintaining place value is helpful in determining whether a final answer is reasonable.

The following table looks more closely at the subtraction strategies for 1000 – 674.

Strategies for 1000 − 674

Strategy: Removal	Observations
1000 − 674 1000 − 600 = 400 400 − 74 = 326	Number sense plays an important role in determining whether an answer is reasonable. Regardless of what strategy they use, students should consider whether their answer is feasible and if it makes sense. Looking at all answers through this perspective establishes a culture of sensemaking. A key piece in this classroom dialogue is not that a student disagrees with another's answer, but that a student is willing to offer a rationale for why an answer is or is not possible. We also see how smaller combinations help students think about applications with larger numbers. Relating 67 + 40 to 674 + 400 shows how bridging mathematical connections from one grade to the next is essential.
Strategy: Adding Up	**Observations**
1000 − 674 674 + 26 = 700 700 + 300 = 1000 300 + 26 = 326	Even with larger numbers, the Adding Up strategy can be an efficient method if students utilize relationships with combinations to one hundred or one thousand to navigate quickly to landmark numbers. The student could initially add six to get to six-hundred eighty, but because the combinations to one hundred were accessible, he was able to add up more efficiently. This strategy also capitalizes on the relationship between addition and subtraction.

Appendix B:
Questions and Answers

How often should I use number talks in my classroom?

Number talks are most effective if they are implemented three to five times a week. This will not only elevate the importance of flexibility with strategies and using number relationships, but it will also support your expectations that mathematics should make sense. Incorporating number talks as a regular math routine will help build your students' confidence in their abilities to calculate mentally.

My number talks take almost half of my math time. How long should a typical number talk last?

It can be easy to let number talks take over your math time, because so many important concepts emerge during the sharing of strategies. However, it is important to make sure your number talk sessions stay focused on your goals. Five to fifteen minutes is the recommended length of time for a classroom number talk for two main reasons: 1) longer number talks jeopardize students' attention, and 2) the majority of your math time should be saved for investigations of big mathematical ideas. Number talks are like a "warm-up" period. You may find that initially setting a timer to help you be mindful of the time will keep your number talks from consuming the majority of your math class.

How can I keep my number talks focused?

Strategically plan ahead of time the sequence of problems you will pose and the strategies you wish to target. When I first began number talks, my problems were unrelated and disjointed; my focus was centered solely on eliciting multiple strategies. Our class discussions were too broad and disconnected from problem to problem.

This is not to say that you should not take advantage of a teachable moment that might arise; however, your talk will be much more effective if you stay focused on your primary objective. Instead, as you see concerns or opportunities for other ideas come up, make a mental note as you craft your number talks for the next day. This will allow you to be more deliberate in using your number talk time.

Sometimes I cannot understand a student's strategy. Why is it difficult to follow students' thinking?

Listening to students' thinking and explanations may be a new teaching skill that takes time to learn. I was accustomed to being the source of answers in my classroom and explaining what I knew. In number talks, teachers listen carefully to students' thinking and understanding, present problems, and ask questions that guide thinking. This is quite a shift. Initially it is hard to listen to approaches that are different from the ones we learned as students and have taught throughout our careers. As you incorporate number talks, you will gradually learn to listen and follow students' thinking. During your preplanning, you will learn how to anticipate what strategies might arise with specific problems. As our own knowledge of mathematics grows, it is easier to predict what strategies students might use and also where we can lead the discussion.

Even when you have begun to follow their reasoning more aptly, students often struggle with articulating their own thinking. This can be difficult to follow, too.

On the following page, you will find some teacher moves that I have found to be effective in honoring student thinking while providing time for me to think through the strategies.

Teacher Moves to Honor Student Thinking

- *Ask for another student to explain the strategy that is in question in their own words.* Sometimes students can more readily follow a peer's thinking or have approached the problem in a similar fashion. This allows you and the other students an opportunity to hear the original strategy from a fresh perspective while allowing you time to think about the mathematics and what worked or what went wrong.

- *Ask the student to reexplain their strategy.* This provides an opportunity for everyone to find a way to connect or ask questions about the parts that might be confusing or difficult to follow.

- *Tell the student that you would like to have time to think about their strategy more deeply and ask if you may talk with them privately at a later time that day.* This keeps everyone from being held hostage while you and possibly other students try to make sense of the thinking, but lets the student know that you are not dismissing or judging their strategy. Using this approach does not imply weakness on your part or lack of preparation—quite the opposite. It demonstrates to the students that you are a learner, too, and are interested in making sense of mathematics.

When I tried a number talk with my class, only one or two students shared their thinking. Why didn't my number talk work?

Be patient with yourself and your students! Sometimes sharing with a whole group can be intimidating, especially for those who are not as confident, so provide opportunities for students to turn and talk to others around them. This will help them learn that you expect them to communicate their thinking and listen to others. If students are coming from classrooms where the emphasis was on using memorized procedures with paper and pencil, they will need time to acclimate to articulating their solutions for problems. Give them time to experience that your classroom is a safe environment and that mistakes and incorrect answers are accepted as an integral part of active learning.

Initially you may need to suggest a strategy used by a student from a previous year to encourage your students to begin thinking logically. Ask them to talk with their peers about whether a particular strategy will work for a specific problem or any problem. Suggest they try using a specific strategy for the next problem. Structuring your talks in this manner is a productive way to build confidence and success.

How can I get my students to use other strategies in addition to the standard U.S. algorithm?

While the standard U.S. algorithm can be a very efficient strategy, it often breaks down for students when they try to use it for mental computation. If we look at the problem $999 + 999$, the standard U.S. regrouping algorithm can be tedious as well as challenging when trying to keep all of the numbers in one's head. As other students adjust both numbers to landmark or friendly numbers ($1000 + 1000$) and then adjust this sum or compensate to make the problem $1000 + 998$, students are quick to realize that more efficient strategies are available. Starting with problems that are one away from landmarks helps bring this idea quickly to the forefront.

Another suggestion is to have students complete an exit problem at the end of the number talk. Requiring them to solve the problem two ways and place a star or asterisk by the most efficient strategy encourages them to test out other strategies and consider efficiency.

Is there a reason you suggest problems should be written horizontally?

When you write the numbers horizontally, you encourage students to consider the magnitude of the whole number, the place value, and the number relationships. This is especially important if the students' primary method for computation is the standard U.S. algorithm. When you write the problems vertically, students can more easily think about each column of numbers as a column of 1s without regard to place value. For example, as students solve the problem 999 + 999, you want them to consider the magnitude of both numbers and that they are close to 1000. When the numbers are stacked or written vertically, students often revert to thinking about the problem as 9 + 9 for the 1s, 9 + 9 for the 10s, and 9 + 9 for the 100s.

As your students develop in their understanding and use of place value, number sense, and number relationships, it is important for you to write the problems and solutions both horizontally and vertically.

Is it ever appropriate to allow my students to use paper and pencil during a number talk?

The main purpose of number talks is to help your students focus on number relationships and to use these relationships to mentally compute efficiently and flexibly. As soon as you allow your students to use paper and pencil, they are not as apt to reason about numbers and will often resort to their former procedural knowledge. You want them to be able to rely on their knowledge of numbers and not a rote procedure.

An exception to this approach is to allow students to use paper and pencil to keep track of their subtotals when calculating problems with large numbers. Since many of these problems have multiple steps, students may benefit from writing down their subtotals for each step instead of holding all of these numbers in their heads.

Do you ever let a student record their strategy while explaining their thinking?

Usually I choose to record the strategies shared during number talks because this

- keeps up the pace of the lesson so that students stay engaged,

- allows for the organization of student thinking to draw out the targeted mathematics, and

- provides an opportunity to model correct notation.

An occasional exception is if the class and I are having difficulty following a student's specific strategy, and then the student may be asked to show us his thinking in a written format.

After I complete a number talk, I'm not sure what problems to give my students the next day. How do I choose the next series of problems?

During your number talk, make mental notes of the issues that surface regarding the following:

Areas to Consider When Selecting Number Talk Problems

- *Overgeneralizations.* When students are investigating which strategies work with different operations, they often overgeneralize and try to apply their generalizations to all operations. An example is when students are convinced that compensation works with addition and then assume it will also work with subtraction or multiplication.

- *Inefficient strategies.* Sometimes students become focused on a specific strategy and ignore efficiency. If you have given them a problem that lends itself to using landmark numbers or compensation, such as $1999 + 1999$, yet the majority of your students solve this either with the standard U.S. algorithm or by breaking it apart into place value, you would want to craft problems to address this issue.

- *Evidence from exit cards.* As discussed in Chapter 2, exit cards are an excellent way to keep a pulse on students' understanding and use of strategies. If students struggle with a specific type of problem or operation on their exit cards, this would guide the types of problems and strategies for the next day's number talk.

Appendix C: Suggested Grade-Level Resources

The following resources are useful for developing math menus and building investigations around math concepts.

Grade	Resource	Author
K	*About Teaching Mathematics: A K–8 Resource, Third Edition*	Marilyn Burns
	Teaching Number Sense, Kindergarten	Chris Confer
	Math and Literature series, Grades K–6	Marilyn Burns, Stephanie Sheffield, and Rusty Bresser
	Contexts for Learning Mathematics	Catherine Fosnot
	Developing Number Concepts series	Kathy Richardson
1	*About Teaching Mathematics: A K–8 Resource, Third Edition*	Marilyn Burns

Grade	Resource	Author
	Teaching Arithmetic: Lessons for First Grade	Stephanie Sheffield
	Teaching Number Sense, Grade 1	Chris Confer
	Contexts for Learning Mathematics	Catherine Fosnot
	Developing Number Concepts series	Kathy Richardson
2	*About Teaching Mathematics: A K–8 Resource, Third Edition*	Marilyn Burns
	Contexts for Learning Mathematics	Catherine Fosnot
	Developing Number Concepts series	Kathy Richardson
	Teaching Arithmetic: Lessons for Addition and Subtraction, Grades 2–3	Bonnie Tank and Lynn Zolli
	Teaching Arithmetic: Lessons for Introducing Place Value, Grade 2	Maryann Wickett and Marilyn Burns
3	*About Teaching Mathematics: A K–8 Resource, Third Edition*	Marilyn Burns
	Contexts for Learning Mathematics	Catherine Fosnot
	Young Mathematicians at Work	Catherine Fosnot
	Developing Number Concepts series	Kathy Richardson

(continued)

Grade	Resource	Author
	Teaching Arithmetic: Lessons for Extending Place Value, Grade 3	Maryann Wickett and Marilyn Burns
	Teaching Arithmetic: Lessons for Introducing Multiplication, Grades 3–4	Marilyn Burns
	Teaching Arithmetic: Lessons for Introducing Division, Grades 3–4	Maryann Wickett, Susan Ohanian, and Marilyn Burns
4	*About Teaching Mathematics: A K–8 Resource, Third Edition*	Marilyn Burns
	Contexts for Learning Mathematics	Catherine Fosnot
	Young Mathematicians at Work	Catherine Fosnot
	Teaching Arithmetic: Lessons for Extending Multiplication, Grades 4–5	Maryann Wickett and Marilyn Burns
5	*About Teaching Mathematics: A K–8 Resource, Third Edition*	Marilyn Burns
	Contexts for Learning Mathematics	Catherine Fosnot
	Teaching Arithmetic: Lessons for Extending Multiplication, Grades 4–5	Maryann Wickett and Marilyn Burns
	Teaching Arithmetic: Lessons for Extending Division, Grades 4–5	Maryann Wickett and Marilyn Burns

Appendix D:
Reproducible Templates

Directions for Making Rekenreks

Materials

10 beads of one color

10 beads of a different color

6-by-12-inch rectangle made from sturdy cardboard or thin plywood

2 pieces of string, each approximately 15 inches in length

Directions

1. Cut two half-inch slits on each short side of the rectangle. Space slits about two inches apart.

2. Place ten beads on each string, five beads of one color and five beads of a different color. Tie each end with a knot.

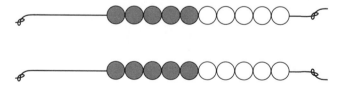

3. Place the knotted ends through the slits so that the beads are on the front of the cardboard or plywood.

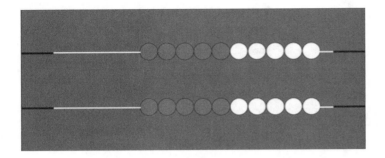

Priya and Alex with their rekenreks in Classroom Clip K.2.

Five-Frame Template

Ten-Frame Template

References

Burns, Marilyn. 1998. *Math: Facing an American Phobia*. Sausalito, CA: Math Solutions.

Fennell, F., and T. E. Landis. 1994. "Number Sense and Operation Sense." In *Windows of Opportunity: Mathematics for Students with Special Needs*, edited by C. A. Thornton and N. S. Bley (pp. 187–203). Reston, VA: National Council of Teachers of Mathematics.

Fosnot, Catherine T., and Maarten Dolk. 2001. *Young Mathematicians at Work: Constructing Number Sense, Addition, and Subtraction*. Portsmouth, NH: Heinemann.

Moses, Robert P., and Charles E. Cobb Jr. 2001. *Radical Equations: Math Literacy and Civil Rights*. Boston, MA: Beacon Press.

National Governors Association Center for Best Practices and the Council of Chief State School Officers. 2010. *Common Core State Standards Initiative: Common Core State Standards for Mathematics*. Washington, DC. www.corestandards.org/assets/ccssi-introduction.pdf.

Pearson Scott Foresman TERC. 2008. *Investigations in Number, Data and Space, Second Edition*. Glenview, IL: Pearson Scott Foresman.

Pearson Scott Foresman TERC. 2006. *Investigations in Number, Data and Space*. Glenview, IL: Pearson Scott Foresman.

Richardson, Kathy. 2002. *Assessment Math Concepts: Hiding Assessment*. Bellingham, WA: Math Perspectives.